PUBLISHING WITH STUDENTS
A Comprehensive Guide

CHRIS WEBER

FOREWORD BY
MARION DANE BAUER

HEINEMANN
PORTSMOUTH, NH

Heinemann
A division of Reed Elsevier Inc.
361 Hanover Street
Portsmouth, NH 03801–3912
www.heinemann.com

Offices and agents throughout the world

The author and publisher wish to thank those who have generously given permission to reprint borrowed material:

Foxfire for Dummies by *Foxfire Magazine* Senior Class Editors: Carrie Allen, John Arthur, Austin Bauman, Kandi Carver, and Samantha Tyler. Summer 2000. Reprinted with permission from The Foxfire Fund, Inc., P.O. Box 541, Mountain City, Georgia. All materials copyrighted.

The article "Tropical Tribune Newspaper: an Interdisciplinary Unit on Rain Forests" was adapted with permission from *Green Teacher*, Summer 1997. Subscriptions are $22 per year from: Green Teacher, P.O. Box 1431, Lewiston, NY 14092. (416) 960-1244.

The article "Type: Doing It Right" by Denise M. Reagan is reprinted by permission of the author. It originally appeared in *Trends in High School Media,* Volume 77, Number 3, Spring 1998. *Trends* is a publication of the National Scholastic Press Association, <http://www.studentpress.org>

"Zdenka Mik's Story," by Gita Webb, is reprinted with the author's permission. It originally appeared in *Kindred*, edited by Judy Barr, 1999.

The excerpt from the interview with Ken Schultz first appeared in "Schultz Lands Winner with Fishing Bible," by Bill Monroe, in *The Sunday Oregonian*, October 29, 2000. Reprinted with permission of *The Sunday Oregonian.*

Library of Congress Cataloging-in-Publication Data
Weber, Chris, 1948–
    Publishing with students : a comprehensive guide / Chris Weber.
      p. cm.
    Includes bibliographical references and index.
    ISBN 0-325-00283-5
    1. Student publications. 2. Publishers and publishing. I. Title.
LB3621 .W39 2002
371.8'97—dc21

                2001039822

Editor: Lois Bridges
Production: Lynne Reed
Cover design: Jenny Jensen Greenleaf
Manufacturing: Steve Bernier
Typesetting: Tom Allen

Printed in the United States of America on acid-free paper
06 05 04 03 02 RRD 1 2 3 4 5

To Mark and Jackson,
my loving sons

You bring me to the top of the world
each and every day.

We will take many of life's treks and climbs,
loving each other every step of the way.

May you conquer any mountain you choose,

moreover,

live life

with open arms.

The Home Team (L to R): Mark, Daddy, and Jackson. Photograph by Jeff Lee.

Contents

Foreword

Marion Dane Bauer

When I was writing *What's Your Story? A Young Person's Guide to Writing Fiction*, I found myself confronted with an important question. Once a young writer has expended the enormous effort required to plan and write and revise a piece of fiction, what comes next? Publication, if by publication one means competing with professional writers for professional markets, is as out of reach as joining a professional orchestra would be to young musicians. Probably more so, because an occasional musical genius is born, but even someone who will one day be seen as a literary genius must acquire years of living experience, not to mention years of learning the craft, before professional publication is a meaningful possibility.

And so I answered the question, "Where can I get my story published?" with complete candor. I said, "You probably can't get it published anywhere." I encouraged young writers to share their work in other ways. But when I was writing *What's Your Story?* I hadn't yet encountered Chris Weber or the many innovative and dedicated teachers whose methods of working with student writers he features in *Publishing with Students: A Comprehensive Guide.*

Reading this book has almost made me wish I could return to my student days and work under one of these teachers. What a thrill it would have been when I was young to have so much demanded of the writing I love to do, to be surrounded by others who had learned to take their writing seriously too, to have my pieces read. Whatever might have come after, I would have remembered that work and that publication for the rest of my life.

This book brings together a group of inspired and inspiring writing teachers who have found practical ways to encourage, demand excellence from, and publish their students. If you are a teacher, it can't help but make you want to emulate their successes. I hope it will encourage you, too, to be teachers who write. In my journeys through classrooms across the country, I have found that no one creates enthusiastic readers more effectively than teachers who are themselves enthusiastic readers, and no one creates stronger writers than teachers who are willing to let their students see them struggle with their own writing.

As everyone knows too well, we have come to a time when there is little place left in the world's economy for people who are not literate. The jobs as ditchdiggers or cogs on a factory assembly line have been supplanted by those in which workers must be able to read and must be able to communicate clearly in writing. This fact alone makes the task of contemporary education more complex and more difficult than educating young people ever was in the past. Few of your students will make a living writing poetry and essays and stories, but all of them will be required, throughout their lives, to write. If under your tutelage they can learn to love the process, they will go into their futures supplied with one of the most important tools for success.

Student publication is more than a fun project, though it can certainly be that for everyone involved. It is more, even, than a way of bringing writers and readers together. It is a way of making genuine literacy—the ability to communicate effectively in writing—the single most exciting goal of your classroom.

Enjoy this book. Be transformed by it. Emulate the models you will find here and see your students transformed.

Marion Dane Bauer is an author and writing teacher in Eden Prairie, Minnesota. Ms. Bauer was first Faculty Chair and continues on the faculty of the Master of Fine Arts in Writing for Children program at Vermont College of Norwich University, a low-residency program in Montpelier, Vermont.

Preface

Picture yourself sitting down at a dinner table with a group of enthusiastic, talented teachers who have been involved in student publications for years. Imagine how much you could learn from them and they from you. Think of the advice you would take away with you, which you could immediately use in the classroom. Moreover, their work would inspire you to help you and your students publish their writing and art. This book is your seat at such a table.

Publishing with Students is a guidebook and not a recipe book. The focus is on the process and other important aspects (for example, roles of students and teachers, overcoming challenges, and so on) of publishing. The teacher-authors share with you what works for them, which may or may not work for you. Sample their work, experiment with it in your classroom, and make the necessary adjustments for your students to successfully publish. Always, always have fun.

For more than twenty years, I have been working with students on their publications in and out of the classroom. These publications have ranged from classroom ones to international anthologies. I founded the Oregon Students Writing & Art Foundation, an organization made up of teachers and students, whose purpose was to publish students' writing and art. So far, we have published four volumes in the *Treasures* series; the latest, *Treasures 3: Stories & Art by Students in Japan & Oregon,* is in both English and Japanese.*

Why have I been so heavily involved with student publishing? What's in it for your students and you? I could have written a chapter about publishing's benefits, but instead, offer some of its key aspects.

---

*Treasure 3 was edited by Chris Weber and published by the Oregon Students Writing & Art Foundation, copyright © 1994.

Forums for Our Young People

Student publications (produced in or out of classrooms) are forums where students' voices are heard. Through them, students communicate their thoughts and feelings about themselves and their lives.

On a visit to Vestal School in Portland, I spoke at a schoolwide assembly about the *Treasures* books. Upon finishing my talk, I introduced one of their fellow students who had been published in *Treasures: Stories & Art by Students in Oregon*. As the Vietnamese girl walked up to the podium and began reading her true story, there wasn't a breath to be heard. No one moved nor said a word; all eyes were upon her. The auditorium came to a complete halt as if it were frozen in time. The student's soft voice and strong story filled the auditorium that belonged to her. As she read her last word, closed the book, and bowed her head, the auditorium sprang to life with applause and cheering.

Students' Work Affects and Motivates Other Students

The staff at Sunnyside School in Clackamas, Oregon, told how a book of students' writing and art touched their students. "Stories have been shared, read and reread, and laughed and cried over. *Treasures* has given our students an awareness of life and the world around them as experienced by children of their own ages."

When students write, their peers will want to read what they have to say. When they read aloud their work, their peers will listen. Published student authors and artists inspire others to write and draw in a more powerful and telling way than teachers can. Adele Cerny, third- and fourth-grade teacher at Seneca Elementary School in John Day, Oregon, has seen this in her students. "This winter, we received our copy of *Treasures*. The students read it constantly and recommend favorite stories to each other. They use *Treasures* to get ideas for topics and styles of writing. It definitely motivates them to write. A frequent comment is, 'A kid wrote this story. I can write, too!' . . . This year, every pupil in my class wants to enter their story in the contest. *Treasures* has provided a tangible goal for my students to work toward."

A Tribute to Teachers

We teach countless students through the years, not knowing how we touched their lives or in what ways we have influenced them. Upon receiving a copy of *Treasures 2* that I sent him, John Wooden, former UCLA basketball coach, wrote, "No material reward can compare with learning you have helped or inspired another to do well."

The following e-mail message reminds teachers everywhere what renews our passion for teaching and student publishing:

It's been about 16 years since my story was published in *Treasures 2: Stories & Art by Students in Oregon*, and I still remember the giddiness that I felt when I received word that it was one of the ones chosen. It was the first proof that I had genuine writing talent. My teachers, parents, and peers had praised my work, but seeing my own words in print somehow made it all real. It gave me the confidence I needed to continue writing and exploring my abilities. Since that time, I have written about 15 stories, 43 poems, 4 songs, 72 miscellaneous papers, and have 22 more stories in various stages of completion. Right now I am working on a series of novels and a special Internet-based, multi-authored book project.

Although I have not tried to get published again since that first success, I know thanks to you that I have what it takes, so I can focus on my own creativity and not whether my work is "good enough" or not. It has made a great deal of difference in my life and will continue to for as long as I still live and write. I can't imagine myself without my writing, and I don't think I would have kept the desire to write in my heart so strongly had it not been for your *Treasures* project and my success with it.

Your efforts in bringing the voices of the children out to be heard in your books have played a tremendous part in the shaping of my own life. With the exception of my parents, I can think of no one whose actions have had a more dramatic effect on my growth. And for someone that I've never met, I owe you a great deal. Thank you, Chris. Because of you, I am who I am today.
Esteem'd Regards,
Aaron Ward

After finishing this book, use our ideas and advice in your own way to publish your students' work so that their voices can be heard. Your publications will all be different from one another. They will probably turn out more beautiful and meaningful than you had originally envisioned. Then sit down with colleagues, tell them about your students' publication, and inspire them to publish with their own students.

Acknowledgments

Chris Weber

A writer couldn't have a better editor and truer friend than Lois Bridges. Time and time again, she went out of her way for me and supported my efforts as this book evolved. In addition to her judicious editing, Lois cared about me and my work. Her friendship is stamped all over *Publishing with Students*. Lois, my heartfelt thanks and love!

I have been very fortunate to have my book in such good hands of other Heinemann staff. Lynne Reed, production editor, has simply been terrific. She has worked so patiently and in such an understanding way with me during the production phase, which means tight deadlines and quality work. *Publishing with Students* is stronger because of the superb copyediting by Jen Noon. When teachers learn that my work is being published by Heinemann, they comment on what an excellent company it is and how lucky I am. I know why—it is because of its top-notch people whom I have been privileged to know and work with.

Aurelia Wight, a dear friend, helped me in so many ways. Her proofing and feedback were invaluable. Whenever I needed help, she was always there doing what she could. I can never thank Aurelia enough for her encouragement and support.

Those who participated in this book worked very hard. These individuals gave more than asked: Lisa Jobson, coordinator for I*EARN, Christy Stevens and Sara Day Hatton of Foxfire Fund, and Sam Swope and Maureen Labrum of Chapbooks.com.

As I worked on *Publishing with Students*, I met and worked with dozens of teachers and students around the world. I was privileged to come to know them, and they taught me so much. Unfortunately and regrettably, I could not include work by most of these fine people. However, I wish to let them know how grateful I am for their effort, time, and superb pieces. Their names appear in Appendix G.

While writing the final revision of this book, I received a letter from Magdelyn E. Hammond informing me that her mother, Elizabeth B. Hammond, had recently died from cancer. Sadly, I read her letter over and over again, remembering what a responsive and caring person her mother had been. Her daughter wrote, "After she got ill, she spoke of how glad she was that she finished the revisions to the chapter before she was diagnosed." I am glad, too, and am including Elizabeth's article "Students Keep Me Teaching" in Appendix H, so that you know why I appreciated her and was so grateful to have known her.

In my final revisions, Marion Dane Bauer made astute observations and suggestions about my writing, which I then worked on and strengthened. Because of Ms. Bauer, I made my last "replay" count and am indebted to her for it. Moreover, her foreword is perfect.

Without the assistance and understanding of Howard S. Johnson, custodian at Atkinson School, in Portland, Oregon, I wouldn't have had a quiet place to work these past summers. Howard, thanks also for the great talks we have every day, and most importantly, your friendship.

My teaching and writing go hand in hand. I have learned so much from each and every one of my students and those student editors with whom I worked on the *Treasures* anthologies. This book is a tribute to them all.

Staff at Atkinson School have certainly made a difference for me. Whether facing a challenge or joining in celebration, Angie, Cecily, Choo Fen, Karen B., Margaret, Raymond, and Stephanie give me their friendship and support each day. They mean so much to me and this book. I am also very grateful to two superb administrators. John Withers, former principal, was genuinely interested in my work and wanted students to improve their writing, so he encouraged and assisted me. John's continual support and caring were gifts of his leadership that I most appreciated. Deborah Peterson, principal, encourages, supports and values my writing.

To write this book, I needed to "adventure travel." Mingma Dorji Sherpa, owner of Last Frontiers Trekking (P.) Ltd. <http://www.lastfrontiersnepal.com/main.htm>, has given me memorable, rejuvenating treks in Nepal. I consider him a friend and brother, whom I will see again on future treks that will uplift my spirit as they have in the past.

Jim Whitney shot the front cover photograph. Rinzin Sherpa, climbing guide on my Island Peak climb, took the photograph of me that appears in the afterword.

Allen Gilbert shot the photograph of a boy interviewing a man, which appears in Chapter 3.

People in my life played a crucial role in helping me write *Publishing with Students*. Gran has been an inspiration throughout my life, deeply affecting my writing. Onpavi, my wife, I am very grateful to you for your love and support as I have toiled these past three years.

Being a father of two loving sons, I needed time away from them so I could finish this book. Alice, our babysitter, and her daughters, Catherine, and Christine took very good care of our boys, and in so doing, gave me the time I needed.

Jeremy Rooper proofread the Afterword manuscript and gave me valuable suggestions that made the piece stronger and more accurate.

Mark and Jackson, my little mountain climbers, you bring me so much happiness and laughter, especially when you invade my office to remind me of what's really important in life. As I have worked on this book, I always remembered with a smile and a hug that you two are the best things I have ever done. Love, Daddy.

Gran (1902–2001)

I learned much about how to walk on life's journey from Gran. As I walk among the mountains of the world, I will always remember her, ever grateful for Gran's stories of faraway lands and peoples that awakened my desire to embrace the world. No one modeled humor, courage, and compassion better than her. I'm sure that my perseverance also came from Gran, and without it, this book could never have been written. There are many other personal traits I needed and called upon to write this book, many of which I learned from Gran.

I'll leave you with a quote from her.

> There's something good in every step from being a child to a youth. Look at the fun they think they're going to have. But there's so much responsibility that goes along with it. If we just realize it, then it's not so hard. It's what we make of it. It's how we take our steppingstones and how we build on them.

1

Writing to Publish Is for Every Student

Publication Is a Powerful Tool

Peter Elbow, one of our best-known writing teachers, writes eloquently about the publication of student writing as a powerful tool in the democratization of writing. He shows how the publication of student writing motivates students to work hard to improve their writing because they have a real audience. Elbow describes how publishing helps student writers enjoy the writing process as a way to communicate with others. He explores that moment when students read their published work, and he examines the effect it has on them and their writing. You will nod your head as you read his strong case for publication as "the single strongest way to help encourage students to revise and copyedit." Elbow also explains how helpful publication is in teaching students about the writer's voice. After reading his essay, you will want to publish student writing as often as possible.

Read more of what Elbow has to say about writing and teaching writing in his books, *Writing with Power: Techniques for Mastering the Writing Process* and *Everyone Can Write: Essays Toward a Hopeful Theory of Writing and Teaching Writing.*

THE ROLE OF PUBLICATION IN THE DEMOCRATIZATION OF WRITING

**Peter Elbow, Author and Emeritus Professor of English,
University of Massachusetts at Amherst, Amherst, Massachusetts**

A thought experiment: Imagine that you had *never spoken a word except to a teacher.* Every time you ever spoke—in your whole life—a teacher would give you either some critical, judgmental feedback or else a grade—usually both. And yet you wouldn't get these responses till a few days or a week after you had uttered those words.

Writing as a Restricted Code-Only for Special People

Try to imagine what it would be like never to have spoken except under these peculiar conditions. Imagine what it would do to your speaking. Yet this is exactly the relationship most students have with writing: they never write except for a teacher—getting evaluative feedback and often a grade on everything they write—but long afterwards. (Even when teachers are overloaded or the writing is informal, they often feel obliged at least to circle a few misspellings.) Paul Goodman once said that if we learned to speak as we learned to write, there would be many more nonspeakers. But most of us speak easily and often enjoy it because we speak from the earliest age to listeners who welcome and applaud all our efforts, and we continue to engage in *interactive* speech throughout the widest variety of circumstances—with many listeners and for many purposes.

This highly restricted, school-based context for writing has led most people to have a vexed relationship to writing—feeling it to be difficult and doing it only when required. For this reason (and others), writing is often felt to be bound up with an elitist, antidemocratic spirit: as though writing is only for special people—people with special talent, special gifts, or blessed with good schooling from an early age. But in recent decades, some teachers have begun learning ways to democratize writing—to help writing burst out of its damagingly restricted, teacher- and evaluation-haunted context—helping all students bring to writing some of the natural, comfortable fluency of speech—helping students feel that writing is for everyone.

Writing Breaks Out

For one thing, teachers have learned to help students use freewriting for exploratory writing and early drafts. Thus students are learning what so many real writers have always known: that they don't have to be organized, careful, and disciplined to *start* a writing project; they can freewrite a disorganized mess and find lots of good ideas—and still end up with a careful, structured, disciplined, final version. Knowing what you want to say and how to structure it is not what you start out with but what you end up with.

Let me turn to a different and perhaps more powerful realm where writing has begun to burst its traditional bounds. Teachers of kindergarten and first and second grade have expanded the very technology of writing by learning to help their tiny students use scribbling and "invented spelling" to get any of their thoughts on paper. It turns out that *writing* is a faster and more powerful entryway into literacy than reading is: children can read only those words they've learned to read—whereas in fact they can *write everything they can say*. We see here the same large principle that we saw earlier: you don't need to master grammar, spelling, or "writing" in order to write good things.

It's interesting to see how much e-mail is now tending to democratize writing—helping so many people in this large cultural shift in their experience of writing. E-mail has led lots of people of all ages to write frequently and easily—often daily!—and in the process to learn that "write" and "right" are not the same words. People are learning to bring to writing some of the informality and fluency they naturally use in speech. More people are learning to use writing to think and to explore. E-mail disasters are also teaching many people the dialectical relationship between generating and revising. That is, if an e-mail document is important or could do damage, we gradually learn to be careful to reread, revise, and be vigilant about how distant readers might misunderstand our words.

I seem to be celebrating wrongness and carelessness in writing. Can I really be writing to celebrate the *publication* of student writing?—when publication requires everything to be careful and right? Yes. I claim that publication too has been proving a powerful tool in the democratization of writing. Let me explain.

The biggest problem in writing comes from the heavily evaluative, school context for writing that I described at the start: students come to experience writing not as a human act of reaching out to say what's on their mind to others. Rather, they tend to experience writing as an attempt to say what they don't understand very well to a teacher reader who already understands it much better than they do—and all for the sake of being graded on how well they did. The mushrooming movement to publish student writing in all sorts of ways has been an enormous help here. It's helped students begin to *reexperience* writing as the healthy, pleasurable process it should be—the process of trying to reach out to communicate to fellows, not just to be tested by an authority.

Publication is so simple. We can link all kinds of interesting teaching activities to it, but I like publication for itself. Indeed, I am nervous about tangling up publication too much as part of a "lesson plan." To do so can obscure and undermine the main thing: writing is an act of speaking out to readers—not an act of being taught and tested. Consider the simple but startling fact that most writing in the world gets no response at all. When people write books, stories, poems, newspaper articles, and memos, the words go out and that's pretty much it. If readers read the words at all, the writer is lucky. Occasionally you get a note back in your mailbox—"Good memo"—but more often it's criticism instead. Sometimes books get a review, but most do not. Magazine articles and newspaper stories, virtually never. Friends may give you responses, but often they are nervous about doing so. My experience as a writer and teacher leads me to this conclusion: what writers need most to help them work on their writing and improve is not instruction or feedback but an *audience*.

Publication in the University of Massachusetts at Amherst Writing Program

Imagine another scene: this is not a thought experiment, but rather something that occurs three to five times a semester in virtually every first-year writing class here at the University of Massachusetts at Amherst for the four thousand first-year students we teach every year. Based on a modest lab fee (why should we expect students to pay only for lab equipment or for books—and not for writing?), each teacher publishes a class magazine three to five times a semester for his or her class. Students simply produce a final, copy edited, single-spaced draft for photocopying. The teacher (or some students) add a cover and a table of contents.

Imagine the moment: I've just handed out copies of the class magazine to my twenty or so students. It's the end of class because I've learned not to pass them out at the beginning of the hour—unless I want to use them right away for a class activity (which, of course, I sometimes do). Once I've passed them out, I see most students leaf through them, but sooner or later—sometimes openly, sometimes surreptitiously—they turn to *their own essay!* Does that seem peculiar? Vain? Think back to some occasion when you first held in your hand a publication containing something you wrote. I'll bet you did what I do: read your *own* essay.

Why? We could give a cynical, pessimistic answer: "Humans are irredeemably fallen, narrow, self-centered, self-absorbed creatures." But that's not a satisfactory explanation of the phenomenon. Is it only vanity that makes us look in mirrors? No. Often we are trying to see how we look to others. Thus we read our own writing when it's published because we're trying to feel how it looks to others. I'd insist that the impulse to look in the mirror and to read over our own published writing is not usually a failure to "decenter" or get out of the self; it's often an effort in exactly the opposite direction: to enter into the view of others.

And so what happens when we or our students read the published version of our own writing? The answer is interestingly mixed. Sometimes we are discouraged. "Oh dear, how did my tummy get so large? My hair so thin?" "I worked so hard on this piece of writing and I finally liked it, but now in this magazine, I notice nothing but faults. And it's too late to make any improvements."

This is sad in a way, but not really. For I find it speaks to the two skills most teachers find it hardest to teach: substantive revising and copyediting. Like most writing teachers, I preach and hector and cajole as well as I can about the benefits of revising and copyediting. I keep devising clever exercises to promote them: "At last. This one will be foolproof!" But they're all remarkably ineffective compared to the simple fact of publishing students' writing so that they read over their own essays in class magazines. I come back to a brute but subtle fact: they *see their own words differently* because they're in a magazine that they see in every fellow student's hand. They have read over their own essay a number of times in the process of revising it, but this subtle and peculiar ability to see your own words as others will see them is hard to learn—for all of us. I believe publication is the single strongest way to help encourage students to revise and copyedit.

I want to point out and stress a practical and concrete principle [that follows]: it's important to publish a *number* of class magazines in a semester. Publishing just one celebratory magazine at the end of the semester is nice, but the main benefit comes from students having the chance to get their writing published over and over and improve their performance.

So far I've stressed the negative reaction to publication: "Oh dear, I don't look as good as I thought." But in fact this self-criticism isn't usually the main reaction most students have to the publication of their writing. The predominant reaction is usually pride (though often disguised—so as to stay "cool"): "This is mine! I wrote this." What a wonderful experience: the gift of actual readers. We teachers stress the importance of audience and audience awareness, but without publication it's hard for students actually to *feel* the reality of audience. Publication of class magazines helps students begin to use writing as an act of reaching out to readers, rather than just trying to figure out "what the teacher wants." In short, there's a nice balance here. Our understandable pride and pleasure in publication offsets the productive disappointment at the problems we see—problems we didn't see when we were actually writing and revising.

The Publication as a Doorway into Literacy

Let me return to the situation of kindergartners and first and second graders learning they can write anything they can say—before they have mastered any of the conventions of writing and spelling. Some observers of this activity have been troubled to see small children being invited to use writing in such a "loose, undisciplined" way. These commentators fear that children will never learn to get writing *right* if they are invited to do so much "wrong" writing. But their worry is valid only if the teachers never explain to children the realities of language and culture: of course important pieces of writing for an outside audience need to be revised and corrected; and, of course, teachers need to work on techniques for making these revisions and corrections.

Publication is an important element in this approach. When teachers use writing in the earliest grades to bring children into literacy more quickly and with more personal involvement, they typically use the following activities. First, the children make a series of drawings and then do some writing to illustrate or accompany each drawing. Then the teacher (sometimes with the help of an aide or a parent) types up the writing in correct spelling and grammar and makes a little book out of the drawings—often with a hard cover with pretty fabric. Thus each child is producing "books." (There is a much-told story of a reporter visiting one of these classrooms where a first grader eagerly offers to show him one of her books. "Have you really written a book?" the reporter asks the child. Her reply puts him in his place: "Haven't you?")

The point is that these books are in fully "standard," correct, conventional English. The students can't do that revising themselves, but they can see in the most direct and palpable way that there is such a thing as a "grown-up" form of writing that they will have to learn. And then they take another momentous step into literacy: these books serve as reading. The tiny children get a big boost in word recognition and sounding out letters when they are reading the standard English form of *words that came out of their own mouths*. And they get a boost in eagerness when they can work on reading the books written by their friends and classmates. (I'm confused when I see champions of phonics labeling these teaching techniques as "whole language" and treating them as the enemy: the use of invented spelling and of reading their own books is nonstop practice in *sounding out* letters and syllables.)

Publication leads most children to *want* to revise and correct their writing for publication. Thus they learn in the most vivid, felt, and realistic way about the difference between exploratory early drafts for themselves and final drafts for a wider audience. It needn't be a matter of puritan struggle: "How can we stop these kids from giving in to the temptation of leaving their writing uncorrected?" Most students naturally want their writing to look its best when it gets published in a magazine.

Publication and Voice-on-the-Page

Finally, let me say a word about how the publication of student writing helps me to teach students about something I've long explored and cared about—but which is slippery and complex: voice in writing. When all the students have copies of class magazines in their hands, it's much easier to explore the mysterious fact that silent words on a page can "have a voice"—and, in addition, to learn how the voice in a piece of writing tends to have a powerful effect on whether readers like it or resist and see faults in it.

Voice may be a slippery concept, but, interestingly, it's a much more productive concept than *style* or *register*. Students are usually more sophisticated in understanding the subtle effects of written words on readers when I ask about the voice in the words—"How does this sound? What kind of person do you hear?" Everyone has had lots of practice in listening for voice quality and describing distinctions between tones of voice. Most students are shrewd and subtle in making distinctions between different voices. "Yes, she sounds mad, but what I hear underneath is that she's discouraged." Furthermore, these voice-oriented perceptions and discriminations make it easier for students to improve and revise their writing than if we talk about style or register. When we talk about the problems of "passive voice" or a "nominalized style," we are stuck hoping students will consciously manipulate their syntax—based on their mastery of grammar. It's much more fruitful to ask them to read it aloud, to get others to read it aloud, and to ask two simple questions:

> First, *What kind of voice or voices do you hear in these words?* This question leads to lovely discussions. Sometimes students agree on the voice, saying that, for example, the opening paragraphs feel stiff and timid. But just as often, there is interesting disagreement: "She's serious." "No, she's pulling our leg." And for the writer, there is always that most productive of questions: "Is this how I want to sound?"
>
> Second, *Has the writer managed to get herself "in" or "behind" what she is writing?* This question leads most students to realize something simple but powerful: they seldom let themselves be as present or alive in the medium of writing as when they effortlessly put themselves into their speaking. And they have no trouble noticing the strength of passages or whole essays where some student really got herself in or behind her words.

After a few weeks, I like to emphasize the word *behind*. That is, I think it's important to show students that you can be "behind" your words and give them the weight of your presence and involvement, even if the writing is not particularly colloquial or personal or autobiographical—or even particularly "sincere." It doesn't take long for students to recognize that a writer can be solidly "in" a piece of writing even if the writing is impersonal. And of course ironic writing can also have a strong voice. Most students have a good ear for language that is actually a little glib or fake or pretending—even when the language is personal and lively. "Yeah, that's the voice we use when trying to get someone to go out on a date."

When students decide that they don't like the way their voice sounds in something they wrote—or if readers convince them that they didn't really let themselves be "in" or "behind" their writing—they don't have to try consciously to manipulate their syntax. They can harness the natural voice skills they already possess and try for different voices without at all having to make conscious choices about syntax or vocabulary. Even our least skilled students know what is involved in trying to say something less timidly—and the syntax and vocabulary change all by themselves.

This approach doesn't require teachers to get into theater games or improvisation exercises (though they are great for writing); it's usually a matter of students realizing that they can *let themselves sound more like themselves* on paper than they had been doing. For example, most students can *feel* what it's like to avoid timidity yet not be dogmatic—or, contrarily, to back away from dogmatism yet not be timid. The concept of voice leads even seemingly unsophisticated students to make wonderfully subtle discriminations such as this: "Yeah, he sounds dogmatic, but it's because he doesn't really believe what he's saying."

Of course it is possible to discuss voice in writing without publishing student pieces: we can have discussions with individual students about their papers; or we can discuss the voice in the literature we are studying. But the publication of student writing makes an ideal forum for discussing this crucial matter of voice in writing. When we look in a mirror, we can't help asking, "How do I look?" When we see our writing in a publication, we can't help asking, "How do I sound?"

When we help all our students publish their writing and think about how they sound on paper, this is a big piece of the larger movement I'm trying to explore in this essay: the democratization of writing through publication.

In the following essays, I have explored more fully some of the complexities of voice in texts:

Elbow, Peter. 1994. "Introduction: About Voice and Writing." In *Voice and Writing*, edited by Peter Elbow (xi–xlvii). Landmark Essays series. Davis, CA: Hermagoras Press (now Lawrence Erlbaum Associates). Reprinted in *Everyone Can Write: Essays Toward a Hopeful Theory of Writing and Teaching Writing*, by Peter Elbow. New York: Oxford University Press, 2000.

———. 1989. "The Pleasures of Voices in the Literary Essay: Explorations in the Prose of Gretel Ehrlich and Richard Selzer." In *Literary Nonfiction Theory, Criticism, Pedagogy*, edited by Chris Anderson. Carbondale, IL: Southern Illinois University Press.

———. 1994. "Voice in Literature." In *Encyclopedia of English Studies and Language Arts*, edited by Alan Purves. Urbana, IL: National Council of Teachers of English. Reprinted in *Everyone Can Write: Essays Toward a Hopeful Theory of Writing and Teaching Writing*, by Peter Elbow. New York: Oxford University Press, 2000.

2

Student-Run Magazines: How to Empower Your Students

Every Kind Imaginable

Magazines are one of the oldest and most common forms of student publications. While they were once the domain of high schools, more and more middle schools are producing high-quality magazines. You might think of only literary magazines, but there are many kinds of magazines being published, such as those discussing the environment and current social issues. Just about every subject is being covered in this kind of publication. School websites display online versions. A few magazines are even on CD-ROMs! Writing forms (such as stories, essays, poems, interviews) in both fiction and nonfiction discuss real-life issues (student violence in schools, race relations, terrorism, and so on).

Foxfire magazines strive to record first-person accounts of local culture. Since 1966, *The Foxfire Magazine* has been produced to preserve the heritage of the Appalachian area, and the Foxfire Fund, Inc., has been training teachers across the country in the Foxfire approach.

Getting your students actively involved in the publication process guarantees success. Teachers know and understand how much harder students work when the publication is their responsibility. The number and complexity of the tasks students undertake vary by grade level, with high school students taking on greater publishing responsibilities than those in elementary school.

Romi Sussman discusses how her students gather submissions and then critique them. Her students develop and carry out different approaches for soliciting submissions. You will learn that there is more to a call for submissions than just sending flyers or putting up posters.

Once the submissions arrive, Sussman describes the critique sessions and informs you about the way in which she models the process so that shortly thereafter students lead the sessions in which they critique and select pieces for their school magazine. ■

GATHERING AND CRITIQUING MAGAZINE OR BOOK SUBMISSIONS

Romi Sussman, English Teacher,
Winston Churchill High School, Potomac, Maryland

Background

Students involved in classroom or schoolwide publications are presented with a monumental task. They must devise a method for tapping in to the talent of student writers at their school and then decide which writing warrants publication in their magazine or book. How is this to be done? Who should be charged with such responsibility? The students and faculty at Winston Churchill High School in Potomac, Maryland, have worked since 1965 to answer these questions for the school's literary magazine, *Erehwon*.

The submission and critiquing processes have gone through many transformations to reach the format that we use today. The school is fortunate enough to have two creative writing classes and two literary magazines, and the ideas set forth below come from these two publications, *Erehwon* and *Polliwog*.

Generating Submissions

Each year, *Erehwon* receives approximately two hundred submissions and *Polliwog* receives approximately eighty submissions from the student body of [1600] students. In order to attract a sufficient number of submissions, the staffs of the two magazines and I solicit writing using numerous approaches. From the beginning of school in the fall, we make morning announcements over the school public address system, reminding students about the magazines and submission deadlines. Staff members visit English classes throughout the first semester to show them the magazines from previous years, to answer questions, and to encourage submissions.

We have a student in charge of public relations for the magazines as well. This student promotes the magazines by creating lively posters and flyers, by organizing unifying events like bowling nights and poetry readings at Starbucks, and by designing T-shirts for staff members. This person also collects submissions from creatively decorated envelopes strategically placed around the school.

The key to our solicitation efforts is our commitment to anonymity. When submitting a piece, an author places two copies of the piece into an envelope or mailbox in the school. The author puts his or her name on the back of one copy. The editor-in-chief (or the teacher) takes the copies with the names on them and remains the only person who knows the authors' names. The other copies are labeled by number only. Transparencies of the pieces are made and will be used for anonymous critiquing at a later date. This process encourages students who are intimidated or fearful about submitting, and it ensures an unbiased selection process.

The Critiquing Process

As submissions begin to trickle in to the classroom in October, we begin our critiques. Critique sessions take place after school two to three days a week from October through January. The entire student body is welcome and encouraged to attend the afterschool critiques. We announce the critiques during the morning announcements, supply light refreshments, and try to create a warm, inviting environment where students feel comfortable sharing their ideas and their writing. Many students who submit work to the magazines do so after coming to critiques and enjoying being a part of the process. Furthermore, much of the magazines' staff is made up of students who attend critiques and then find that they want to become more involved with the magazines. As a result, the critiques serve multiple beneficial purposes.

Each critique session runs for about two hours and includes evaluations of both prose and poetry. Students organize and run the sessions. When they critique poetry, the poetry editor runs the meeting, and when students critique prose, the prose editor runs it. The format that we have created can be used by any age group and for any purpose, whether you are creating a classroom book or a schoolwide magazine.

As we get ready to critique student work, I run a few critiques to model the process for the students. I sit in front of the overhead projector with the piece and ask students questions to facilitate the process. I remind them to start with positive comments and to offer constructive criticism. I ask students to focus on content and style. I will ask them to look more deeply at times and to try to uncover the author's intent. I will point out literary devices such as metaphors, symbolism, onomatopoeia, and alliteration and have them comment on whether such techniques are used effectively. Finally, I will ask them to discuss the line and stanza divisions in a poem or the paragraph breaks in a prose piece and have them discuss whether the author's choices are effective.

I give the students the freedom to make comments and to analyze the pieces, and I only ask questions when there is a lull in the analysis. Furthermore, I try to ensure that the students cover all important aspects of a piece before voting. Such topics include figurative language, symbolism, poem construction, creativity, meaning, author's intent, and personal impact. Once I have used this model a number of times and I feel comfortable with the students' understanding of the process, the students are then given this responsibility. I am always in the room in case there is a problem, but this process gives the students autonomy and makes them feel that they are guiding all aspects of the critiques. With elementary school students, the teacher will probably want to remain the one in charge, but older students are certainly capable of leading the sessions themselves.

To begin a critique, the person in charge puts a piece of writing on the overhead projector and gives the hard copy of the piece to someone in the room. The piece is read out loud one time so that everyone hears it. The session is then open for student comments. The students must always open the discussion with a positive comment, thus creating an inviting and positive atmosphere. All subsequent comments are appropriately sensitive. The students may have criticisms about the piece, but they realize that the author of the piece is probably in the room and treat the piece as if it is their own. Students evaluate for content and style. They discuss literary devices, sentence structure, diction, symbolism, word choice, and meaning. While students comment on the piece, the person in charge writes these comments onto the transparency, and the person with the hard copy writes them onto the hard copy.

Voting on Pieces

Finally, when the group feels that it has adequately discussed the piece, a vote is taken. The person leading the discussion asks the class if there are any further comments or if everyone feels comfortable to vote. If the class agrees to vote, then the overhead projector is turned off, the lights are turned back on, and each student is given a slip of paper. Students then silently write their votes on the slips of paper and have three choices: "in," "out," or "shelved." Voting the piece "in" means it will be published, "out" means it will not be published, and "shelved" means the voter enjoyed the piece, but that the author needs to make some corrections and then resubmit the piece to be critiqued again.

Votes are collected on paper and tallied by the editor-in-chief (or teacher). The name of the author is only revealed to the audience for pieces that are voted "in." The authors are congratulated publicly if they are in the room, and those not present are sent letters of congratulations.

For pieces that are voted "shelved" or "out," the editor-in-chief delivers a letter to the author that explains the decision. In addition, the authors are given copies of their pieces with the comments that the students discussed. For pieces that are shelved, the authors are invited to improve them using the comments and to resubmit them to be critiqued and voted on again. The authors feel that they are part of the critiquing process and have the opportunity to improve their pieces.

Discussion

The critiquing process is extremely rewarding for the students, and we have chosen to keep this process alive by working through the obstacles that we have encountered. The two main problems involve time constraints and egos. Critiquing in this fashion takes more time and planning than having students read and rate pieces individually. As a result of these difficulties, we have learned to set very specific deadlines to ensure that all work is submitted by a certain date and that all critiquing is done in a systematic, time-sensitive fashion. We have found this planning to be well worth the effort. When first reading a poem or story, many students don't understand the meaning of the piece. If left to evaluate a piece by themselves, many would immediately vote it "out." However, given the opportunity to share their thoughts and to evaluate pieces together, students gain a deeper understanding for the meaning of each piece and improve their analytical skills.

The other main difficulty that we have encountered involves the feeling of self-worth of the students who submit work. As a result of critiquing as a group, we have found that students are either too intimidated to submit their writing or nervous about listening to the open discussion of their work when they do submit. We have approached this difficulty in a number of ways.

First, when talking to classes and encouraging submissions, the students emphasize that they are open to all writing and that no one should feel intimidated. We urge all students to attend critiques so that they can see how the process works and how gentle the students are in their evaluations. Finally, I attend all critique sessions to ensure that students are conducting themselves appropriately and showing respect to the authors.

The students take the entire process very seriously, and I am always extremely impressed with the level of analysis during critiques. This process is efficient, engaging, and sensitive. The students are aware of each other's feelings and ideas and they listen and respond with intelligent, thought-provoking comments.

The hallmarks of this program involve encouraging submissions throughout the school, ensuring the anonymity of the authors, sponsoring student-run critiques, and carefully gearing the critique sessions to be positive and constructive. Obviously, every school has its own character and these ideas may need to be adapted for each school. With appropriate adaptation, these ideas should help to create a dynamic and educational submission and evaluation process for your classroom or school publication.

Practical Tips

- Create anonymity for student writing; this encourages students to get involved and dissuades bias in the selection of pieces.
- Teach students how to critique a piece of writing; start with positive comments and always maintain the nurturing feeling in the classroom.
- If age appropriate, allow students to run critique sessions and to feel a sense of ownership over the process.
- Discuss pieces one by one on an overhead projector—look at language, meaning, and overall feeling for each piece.
- Vote on pieces using secret ballots—vote "in," "out," or "shelved."
- Maintain anonymity; only reveal names for those pieces voted "in."
- Inform authors of the status of their pieces.

State Scoring Guides as Rubrics

In developing a rubric for rating student's work, you might take a look at your state's writing scoring guide (if it has one). Teachers and student editors used the Official Oregon State Writing Scoring Guides located at Oregon Public Education Network's website <http://www.open.k12.or.us> for selecting stories and poems that appeared in *Treasures 3*. It is a well-developed rubric that is divided into these writing traits: Ideas and Contents, Organization, Voice, Word Choice, Sentence Fluency, and Conventions.

In the following piece, Matt Cohen, the editor-in-chief of the 1999–2000 edition of *Erehwon,* shares his views about the magazine process and product. He brings us the student perspective, which we want and need to hear. Cohen shares with us the lessons learned and the lifelong impact of his work with *Erehwon.* You get a clear sense of how much this experience meant to him and other students. ■

A STUDENT'S PERSPECTIVE

Matthew Cohen, 17, Winston Churchill High School, Potomac, Maryland

Our magazines have arrived fresh off the presses in large brown boxes. As my classmates and I anxiously tear them open, waiting to see the result of our yearlong project, I am reminded of all the long hours of hard work that it took to produce this year's *Erehwon*.

In each page, I picture the design meetings and the seemingly never-ending afterschool critiques. All the hours of production, during which everyone remained dedicated to ensure that the magazine would continue its tradition of excellence, seem worthwhile when I get my hands on the magazine.

Working on the *Erehwon* and *Polliwog* staffs has been a tremendously gratifying and enriching experience. The individual responsibility of meeting deadlines and fulfilling requirements has taught me a great deal about being organized and staying focused on goals while leading a group of my peers. Working with others on such a creative project has given me the ability to make all the members of the magazine feel that they are making a valuable contribution and that their voices are being heard.

As I view the final magazine that I will be a part of at Winston Churchill High School, I am reminded of how frightening I once found the endeavor of producing one magazine to represent the best our school had to offer. But now, I look back at all the problems that came up along the way and am pleased how as a staff we found innovative solutions that redefined the production process.

It will not only be the magazine, the physical result of our hard work, that I will take with me for the rest of my life, but also the lessons working on the literary magazine staff taught me and the feeling of camaraderie that we created.

Eliot Wigginton, the founder of the Foxfire Fund, and I met after I sent him a copy of *Light of the Island,* a middle school book I had supervised. Learning how his students worked on various aspects of publishing *Foxfire* influenced the way in which I worked with students on publications. Knowing that the *Foxfire* project had changed the lives of thousands of teachers, I wanted to mention the magazine in this book.

In the following article, you will discover that the *Foxfire* process requires many key ingredients, teamwork among them. Team building begins in the summer, bringing together teachers and students who later on in the school year work as a team to solve problems and overcome challenges.

If you have read any of the *Foxfire* magazines or books, you will have read engaging interviews of local Appalachians. Sections of this article provide detailed instructions so that your students can prepare their own questions and conduct interviews of people in their local community. ■

THE FOXFIRE MAGAZINE

Angie Cheek, English Department Chair/Foxfire Facilitator, Rabun County High School, Tiger, Georgia

For two years I was a part of the magazine class, and, as a result, I have experienced all the emotions that go along with it—the tears of angst that come with lost or crashed disks, the frustrations of a computer that just won't cooperate, the nerves before the first interview, the thrill of a good interview, and the incredible pride after seeing your name in print for the first time. Working on the magazine has also given me several opportunities to give presentations about the class at several colleges, universities, and conferences. With each interview and speech, I have gained something that no other class could have given me—the confidence and assurance I needed to go from being the most timid, shy person in my class to being a leader among my peers. The skills and opportunities I have obtained through working for *The Foxfire Magazine* are assets that will help me throughout my life.

Lacy Hunter, former *Foxfire Magazine* student

Evolution of the Magazine

The Foxfire Magazine has evolved as times have changed. Originally, the students solicited donations to publish the first issues; later, the magazine received grants. Today, the magazine budget is based on subscriptions sold and donations received. Gone are the layout boards, unusual size, and one-column format. The students changed the publication (after surveying subscribers and ascertaining their support) to a more modern look. It includes a two-column format, 10½ x 7¾ inches, glossy paper stock, and coffee-table–quality cover photos. While many changes have occurred over the years, one aspect of the magazine that has not changed is the focus on recording and preserving the culture, heritage, and language of the people of the Appalachians.

The Program

The magazine program provides students with many opportunities. The following are our goals:

- to give all students, despite different abilities and interests, the opportunity to discover their rich heritage through connection with their community and its people
- to provide students with the opportunity to learn to use technology and acquire skills necessary for today's workforce

- to help students gain and hone their communication skills (reading, writing, speaking, and listening)
- to provide students with opportunities to develop collaborating, time-managing, decision-making, and problem-solving skills
- to guide students in the acquisition of leadership skills
- to teach the Georgia state curriculum mandates through the production of the magazine

By meeting the demanding publishing schedules of a quality publication with an audience beyond the classroom, intrinsically motivated students learn teamwork as well as self-discipline and responsibility. Students' motivation comes not only from receiving a grade but also from wanting to produce a well-written article about their neighbors, family, or friends. They feel an obligation to do their best for the person featured in the interview, for the readers of the magazine, for themselves, and for the magazine class.

Working as a team, Angie Cheek, an English teacher, and Joyce Green, a business teacher, serve as the magazine facilitators/advisors. Senior editors work closely with the advisors to train, mentor, and guide fellow students. The facilitators design a summer program to train senior editors in leadership, communication, collaboration, and team building, as well as computer and article-production skills. The team of editors, the facilitators, and staff from The Foxfire Fund, Inc., work to become adept at using software programs, discuss and demonstrate aesthetically pleasing layouts, and even face seemingly death-defying feats in completing a team-building ropes course.

Students and facilitators bond into a team. The senior editors use the skills learned during the summer to assist and advise other students, to edit and proof student work, and to help manage the day-to-day activities of the magazine's production. Once other students become accomplished at a skill, they train their peers; some become associate editors and will eventually become senior editors.

Magazine Teams

Students may select Foxfire Magazine/Integrated Business for either a one-hour class or two-hour block. Three teams make up the magazine staff: writing, marketing, and handling subscriptions.

The Writing Staff

Most students are members of the writing staff. They interview, photograph, transcribe, write introductions, crop photos, choose quotes, design article layouts, and proof and edit their articles and those of others. The classroom can be a hectic place at semester's end as the deadline for finished articles approaches. *The Foxfire Magazine* is published twice a year (double issues), with subscribers from all fifty states and numerous foreign countries. Seeing the finished article in print gives students a feeling of elation and a sense of pride.

The Marketing Staff

The marketing staff formulates and implements national and local marketing strategies (often meeting with local marketing experts), creates marketing tools, and works with local businesses to sell the magazine. They design flyers, brochures, posters, displays, and other marketing ploys. They know they have accomplished their goals when they see increased magazine sales.

The Subscription Staff

The subscription team maintains a database to keep current records of subscribers, handles all correspondence and magazine mailings, and works closely with the marketing team to increase subscriptions. Their job also includes handling customer problems, suggestions, and complaints. The team accomplishes its goals when the customer is satisfied.

The Challenges

Facilitators and students work together to create solutions to the magazine's challenges. The most frequent challenges we face are class scheduling, learning how to create a backwards timeline, assessing and evaluating learners' work, and having enough time to accomplish our goals. For many years, the magazine was a fifty-minute period. By the time students readied their equipment to work, the bell would ring, and students would pack up and rush to their next class. The facilitators and students asked the administration for, and received, a block schedule (two periods) as an alternative to the fifty-minute class.

To ensure that students meet deadlines, the facilitators, senior editors, and staff created a magazine timeline with specific assignments that must be completed by a specific date. This timeline helps keep everyone focused on what needs to be accomplished and has resulted in publication deadlines being met ahead of schedule.

The facilitators and senior editors also created a fair assessment tool for evaluating students during grading periods. It lists what is expected of a student during each six-week period. The students know that in order to receive a good grade, they must accomplish the listed goals for that period of time.

Because senior and associate editors are busy helping other students, working on their own articles is sometimes a time challenge, so one outcome of the summer program was the *Foxfire Student Handbook*, which gives step-by-step instructions in the basic skills of magazine production. This handbook is revisited and revised each summer.

To ensure that students and their parents know that the class requirements are rigorous, at the beginning of each semester, the students and parents receive a letter from the facilitators and senior editors delineating what is expected. At the end of the semester, all then know whether or not the student achieved the goals.

Conducting Interviews

If you wish to include *Foxfire*-style interviews in a magazine of your own, you may find helpful the following instructions from the *Foxfire Student Handbook, Foxfire for Dummies.*

Interviewing

Prerequisite: You must already know how to use the microphone, camera, and the tape recorder before you go on your interview.

- After finding an interview topic (one that has not been published in the past five years—different angles are okay), locating an interviewee, and making questions, set up the interview time and date. You must keep up with his/her phone number in case of an emergency (reason to cancel). You must also be sure that your interviewee has the school's telephone number as well as your full name.
- To make yourself aware of your topic, you may go to the library, historic society, chamber of commerce, courthouse, or the *Foxfire* archives. Research information can be used in the article with the proper citation and written permission from the publisher.
- Next, make up a list of questions that are suitable for your topic. DO NOT use words that give you only a short (yes/no) answer. You want the interviewee to talk as much as possible.
- In the days before your interview, make sure you have transportation to the interviewing location. Inform the equipment manager when you will need the proper equipment so he/she can be prepared.
- On the day of your interview, obtain your equipment from the equipment manager. Making sure the equipment works before you leave is your job. Load the film into your camera and take another roll in case you need it. Also, bring two tapes and extra batteries.
- When going out to do an interview, you must have someone with you.

(Note: At least two pictures need to include you with your interviewee—no posing!)

- Take a pencil and paper to write down important facts such as appearance, personality, the surroundings, etc. (This can be used in your introduction.)
- Take your curiosity on the interview. Nothing encourages any of us to talk more than to know that we have an interested listener.
- Let the person talk about what he/she wants to; when the interviewee is finished, you can direct him/her back to your questions.
- Keep in mind the limitation of your equipment. Position the microphone so that it will capture the voice you desire.
- Remember tape recorders capture sound, not gestures. If someone nods his or her head yes, you are not going to get that on tape. It is up to you to translate that gesture into words: "So, it was four feet long?"
- Set up your equipment and begin interviewing. At the beginning of your interview, say the following:

    This is (your name), interviewing (name of interviewee), about (subject), on (date), tape (#).

- If you come up with more questions during interview, USE THEM! By listening to what the interviewee is saying, you can come up with other questions.
- At the end of the interview, turn off the recorder, take some pictures that pertain to the subject, and fill out an interview control sheet. (An interview control sheet aids in archiving materials. Students list important data: names, addresses, dates, interviewers' names, and so on.) When you leave, be sure to thank the interviewee; tell him/her you will call when a copy is ready to be reviewed. The interviewee will need to edit this copy.
- When you return to school, return equipment to the equipment manager. Label your tapes. DO NOT leave tapes or film in the equipment! Continue with the process of following the subsequent steps to completing the article.
- Sometimes you may find that a follow-up interview is necessary to finish the article.
- Thank your interviewee sincerely after any follow-up.
- Get his/her mailing address to send a thank-you note, to send a copy of the finished transcript with a publication release form, and to send copies of the magazine when his/her article is published.
- Make sure he/she completely fills out the publication release form and signs it on the appropriate blank on the bottom. Have a witness's signature.

Preparing Questions

- Ask questions that are appropriate for your topic. Research if necessary (not personality articles because they record the personal history of a contact's life; the contact tells his/her own personal story, and we record it). Come up with at least 10 questions. Do not ask vague questions.

- Use words like *how, tell me,* etc.
- Do not ask yes/no questions.
- Get your questions checked by a senior editor before interviewing.
- Make changes if necessary.

Sample Personality Questions

- Tell me about when you were a child.
- Tell me about your earliest memory.
- Tell me about family life when you were growing up.
- Tell me about things you did for fun when you were a child.
- Tell me about what you did with your parents that you remember best.
- Tell me about times with your parents that you enjoyed the most.
- Tell me about advice or training that your parents gave you that has helped you to lead a better, fuller life.
- Tell me about some examples that your parents set for you.
- Tell me about your social life as a teenager.
- Tell me about when you moved out on your own.
- Tell me about some of the jobs that you've had.
- Tell me about the role religion has played in your life.
- What advice would you give to people today?
- Tell me about what is different from the way it used to be when you were growing up.
- Tell me about the difference in people today from the way they used to be.

A Bit of Advice

Folks across the country have tried to create *Foxfire*-type magazines. They have implemented programs that require products. The best advice we can give is to focus on the process and not the product. The Foxfire process is *not* a product: it is an approach to teaching and learning. Yes, our product is a magazine with deadlines and commitments, but in the hustle and bustle of magazine production we try never to lose sight of why and how we are doing this work.

Plans for the Future

Since future students will have a large voice in how the magazine operates, to imagine how the magazine might change proves difficult. We are constantly evaluating our efforts—what works and what doesn't—and implementing changes. Our immediate plans include contacting all former subscribers and enrolling new ones in the hope of increasing our subscription base. We want to reach our elders and record their stories before it's too late. Furthermore, we have been a laboratory classroom, and several groups of high school and college students, as well as teachers, have visited us. We hope to enlarge this aspect of our program. We also have a dream of purchasing graphic arts equipment so students can print their own magazine. If you dream it and believe it, it can be!

For more info:

During the summer:
The Foxfire Magazine
P.O. Box 541
Mountain City, GA 30562
706-746-5828
Fax: 706-746-5829
<www.foxfire.org>

During the school year:
The Foxfire Magazine
Rabun County High School
230 Wildcat Hill Dr.
Tiger, GA 30576
706-782-6355
Fax: 706-782-0753

3

School Newspapers and Newsmagazines: Tips for Getting the News Out

Today's Fine Student Journalists

It's almost impossible to keep up with breaking news all over the world every second. People often question journalists and wonder just how responsible they are. Yet the profession is in good hands with our young journalists. They take their job seriously, reporting on a wide variety of topics, some school- and community-related. Other articles focus on national and international news.

There are numerous categories in school newspapers and newsmagazines. Students are engaged in writing news, editorials, sports, and features. Personality profiles reveal important people in their lives. Their entertainment reviews cover books, plays, and movies. Columns are devoted to humor, personal experience, sports, and on- and off-campus concerns. Student journalists report on health news and express their opinions on health issues.

Graphics and photographs are equally important in transmitting the news. Black-and-white or color art illustrations and cartoons (e.g., comic, editorial, and sports) are integrated into the text. Photographs and photographic essays accompany articles or stand on their own.

The world of student newspapers offers variety in size and design. You can read newspapers as small as 1–8 pages; others are 9–12 or 13–16 pages while the largest are 17+ pages long. They come in the forms of tabloids, broadsheets, and newsmagazines. Some school newspapers publish magazine supplements. More and more online versions are displayed daily, weekly, or monthly.

After reading the following piece by Katia Fedorova, a young Russian journalist, I was immediately struck by the notion that an American student might well have written similar feelings and thoughts about the subject. Yes, her voice is her own, but she touches upon such universals as communicating to the readers, the planning process, constant revisions, and the reward of seeing and reading one's words in print. When Fedorova writes, she speaks so well for many of her peers around the world, and you can't help but listen. ■

The Pangs of Creation

Katia Fedorova, 17, Practice-Educational Complex 18-13, Moscow, Russia, Student of Tatjana Gorshina, English Language Teacher

I have always been attracted by such professions (jobs) in which one can show one's abilities and state one's attitude towards life and people. Journalism, I think, is a whole world where each of us finds a place for oneself. We are all different in our positions, thoughts, and emotions. People's relationships vary. It is important to understand the laws that govern relationships, to see the truth, to grab the idea and carry it across to the reader. It is a very hard and a very important task. In order to become a good journalist, one has to study a lot.

My first attempt occurred when I was twelve. Before that, I'd never even thought that it was so difficult. My first thought had been, "How should I begin?" I couldn't sleep. Gradually, my thoughts began to arrange themselves into a logical chain, to shape them into words.

A good beginning is a guarantee of success. When you finish the last sentence, you think, "Shall I reread it or not?" When you see that you have used the same word in five consecutive sentences, you feel sad. Having reread your writing two or three times and having corrected everything you could, you take it to the school newspaper. The editor-in-chief is sure to find some stylistic inaccuracies. You listen to all his remarks, and your brain keeps working feverishly. "Why didn't I notice all of that myself?"

Finally, it's over. The school newspaper is out—that's your best reward. There are lots of materials in it, but you find your own quickly. Your article looks much more beautiful and intelligent in a newspaper. You can't believe it's the same article that gave you so much suffering. If you ask me why one should spend so much time and effort on writing, I'll give you a confident answer. "I like to feel those pangs of creation; I like to meet interesting people and tell about them in my beloved newspaper."

When planning a school or community newspaper, you want to consider certain general questions. Joe Brooks, a member of the teaching staff for the *Guilford Gazette,* lists key questions and includes pertinent, helpful tips about some of the questions to give you better understanding as you begin your own paper. For example, after the question, "How many issues do you want to publish per year?" he notes that newspapers do not have to be published daily or even weekly. Brooks points out that the *Gazette* is published three times a year.

As this publication has evolved, critical components stand out, and he provides a list of them, many of which will be key in any student-run newspaper. Pertinent information explains in depth their student training, orientation, newspaper staff meetings, and weekly reflection activities. ■

KEY TO OUR SURVIVAL

Joe Brooks, Guilford Central School/Community Coordinator,
Guilford Central School, Guilford, Vermont

The *Guilford Gazette*

The *Guilford Gazette* serves a population of more than 1,900 people in rural Guilford, Vermont. Adult advisors include a community member and a diverse team of teachers who work with the middle school student staff.

Here are a series of questions, ideas, and comments that we have developed to share with schools who are considering starting up community newspapers:

Starting a Newspaper: Ideas to Consider
- Are you interested in starting a school newspaper or a town newspaper? Students can learn a lot from either experience. A town newspaper is more ambitious but produces larger rewards (for the school, the town, and the students) in the long run.
- How many issues do you want to publish per year? Calling it a "newspaper" doesn't mean it is published daily or even weekly! We publish the *Guilford Gazette* three times a year!
- What kind of support can you count on from your school administration? Administrative support is very important and may have to be built gradually if it is not already there.
- What age group/grade will publish the paper?
- Which standards does your school curriculum focus on for that age group/grade?
- Do you have regular school volunteers? Would they be willing to help on a regular basis? What skills do they have (e.g., writing, editing, publishing experience, patience, typing skills, community awareness, connection to community)?
- Are there other people/organizations in your community that you could

approach for help (e.g., printers, newspaper editors, community groups, senior volunteers)?

- Think about how large a part of the curriculum you would like the newspaper to occupy eventually. Journalism is a great way to teach writing skills, editing, grammar, vocabulary, spelling, computer skills, current events, and other topics.
- The entire school could eventually become involved. Different grades/age groups could be responsible for stories, artwork, photos, folding, and collating, and so on.
- How will you involve the students in the process of decision making (about whether to publish, what to publish, how the paper will look, etc.)?
- How will newspaper skills be taught—through regular class work and curriculum, through special minilessons, by inviting outside experience into the classroom, or . . . ?
- How will the students' work be credited and assessed (report card grades, written feedback)? Who will do the assessment (teachers, volunteers, peers, reflective self-assessment by students)?

Survival

One thing the *Gazette* has going for it at this point is that it is a given for our school. This helps us do whatever it takes to make it work. It is critical for an activity like ours to have a partnership of teachers and/or community volunteers involved to share the load and offer the opportunity of dialogue and perspective around what is happening with students. Hard work and patience with a long-term view of growth is an important part of success. It takes complete commitment on the part of adults and students.

We have gotten a wonderful response from teachers with whom we have shared the *Gazette* at conferences and workshops. We have never advocated imitating what we have been trying to do in more than such general terms as sharing our school's approach to community-based or service learning and trying to show where the *Gazette* fits in that schematic.

Gazette Curriculum Components and Supports

In order that the *Gazette* survive, we have identified and put the following pieces in place:

- written policies addressing work accommodations, student contracts, and so on

- job application and orientation procedures
- student contracts (signed by parents, teachers, and any others, if necessary)
- clear definition of advisors' role
- written job descriptions for various departments (e.g., editors, business)
- school-year publication schedule
- clear process for student decision making (staff meeting protocol)
- structured student reflection component every week, plus eight extended sessions
- minilesson approach to teaching publishing-oriented skills
- written assessment that responds to student self-assessment
- letter grades, corresponding to school academic policies
- inclusion of the *Gazette* in school reporting and orientations
- regular paid planning time for advisors

Some of the components are discussed in greater detail.

Job Application and Orientation Procedures

Each fall at the beginning of school, students apply for a variety of *Gazette* positions. The advisors review these and try to match interests and experience.

A new production assistant will be trained by the production manager, who is usually a returnee from the previous year. This works a little better each year. The same process is used with editors and especially with our business and advertising department. Generally, students get the jobs they want. We ask applicants to tell us why they want to work for the *Gazette*, what they have to offer, and why they think that the *Gazette* is important to the community. We encourage a year's commitment, unless it really does not work out. We also have students, parents, and teachers sign a contract of commitment. Most students stay with us. We have a process for entering and exiting during the year.

Orientation is conducted jointly by advisors and by returning staff. Orientation includes information about policies, editorial, formatting, computer procedures, classroom exemptions, and so on.

Clear Process for Student Decision Making (Staff Meeting Protocol)

We use Roberts Rules of Order to conduct staff meetings each week. That is how we begin *Gazette* sessions. Anyone can add an item to the agenda, and minutes are kept and read. Students take turns doing minutes and facilitating the meeting. Other decisions are made by consensus in various departments. If an issue is larger, it is brought to the whole staff for discussion and approval. One issue was whether the *Gazette* should participate in a fundraiser with McDonald's. After lengthy

Figure 3–1. *Guilford Gazette* reporter interviews local farmer Bob Gaines, who owns the oldest land grant in Vermont. Photograph by Allen Gilbert.

discussion and debate, the students actually decided that the McDonald's deal did not include enough benefit for the *Gazette*. The motion was voted down.

The advisors vote, too. One person, one vote. This is not to say that advisors don't step in when needed. But we adhere to the notion that we are, in *Foxfire* language, "guides on the side."

Structured Student Reflection Component

The advisors step out of role about once each month to conduct a reflection activity. We use a series of questions that address learning and enjoyment of each person's role. The advisors also participate in sustained reflection writing for twenty minutes or so. In addition, each student has a *Gazette* binder containing a calendar, policies, contract, and other information related to his or her job (provided by advisors at the beginning of the year). In this binder is a setup for weekly reflection. We try very hard to have everyone reflect on what we have done, learned, and need to do.

Emily Coutant, a regular contributor, wrote the following piece for the *Gazette* while working on a local farm. She wonderfully captures the feeling of hard work and sometimes magic involved in a dairy farmer's everyday life. She does this, of course, through the eyes of an adolescent, which makes her work all the more special in these days of fast-paced lifestyles and media-saturated young people. Emily has always had a gift for writing, but I think this piece remains somewhat unique and quite special for those of us at Guilford Central School.

—Joe Brooks ∎

DOWN AT THE FRANKLIN FARM

Emily Coutant, 13, Guilford Central School, Guilford, Vermont

I remember walking into the milking barn in full swing. The steady buzz of the milking machines and the hokey twang of the country and western station comforted me. David Franklin and some of his buddies were standing in a circle gossiping. David handed me a coarse, stiff paper towel. He asked me to wipe a cow. Wiping means getting the manure and dirt off the teat. Wiping also involves stripping. Stripping means squirting some milk out by hand so the cow knows she will be milked soon. She can then let down her milk.

"Oh gosh, I can't do this. It's hard. I'm going to look like an idiot in front of all his friends," I thought. I bit my lip, squeezed the teat, and prayed. My freezing hands shook with embarrassment. All of a sudden, I felt something warm trickling down my numb, red fingers. Could it be? I looked with wide eyes and the milk was flowing in a steady stream. I wanted to holler, to draw attention to myself. That moment was my first victory in the barn.

Since that day in October, I've become a part of the amazing Franklin Farm. On a typical day at the farm, I drop my bag and my whole school identity. I become a smelly barn girl. Like Superman, I slip into my red and blue coveralls, my red boots, my fuzzy green gloves, my neckwarmer, and hat.

I march into the milking barn and herd the cows into the barn and their stanchions. Some of them need you to guide them into their stalls with a "dainty" tap.

Then I drag the wheelbarrow out to the bunk to get bunk mix for the young heifers. Bunk mix is a combination of haylage and silage. It smells like sour salad dressing. I spread the bunk mix around their feeding place. The young heifers don't like to be seen eating, so they wait until I'm out of sight.

Next I heat the milk for the calves or hutch babies. I pour four scoops of milk into a bucket and put it into a bigger bucket of hot water. After that, I give grain to some older heifers. When they see me coming, they get all rambunctious and start jumping around. They're not shy at all about eating. They fly right in.

The fresh cows need to have their stalls bedded and must be fed hay. They sway their heads from side to side as if to say, "I hate being pregnant. Get me out of here!"

The older heifers need bunk mix and bedding. They're pushy and they talk back like ninth-grade girls. The next and last of my chores is the calves. They are all old enough to drink warm milk out of a bucket. When they see me coming, they start to chirp like toddlers saying, "I want it. Gimmee milk." After I feed them, they suck on the bars of their hutches. Sometimes I let them lick my salty hand.

On Fridays, I stay late to help Asa, one of my barn friends, finish the milking. We chat about music and snowboarding while floating around the barn, wiping, milking, and dipping cows.

You've never seen teamwork 'til you've been at the Franklin Farm. David and Mary Ellen Franklin keep the whole system going. They work things out even if it's hailing dinosaurs. While I'm busy with my chores, John and his twin brothers, Neil and Paul, are tearing around the barn on their tricycles, laughing. Half a dozen barn cats huddle together on their crate waiting for a plump barn rat to scurry by. David or Mary Ellen work through their milking pattern. They have to concentrate on their task.

Lots of kids hang out and help at the Franklin Farm because they're such a happy family. There are always projects to complete. David and Mary Ellen always say, "Well . . . what will our strategy be tonight?"

I wanted to work at the Franklin Farm because I saw how healthy, strong, and content the Franklins are. I thought that I was everything but that. Being at the farm has taught me alertness, responsibility, and to expect the unexpected. It also feels great to be needed. Once two unmilked cows made a run for it. I was at the bunk. Mary Ellen was yelling, "Cows are running out the other side of the pole barn. Emily, where are you?" I got this surge of adrenaline and galloped down to head them off. Mary Ellen was shouting, "Perfect, perfect, that's just perfect!"

It was also perfect the night the calf was born right in front of me. The cow, #11, was wide eyed and breathing heavily. After a while I saw two perfect hooves shoot out, then a nose. I was cheering her on, "Go, 11, just a little bit more!" The calf looked like a perfect little diver riding a wave into life. What can I say? The barn is my connection to the real ways of the world.

Mark Levin asks the same question teachers ask the first time they turn the reins over to the students. "Can they really do it?" You'll find out how he and his students did as Levin takes us through his journey in transforming his newspaper from a teacher-centered to a student-centered publication. He tells you how he prepared himself and them for this monumental change each step of the way. Throughout the process, Levin manages to keep his sense of humor and not take himself so seriously. It's clear why students would have fun working with such a teacher. After "walking" with him, you'll not only know that his students successfully ran their newspaper, but also discover how your students can, too.

If you're interested in learning more, you can check out his website: National Elementary Schools Press Association <http://www.nespa.org>. ■

PUTTING STUDENTS IN CHARGE

Mark Levin, Director of the National Elementary Schools Press Association (NESPA) and Teacher, Carolina Day School, Asheville, North Carolina

I didn't think they could do it. I didn't really believe my students would be able to publish a twenty-four-page newspaper on their own. After all, I was used to perfection (well, maybe near-perfection) and I hated to see that compromised—even if that meant I did most of the work. My students eventually came to change my way of thinking and proved that they could give new meaning to real-world learning experiences. And in that process my students came to earn my respect for being more-than-capable kids.

The idea to start a class newspaper was borne out of a desire to put some excitement into the writing component of my fifth-grade language arts curriculum. I decided that having a school newspaper would make writing more educationally meaningful *and* fun for my students. I was definitely right on that account. But I knew that ten- and eleven-year-olds would not be capable of publishing the paper on their own. In fact, I would be happy and satisfied to just have them turn in their articles on time. My expectations were lower than their collective desires to be real-world publishers.

The kids were excited about writing and I was pleased that some of them turned in articles, and generally on time. I figured that was indeed a real-world learning experience right there. I accepted whatever they gave me, took their articles home (almost always handwritten), and spent entire weekends editing, proofing, and laying out the newspaper. When I was finished, the paper went to the printers and *Carolina Kids' News* made its debut. We were all excited to see that first issue arrive, and I was pleased that "we" had somehow managed to publish a perfect paper.

Perfect It Wasn't

It was perfect if one counts perfection as error-free. But something was missing from our experience—the students. I had taken over the roles of typist, editor, proofreader, layout artist, photographer, and publisher. While we were all proud of that first issue, and all the subsequent issues published that year; it was my wife who suggested "Maybe, just possibly, couldn't the kids do it themselves?" My gut reaction was an emphatic "No." Then wishful thinking started to enter my mind. I contemplated freeing up those weekends for ourselves. The idea of students doing it all became appealing. I still didn't know how they would manage, or believe that they could.

Unveiling the "New" Plan

The students were excited about the new plan, but hardly ecstatic. And I'm sure there were more than a few skeptics in the group. After all, it meant more work for them. I explained that with this extra effort on their parts would come extra *honor and glory* that they would truly deserve. It only took one pep talk to get them pumped and ready for the new era. They came to like, then love, the new plan.

The first step in transforming our newspaper from a teacher-centered to student-centered publication was to practice what I had been preaching. I had often mentioned to my young charges how newspapers lived by a stylebook, but there really hadn't been a need to develop one since I took care of any style issues as I typed the paper. Now it was time to rethink the whole process, and in that process, learn just how capable students could be.

I developed our newspaper's first stylebook, or actually a style sheet. I came up with style rules the students would use to help as they themselves typed the articles. But this was only the beginning. I decided that the students would not only type, but lay out the pages as well. Our style sheet dictated things such as:

- what fonts to use for story copy, headlines, and captions
- which point sizes to use
- margins (all sides, plus space between columns)
- how we would list titles of books, movies, etc.
- how teachers would be listed

and just about every other formatting situation I could think of, including placement of page numbers and section titles.

Much to Learn

Unveiling a style sheet was the easy part. Teaching my students how to use a desktop publishing program was a little harder. But they were eager learners and ready to try anything. They learned how to draw text blocks, insert clip art, apply text wrap, add captions, rotate text, and type. My students all had some keyboarding experience, but typing still remained a weakness. Even to this day, while typing speed has improved as students become more efficient at keyboarding each year, it's still the only thing that slows down the process. Over time, everything else becomes second nature to my young journalists.

Completing the Picture

I still had to decide how to get the whole paper to come together as one. The answer for us was to assign two students per page and have them be completely responsible for turning in a camera-ready page. After receiving their "beat assignments," they would be completely free to develop their page. The style sheet would help guide them in using the same design elements on each page. The page layouts would then appear to have been completed by a single individual rather than an entire class working as one. The plan worked, and the beginning of our transformation was a success.

Students will always need some direction and constant monitoring. They aren't used to being in charge and making most of the decisions. Occasionally I would find myself settling problems that would have been best solved by the student staff as a group or by my student editors. As a teacher/advisor, I learned to step in when needed and step back whenever possible. Over the years of using our "new method," I've had some editors who would amaze even me and others who had limited leadership abilities. But everyone learns from experience, including teachers. Let students learn from their mistakes. It makes for a better learning experience.

Becoming a True Real-World Experience

My students were now publishing a real newspaper on their own, but there was still one more bit of responsibility I had yet to give up: the administration aspect of the publishing process. We had always had student editors, but their roles had been more as figureheads than as working editors. I decided to turn over the entire newspaper operation to students and I would serve only as advisor, a respected term familiar to high school journalism classes across the nation. I would be the one who would have to get used to this backseat role. Understand that there still remains much

Figure 3–2. Senior editor shows fifth-grade student photographers how to use the newspaper's new digital camera. Photograph by Mark Levin.

for the advisor to teach, and there always will be, but the first step is a willingness to let students learn by doing.

Sure, there might be mistakes. All papers have them—even those put out by the professionals. But we learn from our mistakes and strive to try harder the next time. With newspaper publishing, there will always be another chance to improve. And besides, as famous publisher William Randolph Hearst once said, "Don't be afraid to make a mistake, your readers might like it."

Everyone Has a Job

On the new *Carolina Kids' News*, everyone has the most important job of any newspaper—that of reporter. Every student in the class has at least one article in every issue of our newspaper. They work by themselves, with other students, and with student editors to do everything they can to see that their individual articles are perfect. They also have the second job of layout artist, because each pair of students is responsible for completing a camera-ready page. But there are other job possibilities open for those students ready and willing to take on more of a leadership role.

Editors are important in all publications, and my students volunteer for this position with gusto. The job could become overwhelming, and sometimes does—but we divide and conquer by having four editors per issue and each editor responsible for one-fourth of the newspaper. Though all students help peer edit each other's articles, the editors help with additional editing. The editors have quite a bit of autonomy. They help settle disputes, decide on article importance and headline point-size assignment, and make lots of other real-world decisions. When I find a particularly adept editor or editors, I'll ask that person or persons to remain on throughout the year as senior editor(s). It's quite an honor. The regular issue editors usually change with each issue.

We have other jobs that are very important to our total operation. The business managers are in charge of our finances. The school provides about 75 percent of the paper's funding, and we have to raise the other funds ourselves. The business managers raise money by sending out letters soliciting underwriting and then keeping accurate records when money does come in. They send thank-you letters to the donors and make sure that all underwriters are listed correctly in each issue of our paper. The business managers also keep a simple ledger showing newspaper income and expenses throughout the year.

Circulation managers have several duties. Their year starts by sending letters to parents inviting them to sign up grandparents and other relatives as subscribers. All families in our school, as well as staff, receive each issue for free. But other relatives and friends can sign up for a nominal subscription fee that includes delivery by first-class mail. As subscribers send in their forms, the circulation managers add the names to our subscriber database to help in printing mailing labels later.

The real work for the circulation managers starts the minute the newspaper arrives from the printer. These students divide the rest of the class into a delivery team to rush the class sets of the paper to each teacher. They also deliver a copy to each of the staff mailboxes and get the envelopes ready for subscribers. In addition to mailing issues out to subscribers, we also participate in a newspaper exchange with about twenty-five schools across the nation. Students are responsible for seeing that these papers get mailed as well.

It seems that I always have 90 percent of the class wanting to be a photographer, and we make that possible by choosing four students to serve as head photographers. I give them basic (very basic) training in the use of our cameras, including a ten-minute course in composition. The composition hints I teach include: come in close, watch for distracting backgrounds, and don't shoot directly into glass or other reflective surfaces. Our photos will never win the Pulitzer Prize, but they do serve the purpose of making the newspaper and news articles more interesting and real.

Then, when photo time comes, either the head photographers take the pictures or they train the reporter to take his or her own photographs. We generally use a Polaroid camera for our photos so we know instantly if the picture is truly worth a thousand words.

A Real-World Activity at Last

We've come full circle from my first days a decade ago as a teacher-turned-publisher. I've seen my classes of young writers become journalists and business executives. They've learned how to manage the business of publishing in spite of me or because of me. Every year they impress me, others at our school, and their parents. I take pride in being able to say, "They did it themselves." It's a wonderful feeling to be able to turn over the work to such capable students—knowing that the work will get done. Ten years later, I still have my weekends free. (Well, at least free from newspaper work.)

In a Nutshell

To summarize, here's a list of the steps I would use to help streamline the process of putting students in charge. You should be familiar with all the steps you wish to use before unveiling them. Your students will be quick to learn, you need to be quick to teach.

1. Develop a master plan for your newspaper. Decide just what and how much you wish to teach. This will include: headline writing, article development, interviewing techniques and etiquette, and so on.
2. Develop an "Earning Your Credentials" list. Here you can have a master checklist of all those items you want to cover in the early stages of your newspaper's organization each year. Once my students have learned most of the items on this list, they're ready to receive their press badges.
3. Have students apply for various "administrative" positions, including: editor(s), business managers, circulation managers, staff artists, photographers, or reporters covering specialized beats such as sports or entertainment reviews. Plan some training for each of these positions.
4. Develop a style sheet for your students' use. Teach the material it covers to your student staff and make sure they understand the importance of following it.
5. Teach the basics of desktop publishing so that your students understand how page layout comes together. Students should know how to create text

blocks, add graphics, move objects around, apply text wrap, and resize everything to fit their allotted space.

6. Have a staff meeting to pick and/or assign articles.
7. Get started.

I'll tell you right now that none of this is going to be easy. Starting and maintaining a class or school newspaper could be one of the most challenging jobs you'll ever volunteer for. It could also be the most satisfying. You'll find your students asking, "Can I have a whole page?" instead of "How long does this *have* to be?" Now that's an educational breakthrough!

Don't get discouraged. Publishing a student newspaper, regardless of size, takes lots of time and effort. You and your students will find ways to make each issue better. By putting your students in charge you'll be able to accomplish most of this during class time. And it will be meaningful instruction. Students will come to learn how important their jobs are and that it takes teamwork to put out a paper. They will be learning real-world skills.

Your students will beam with pride every time a new issue hits the newsstands. Younger students will be clamoring to get signed up for the next year. And you'll be able to sit back and say with pride, "We did it!"

Believe me, it will happen.

Happy publishing.

Student editors who work with computers have dozens of typefaces available to them. They need to know and learn how to use them effectively. Denise M. Reagan's article lists essential tips that are useful for upper elementary students, middle schoolers, and high schoolers working on newspapers, books, and magazines. While most high school student editors will be able to understand her guidelines, younger students will benefit from their teachers' instruction and assistance.

One of her points, "Get to Know Your Faces," was the first item I covered and explored with a group of fourth and fifth graders working on book design and layout. In doing so, I provided them with plenty of actual examples of typefaces. We spent hours examining sans serif and serif typefaces in printed matter, mostly books. After trying out various typefaces, we selected the serif typeface for our class book.

Every tidbit of advice in "Type: Doing It Right" is accompanied by Reagan's equally helpful observations, suggestions, and questions. As you and your students follow her advice, you will be well on your way to selecting a type that will fit the nature and personality of your publication. You will then design each page with spacing that makes the text legible and is easy on the eyes. The look and feel of your student publication will bear your personal stamp. ∎

TYPE: DOING IT RIGHT

Denise M. Reagan, Designer,
Minneapolis Star Tribune, **Minneapolis, Minnesota**

Please the Reader's Eye

Limit Your Typefaces

Pick two or three type families (consisting of all the weights and styles of a type-face) and stick with them to develop an identity for your paper. This also forces you to be creative and not to rely on gimmicky fonts for variety. Once you truly know a typeface, you can use it at its optimal strength.

Use combinations of these families in different weights and sizes for body copy, bylines, cutlines,[1] photo credits, quotes, pull-outs,[2] and other displays type treatments.

Get to Know Your Faces

Print out typefaces in all kinds of combinations and sizes and study them. How do the letters relate to each other? How are the serifs shaped? Notice the thick and thin parts of each letter. What do the lowercase letters look like? The capital letters? The punctuation marks? How do the letters change with each weight (light, book, roman, bold, and extra bold are all weights of a typeface)? What does it look like in italic? How about when you increase the point size?

Even if your publication already has its typefaces in place and no plans to redesign, you should still examine the typefaces.

Play with Your Faces' Cases

Think about the shapes of letters in both upper- and lowercase. Does it make aesthetic sense to use a capital letter where a lowercase one would normally go? How about all uppercase letters? Warning: These kinds of combinations can be tricky and sometimes become illegible.

Headlines

Know what the headline will say before you design the page. Do not design a page and leave a space for a headline that will come later. A good headline will marry the story and the image. Read the story yourself to assess its tone, and recognize

---

1. A cutline or caption is the type that explains what is happening and identifies the subjects in the accompanying photo.

2. A pull-out is any information pulled from the story or additional information that could be printed at a larger size or in bolder type to highlight its importance and help create a point of entry into the page.

the visual cues the photo or illustration provides (often the headline type itself could be used to create an image). Avoid overusing puns.

Kerning and Tracking

Kerning is altering the fit of certain letter combinations so that the limb of one character projects over or under the body or limb of another, or so that parts of letters don't touch. Tracking is adjusting the letterspacing and word spacing of a range of characters. Kerning and tracking can help you adjust awkward spacing between letters, especially at larger point sizes. Both PageMaker and QuarkXPress have tools for custom tracking and kerning of type.

Leading

Vary the vertical distance between lines of type to create a texture on your pages. Extra leading can create a quieter, stylish, or classy look.

Avoid Bad Breaks and Widows

Breaking words at the end of a line in display type (headlines, subheads, or anything besides body text) is usually unacceptable. Also avoid awkward phrasing caused by line breaks in headlines—reword them or force returns to get them to flow the way you want. Sometimes, however, you might break a word on purpose to create an effect. A widow occurs when the final line of a paragraph appears at the top of the next column. Avoid these at all costs, especially if the widow is a syllable of a paragraph's last word.

Use White Space

Give readers areas to rest their eyes, to pause between stories or thoughts. White space can create drama and can help balance a page. Lack of white space creates tension. The presence of white space imparts a relaxed, almost tranquil feeling. Miniature components of white space, such as paragraph indentations, leading, or vertical column space are powerful in their repetitiveness. Dynamic headlines, photos, and illustrations benefit from liberal white space around them. But even the most generous use of white space will only magnify a feeling of dullness if there is nothing to contrast it. Watch out for trapped white space.[3] It will segregate elements, making them appear disjointed.

---

3. Trapped white space occurs when elements on a page are arranged awkwardly, leaving a large area of dead space toward the center of the page. White space is crucial to a page to aid in organization and readability, but it must be balanced throughout the page.

In his essay, Harold "Butch" Beedle shows how interdisciplinary education plays a role in publication. His students' *Tropical Tribune* newspaper is a perfect model. He makes it easy to see how other teachers and their students can publish newspapers based on their own interdisciplinary themes.

Beedle takes us through the seven steps he and his students use in making their newspaper: teaching the background material, researching, writing, proofing, laying out, printing, and distributing.

When his students are engaged in the writing process, they learn how to ask questions and try to find answers. Beedle discusses how his students research and interview such newsmakers as authors, filmmakers, and TV hosts. Along with developing solid articles, students want to inform readers and move them to act so that other schools will become involved in environmental issues like saving the rain forests.

When students are given such an opportunity, they make changes not only for themselves but also for others. ∎

The Tropical Tribune:
An Interdisciplinary Unit on Rain Forests

Harold "Butch" Beedle, Sixth-Grade Teacher,
J. C. McKenna Middle School, Evansville, Wisconsin

In 1988, when sixth-grade students at J. C. McKenna Middle School wanted to buy acres of rain forest, their teachers created a unit about rain forests to accommodate their interests. Four years later, the teachers added a newspaper project to the unit to enable the students to practice a multitude of journalism and writing skills and to inform others about tropical rain forests. Since its inception, the *Tropical Tribune* has grown into a nationally recognized student newspaper, and thousands of copies are used by students and teachers in all fifty states and as many as nineteen countries.

Many schools are examining the role of interdisciplinary or integrated education. Interdisciplinary education is an instructional process that connects all the fragmented subjects into a cohesive unit, curriculum, or theme. Environmental topics, like the rain forest, are natural topics for interdisciplinary units. They comprise high student interest, current events, civic responsibility, science, math, and a host of research, language arts, reading, and higher-order thinking skills.

Many interdisciplinary programs suggest a culminating activity that gives the students the opportunity to demonstrate what they have learned or to act positively on their new knowledge. Publishing a student-created newspaper has proved to be an excellent culminating activity. Newspapers are wonderful vehicles for putting writing and research skills to use.

Writing for an audience teaches the students to be precise and clear. They must look for main ideas in the *who, what, where, when,* and *how* of a story. Their writing must incorporate proper grammar, thorough research, and a well-developed understanding of the material if they expect others to understand and use their articles. Writing for others gives students an opportunity to use their skills and share their knowledge in a realistic and meaningful way. Students will work tremendously hard on a project they believe is important and that is of their own creation, rather than a workbook-driven lesson. Brad Sigmund said, "When I looked at the finished product, I realized it wasn't just a newspaper, it was OUR newspaper."

A newspaper could be used as a culminating activity at the end of any unit. There are endless topics, themes, and ways a newspaper can be created. Each would be unique to the interests of the school and resources available. Through the years of trial and error, we have learned a few lessons that could help others develop an interdisciplinary newspaper.

The most important lesson is to keep it simple. Try to break down the procedures into their simplest forms. We generally use seven steps in creating the newspaper. Sequentially, they are the teaching of the background material, researching, writing, proofing, laying out, printing, and mailing or distributing. The process described here is used at J. C. McKenna and is specific to our needs, schedule, and abilities. It may not pertain exactly to other schools, but you should be able to find enough information here that you can begin to create your own individual class newspaper.

Background and Research

An in-depth background is essential to creating a high-quality newspaper. To lay this foundation, we use a multidisciplinary approach with our sixth-grade classes. In an extensive unit on rain forests that incorporates social studies and science, students learn about ecological features of the forest, biodiversity, food chains, animal classifications, pollination, seed dispersal, indigenous people, and the issues facing tropical rain forests and the people who inhabit them. At the same time, in reading and language arts classes, students learn about the sections of a newspaper—such as editorial, news, features, entertainment—and practice the different writing styles needed for each.

During the unit, students are expected to take notes about what they are learning in class. We emphasize that journalists must have accurate and reliable notes on which to base their stories. In this way, the skill of note taking becomes relevant and students pay closer attention to it.

After the unit is taught, the students sift through their notes, looking for topics they believe would make interesting stories. The story ideas come from lectures, videos, guest speakers, slides, books, class discussion, and current events. Each social studies class brainstorms a list of potential topics; the classes' lists are combined into a master list for the entire grade to use.

At this point, one day is block-scheduled for the entire grade (approximately a hundred students). Based on their previously stated interests, the students are divided into four groups for researching and writing the four main sections of the newspaper: news, features, entertainment, and editorial. Each group is assisted by a core teacher and, if possible, at least one parent or community volunteer. These groups begin by prioritizing the suggested story ideas on the master list. They assign themselves stories.

The rest of the day is used for the important work of researching and writing the rough draft. To facilitate this, the staff assembles all of our resources into one central location. These resources include all the relevant school library materials and a vast number of books, magazines, videos, and articles that the staff has collected over the years. We currently have more than one hundred files on topics such as medicinal plants, mammals of the rain forest, logging, and indigenous people. Putting all of these resources in one spot speeds up the research and allows teachers to better assist and monitor the students' progress.

Interviewing the Newsmakers

In order to keep our readers current on important rain forest events, we, like most newspapers, try to interview the newsmakers themselves rather than rely only on information from books or magazines. A priority for our staff has been finding scientists, environmentalists, authors, businesspeople, and adventurers for our students to interview. Recently, for example, the students interviewed Mark Plotkin, author of *Tales of a Shaman's Apprentice*; Dan Janzen from the Institute of Biodiversity; TV host Jack Hanna; Judy Kimerling, author of *Amazon Crude*; Joe Kane, author of *Savages* and *Running the Amazon*; undercover fish and wildlife agents; and Neil Rettig, a *National Geographic* author and filmmaker. Contacts like these have often proved to be so exciting and educational that the whole sixth grade takes time to learn about these people and their work. "I got a whole different view than just reading a book. I got to know for sure what was happening," Gina Kaiser proclaimed.

Most interviews are done by telephone, and we have learned to use speakerphones and tape all the interviews. This way, students find it easier to listen and think of follow-up questions rather than madly try to write notes while the person is talking.

A new and rich source of information is the Internet. Most major rain forest organizations maintain a website, posting information about rain forests and current events. There are also listservs on particular topics that will send regular updates to anyone who wishes to receive them. These sources can keep students as current as the mainstream press. The advance of telecommunications also makes it possible to conduct electronic interviews with people far away. Recently we interviewed author Mike Tidwell about his book *Amazon Stranger* while he was living in Kyrgyztan. E-mail interviews also have one distinct advantage: they give students a written transcript to work with.

We found that the academic staff of universities, museums, and zoos are also eager to share their expertise. Many are willing to come to school, show slides, and visit with our students free of charge. The teachers make these visits into a mock press conference. The students listen to the presentation, ask questions, gather notes, and write a practice article with direct quotes. This is an excellent opportunity to fine-tune their writing skills. The students have found it invaluable to listen to visitors describing their work with Amazon river dolphins, mountain gorillas, Yanomamo Indians, howler monkeys, and valuable tropical plants. By learning from actual frontline experts, students see firsthand that real people are working to make the world a better place.

Some of these encounters have also led to exciting side projects. We now keep in contact with researchers in Belize, Peru, and Ecuador. One scientist in Belize, known as our "adopted scientist," writes letters to us each year explaining her research and problems she has encountered. She usually creates a special problem for the students to solve each year. In response, our students have gathered much-needed school supplies for her to distribute to rain forest schools. Some students now have pen pals in Belize.

Not to be forgotten are the environmental groups that focus on rain forest issues. Besides sharing information, they often offer programs that encourage school participation. One important function of our newspaper is to share the work these groups are doing and to show ways schools can get involved. Sharing this information with other students through a newspaper serves two purposes. It shows once again that people are aggressively and conscientiously working to solve environmental problems, and it may encourage others to get involved with an environmental group's project. The director of a project helping the Yanomamo Indians in Venezuela reported receiving over $1,000 in donations after we ran a story about his school in Maine that was helping to buy medical supplies for the Yanomamo.

Finding an ever changing pool of adults willing to be interviewed by a student newspaper can be challenging. One method we use is to distribute extra copies of the *Tropical Tribune* to groups or individuals that we might want to use as a resource

Figure 3–3. These sixth-grade students still use the labor-intensive method of laying out the *Tropical Tribune*. The student on the left is using a waxer to apply a thin coating of wax to the back of a typed article. The students on the right are responsible for the page layouts. The waxed articles can be easily placed and moved as the students build the paper. The light box allows them to see the blue grid lines on the paper through the article and line up the items accurately. Photograph by Harold "Butch" Beedle.

in the future. After seeing an issue, many of them enthusiastically embrace the goals of the newspaper and want to become involved. Of course, it doesn't hurt that we are often promoting issues important to them and to an audience that they might want to reach. These contacts have developed into some interesting working relationships between our school and many other schools, organizations, scientists, and environmentalists.

Kimberly Beedle recalls, "One special moment I had with the *Tropical Tribune* was when my dad took me to listen to a speaker that wrote a book about her life in the rain forest. Her name is Dr. Linnea Smith. She is an American doctor in the jungle of Peru. I got a book signed by her and shook her hand. It turned out I wrote a story about her for the paper. We sent her a paper in Peru. She e-mailed us and said she liked the story. Now we e-mail back and forth."

Organizing the Research

When students are finished gathering information and taking notes, they complete a web that serves as a graphic organizer of their main ideas. Then they use the web to create an outline, and beyond that, a rough draft of their story. Once a student has written a rough draft, she submits it to be proofread and edited by her peers using editing techniques they learn in class. Thus begins the process of refinement and improvement that middle school students hate, but which is essential to their success. Only after their work has been proofread and corrected can students type the piece on a computer. Then the students work individually with a teacher to do the final edit of their stories on the computer.

A newspaper is a collective effort of many individual talents. Producing a paper involves variety of skills, including writing, editing, proofreading, photographing, word processing, drawing, and decision making. Gathering news is just a part of the picture. Not all the students participating must write a story with hard facts. We encourage fiction, poetry, drawings, political essays, and book and movie reviews. Offering a variety of creative options ensures there is something for every student to do at any level. Eric Nelson said, "In doing the *Tropical Tribune*, students got paired up with people they didn't know. You discovered hidden talents that you didn't realize people had."

While it is our goal to get the work of every student published in the paper, the major criterion for publishing a student's work is that it be their best. "I tried a lot harder to write better because I wanted my story to be in it," maintained student Miranda Hall.

Finding an Audience

Producing a newspaper on a environmental theme can be a powerful motivator for students to learn the issues and teach others, but this occurs only if there is an audience, whether it is classmates, parents, community members, or national readers. "The most special moment I remember is when the *Tropical Tribune* was 'hot off the press.' It was fun to see people's eyes light up at the sight of their story printed in the paper. We were all very proud of it. The hard work had really paid off," stated Leah Olson.

Fortunately, our students have a tailor-made audience. Save The Rainforest, Inc., does not have the resources to send information to each student who writes to them about rain forests. We have worked out an agreement that allows our students to respond to their student mail by sending a free copy of the latest *Tropical Tribune*. This partnership is a perfect arrangement for both parties, guaranteeing readers for us and enabling Save The Rainforest to provide appropriate information to students.

Distribution

In past years, we printed about a thousand copies of two issues of the paper on 11 x 17–inch newsprint. Due to the time commitment involved we now publish only one expanded edition. Looking like a real newspaper, each issue costs us under $500 to print and mail. We cover most of this cost with a $2 subscription fee. In addition, a local grocery store gives us 1 percent of the cash register receipts of customers who signal their support for our project by dropping their receipts into a container in the store. This money easily pays for any cost overruns we may incur and gives us an operating budget to pay for guest speakers, special programs, and field trips related to our journalism.

After the papers are printed, they are labeled, addressed, and sorted for mailing or distribution. This requires a great deal of student involvement, but sixth-grade students seem to enjoy the hands-on cooperative effort it takes to get the papers ready for mailing. We use the school's nonprofit mailing permit to mail the newspaper in bulk, which saves us a considerable amount of money each year.

Ordering Information

To order a copy of the *Tropical Tribune*, send $2.00 to:
Tropical Tribune
J. C. McKenna Middle School
307 South First Street
Evansville, WI 53536
or e-mail: bbeedle@ehs.k12.wi.us

It is difficult to tell if the program has had a long-term impact on our students. But a small sampling of students revealed some subtle influences. One student is now a student writer for a large newspaper and attributes part of her success to her first newspaper experience. Several have learned to monitor the Internet to keep informed, and others talk about career options in science or journalism that they had never considered before. Typical are comments like Jeri Schnabel's: "I felt like I had accomplished something by informing kids and having a voice," or Brad Sigmund's: "It's amazing what some sixth graders can do when they put their mind to it."

Another exciting development is happening in our very small rural town in Wisconsin's dairy country. Three families have recently taken their middle school children on extensive ecotourist ventures into the rain forest. The high school is planning on taking a class to the rain forests of Panama. That is not the type of trip that people around here usually take. Maybe the *Tropical Tribune* has not opened only the readers' eyes to the world, but also the eyes of some of our writers.

4

Keys to Successful Bookmaking

Advice to Get You Started

After more than twenty years of helping students make books, I realize that there's much more to say about making books than can be shared in one chapter. I have included pieces that I feel might benefit you the most. The importance of the book-making process is discussed in the first piece of this chapter. In the next, you will learn how to make accordion, fan, and flag books. In the concluding piece, the author writes about chapbooks and the way in which they are revolutionizing how books are being produced.

THE PRODUCTION PROCESS AND SCHEDULE

Chris Weber

A good traveller has no fixed plans
and is not intent on arriving.
—Lao Tzu, 570–490 B.C.

I have helped students make books of all kinds and sizes. My work has included international collections and dozens of classroom anthologies. Tucked in between are citywide and statewide anthologies. While some have won awards, all have won the hearts of the students and parents. I have written about many aspects of book publishing, but none more important than the process itself. Bookmaking begins and ends with process.

To give you an idea of what students are capable of, I have included student writing and art from the *Treasures* series, which I supervised.

The Importance of Process

In publishing, the process is just as important as the product, and it is essential that students and teachers believe in and act on this notion. What you go through together is similar to what authors, editors, copy editors, layout artists, and book designers experience when publishing a book. The process is ever changing and filled with questions and challenges.

Nonetheless, you and your students will answer those questions with creative solutions to unforeseen problems, and you will successfully adapt to daily changes. Students will push themselves harder and farther than they thought was possible. You will discover new roles for yourselves and see what you are capable of accomplishing. You will appreciate and understand what kind of teamwork it takes to publish writing and art. When I describe what it is like to work with students and teachers on various publications, one image comes to my mind: It's like taking part in a barn raising.

Do What You Can

You know your students and what they can accomplish. You want them to succeed and they will—just go slowly at first and take small steps. In your first class project, you might consider just involving your students in a small portion of the process. The students might design illustrations for the cover, vote on the layout of the front and back covers, and form teams to proofread drafts of the publication. Use the knowledge gained from your first experience to improve upon your second project. During that project you could have students take on an additional responsibility, but you do not have to. It is more important that you take time to feel comfortable and accomplished at doing what you are already doing.

Just Ask

Do not hesitate to call on older students or parents to help complete a class publication. Older students will be delighted to have the opportunity to work with younger students and help them with conferencing, proofreading, inputting stories, or any other necessary task. Over the years, I have seen to what amazing lengths parents will go for their children and other children. Parents have helped by inputting and proofreading stories for first and second graders. The PTA at Atkinson (the school where I teach) has given financial assistance to help pay for class publications. When I was working on *Treasures 3: Stories & Art by Students in Japan & Oregon,* one mother drove her daughters forty miles two to four times a week so that they could work with me. Parents will do whatever they can to help. All you have to do is ask.

Figure 4–1. Front cover art for *Treasures 3: Stories & Art by Students in Japan & Oregon.* This watercolor, titled "Father and Daughter at Ueno Zoo," was painted by Justin McHenry, 17, Stayton Union High School, Stayton, Oregon. Judith Frohreich, teacher.

Profiles in Production

How much of the production process should the teacher take on? The answer varies from teacher to teacher. I have worked with several teachers, and each one has

Figure 4–2. "Let's Play," a watercolor by Nobuyo Aimoto, ninth-grade girl, Shuyo Junior High School, Tokuyama, Yamaguchi Prefecture, Japan. Kimiyo Sawa, teacher. This artwork first appeared in *Treasures 3*.

assumed a different amount of responsibility during the production process.

In a fifth-grade class, the teacher chose the kind of publication and the role her students would play. Her students interviewed special people in their lives, wrote down transcripts of their interviews, and wrote a story about an event in that person's life based on information gained from the interviews. Then the class was divided into six proofreading teams, and each member proofread at least three stories. Their teacher and a university practicum student input the stories onto floppy disks. The teacher wrote the front matter, determined the order of stories, and created the book design and layout. Afterward, students drew illustrations on their covers, painted on the insides of the covers, and hand-sewed their books together.

Did it make any difference that teachers varied in the production responsibilities they gave to their students? No. Even though I personally feel that students learn more when they're doing the work, I also respect my colleagues' judgment. The teachers and students did what they could and were ready to do. From class to class, students took their tasks to heart. In the end, their teachers and I were proud of all of them and their publications.

The Production Schedule

Before production begins, I present the students with a general overview of the production schedule and explain the tasks involved. I include approximate deadlines for student writers and the production teams in this schedule.

In planning schedules, I take into account assemblies, field trips, and other school activities that steal time. I adjust the schedules accordingly by lengthening them one day for each day lost. As I am an ESL teacher who coteaches with other teachers at specific times, my schedule is not very flexible. Classroom teachers might be able to reschedule their planned production time so that it does not conflict with assemblies or field trips.

Sample Production Schedule for Class Book

I have deliberately not broken this sample down into individual weeks because the process and time requirements vary from class to class. Instead, I have organized tasks into three production stages: planning, production, and printing and post-production. I have found that students and teachers generally take nine to twelve weeks to put together a book.

Planning Stage (1–2 weeks)

1. Class decides what the class project will be (anthology, calendar, etc.) through discussion.
2. Students think about and list title possibilities.
3. Teacher discusses production schedule and answers questions.
4. Teacher describes different editorial teams and their work. Students self-select teams, using whatever method is most appropriate for the class.
5. Class decides team rules. They are written on poster-sized paper and displayed in the classroom.
6. Teacher explains criteria for how students select which piece(s) of their writing and art to include in the publication.
7. Students tell teacher which pieces they want included in the anthology.
8. Class votes on book's title.
9. Teacher discusses how front and back covers should reflect their title and uses examples of previous publication covers to illustrate this point.

Production Stage (7–8 weeks)

1. Students begin creating cover(s) by hand or on the computer for the class to vote on later.
2. Teacher holds publication conferences with students. Students write down their teacher's questions and suggestions as they are made.
3. While revising, students assess their teacher's comments and act on only

the ones they feel will improve their piece. Students also include self-corrections and those made by their teacher. Peers can assist with proofreading and checking the final copy of the piece(s).

4. Students continue working on possible illustrations for the class book.

5. Students turn in summaries on 3 x 5 cards of stories they want included in the class anthology. Later the teacher gives these cards to the team that decides the sequence of the stories that will appear in the publication.

6. Students continue to revise and proofread their stories; this can be done in pairs.

7. Teacher conducts remaining publication conferences.

8. Students submit illustrations for front and back covers, and the class votes on the covers.

9. Students and teacher decide what kind of binding to use and whether the class can afford color or black-and-white covers.

10. Teacher goes over tasks and answers questions in meetings with the proofreading team(s) and the team that will determine the order of stories.

11. Students turn in drafts of their piece(s) for additional proofreading.

12. The designated team determines the order of stories using 3 x 5 cards containing story summaries and gives a draft of the story order to the teacher.

13. Students input stories onto disks and print out hard copies.

14. Proofreading team(s) proof drafts and return them to student writers, who will input changes and corrections and save the revised stories to disk.

15. Students begin working on illustrations for their stories.

16. Proofreading team(s) proof the next set of stories.

17. Teacher and/or student(s) write introduction to the anthology.

18. Students finish illustrations for their stories.

19. If there is time, proofreading team(s) proof the stories once again and return them to student writers.

20. Students give the teacher disks containing final versions of their writing(s). Teacher copies the electronic version of each story onto a master disk.

21. Teacher and a small group of students input final version of front matter (e.g., title page, copyright page, introduction, table of contents).

22. Teacher, parent volunteer, or small group of students checks final copy that includes front matter and text with illustrations.

Printing and Postproduction (1–2 weeks)

1. Teacher has copies of text run off in school workroom on copying machine, gives it to parents who might run a school publishing center, sends text to school district printing shop, or takes text to local copy shop.

Figure 4–3. "At the Dentist," watercolor by Masato Watanabe, kindergarten boy, Narusawa Kindergarten, Narusawa, Yamanashi Prefecture, Japan. Haruko Watanabe, teacher. This artwork first appeared in *Treasures 3*.

2. Teacher has covers printed. (If the covers are to be in color, they will most likely need to be taken to a local copy shop for printing.)
3. Teacher has books bound. Simple types of binding (e.g., staple, comb) can usually be done at school or at a copy shop.
4. Students and teacher plan publication party and invite others, such as parents and the principal.
5. Everyone celebrates the work at a publication party. Many parties include readings and signings. Consider taking photos or videotaping this event.

Use this schedule as a rough guide and remember that the process is not like following a recipe for baking a cake. Do not worry if students spend what appears to you as an inordinate amount of time on some tasks and too little time on others. Each class is different, and students will be drawn to particular activities and engrossed in them for great lengths of time. On the other hand, they might get easily bored with other jobs and cannot abandon them soon enough. As long as students give enough of themselves in each task to produce a publication that will satisfy you both, do not worry how long or little they spend on each job.

When it seems that the class is just starting to make real progress, often something happens that causes the process to stop or even reverse itself. This has happened every time in my publications, but when this happens, I am reminded of a Japanese proverb that says, "Fall down seven times, stand up eight."

Most of the time, many of the stages occur simultaneously, and your classroom becomes a sea of activity. At desks, in front of computers, in corners, and on the rug, students revise their final drafts; one team is editing stories while another is deciding in which order the stories will appear; cover artist(s) put on the finishing touches to their illustrations; teacher meets with a student; and so on.

Keeping the Teams on Schedule

Near the end of each production week, the students and I meet, look over the schedule, and review our progress. We discuss what we have accomplished, assess the remaining work, and make any necessary changes to the schedule. If some are falling behind schedule, we discuss how they might possibly alter their work habits. Teams fall behind for several reasons. Some teams work very methodically, do more than asked, and are almost perfectionists in their efforts. These teams just need more time, and I accommodate them by providing them with extra time during their recesses or before or after school. Other teams may have internal problems (e.g., personality conflicts or disagreements). I help such teams address these problems, solve them, and get back on track.

Students' questions take up most of our meetings. They want to have a clear picture in their minds as to exactly where they are in the scheme of things. I listen patiently and answer as calmly and as encouragingly as I can. I wrap up each meeting assuring them, "You will create a wonderful book that your parents, you, and I will be very proud of. Keep up the good work."

Students' books will be made up of beautiful stories, which capture the students' lives and those of the people around them. Whenever I leaf through copies of the *Treasures* books, I am always amazed at the student authors' heartfelt sincerity, depth, and wisdom. I am moved as I glimpse moments of them through their words. Sometimes, I am transported to distant lands when reading narratives written by ESL students about their native countries and cultures.

Anytime I want to visit Laos, I read "The Rising Moon," by Sou Fou Saeturn, which first appeared in *Treasures 2: Stories & Art by Students in Oregon*. You can't help but be there with Saeturn and see what he sees through his rich, photo-like imagery. Reading this piece aloud brings alive the song in the words. "The Rising Moon" is one of the most beautiful student pieces I have ever read. ∎

THE RISING MOON

Sou Fou Saeturn, 17, Portland, Oregon

There is a hill near my house that I often climb at night. The valley is full of the noise of animals that often come out and watch the moon at night.

From this hill I have watched many moons rise. Each animal has its own family and home. The trees are full of owls and all kinds of animals that watch the moon. These animals settled these hills before we came.

There have been broad, confident harvest moons in autumn, shy misty moons in spring, lonely white winter moons rising into the utter silence of an ink-black sky, and smoke-smudged orange moons over the dry fields of summer.

Every night I go out of my back door and see all these animals watching the moon rise as I watch. But we, who live indoors, have lost contact with the moon. The trail is dark and it is hard to see the barn down near the pond.

Every hour the moon gets brighter and brighter, and my mind and my heart are feeling hopeful and happier.

Moonlight shows me none of life's harder edges. Hillsides seem silken and silvery, the river still and blue in its light. In the moonlight, I become less calculating and more drawn to my feelings.

And odd things happen in such moments. On this July night, I watch the moon for an hour or two and then go back to the mountains with the moon on my shoulder and peace in my heart.

Figure 4–4. This untitled watercolor by Sao Thong appeared on the "Refugee" section title page of *Treasures: Stories & Art by Students in Oregon*.

I turn often to the rising moon. I am drawn especially when events crowd ease and clarity of vision into a small corner of my life. This happens in the fall. Then I go back to my hill, await the moon, enormous and gold over the horizon, filling the night with visions.

An owl swoops from the ridgetop noiselessly but bright as flame. How sweet the moonlight sleeps upon this bank. Here will I sit and let the sound of the light winds blow across the hills.

At moonrise as I slow my mind to the pace of the heavens, enchantment steals over me. I open the vents of feeling and exercise parts of my mind that reason locks away by day. I hear across distances from below the hillsides.

By the time the moon stands clear of the horizon, full-chested and round and the color of ivory, the valleys are shadows in the landscape.

And then I turn back home and get a good night's sleep, for the animals are peaceful and quiet and have gone back to their nests to rest.

When one thinks of a class book, the first image that probably comes to mind is a rectangular book with a comb or staple binding. Yet books come in many different shapes and bindings. Go to the children's section of a bookstore and you will see how creative authors are becoming. We can be just as imaginative! Louise Parms presents some of the ways your students can make and design books to bring fun and meaning into publishing.

Parms introduces the art of making accordion, fan, and flag books. In her essay, she gives a detailed account of her students making each kind of book—what the steps are, and when and how they carried out each one. Parms provides possible projects for each book structure along with suggestions she passed on to her students. Her observations of students at work will help you see your own students and better understand their attitudes, approaches, and concerns so you can guide them.

To get you started, Parms provides step-by-step directions for each book type, including a list of materials, along with illustrations.

Once you have tried these book arts approaches with your students, explore other book construction shapes and binding techniques. You might never go back to the more traditional forms. ∎

THE BOOK ARTS APPROACH TO PUBLISHING WITH STUDENTS

Louise Parms, Teacher, Horace Mann School, Riverdale, New York

One of the challenges I face when publishing with students and collaborating with teachers on book projects is stretching students' and teachers' imaginations about how a book takes its shape. I try to encourage them to go outside the box, outside the traditional mass-marketed book form that we encounter every day, by exploring the creative possibilities of the book arts. These may incorporate interesting binding techniques, unusual design layouts for text and graphics, and different kinds of cover materials; these elements can be combined to complement the context and content of the books. When students and teachers take inspiration from historical as well as contemporary sources, the book design possibilities for student publishing become rich and varied.

The Accordion Book

One of the simplest and most easily varied book structures is the accordion book. It is well suited to younger students as well as older children and adults. In both social studies and language arts, students are exposed to ideas that include both individual and cultural diversity, encompassing areas within and beyond their own experiences. In the following description, I explain how the accordion book structure was used with second graders in a project designed to celebrate individual differences as part of a larger curriculum that explores the individual in relation to friends and family before moving on to the larger community.

As an introduction and motivation for discussion of individual diversity, the book *Nappy Hair,* written by Carolivia Herron and illustrated by Joe Cepeda, was presented to the students in a dramatic choral reading by several faculty members during a social studies period. This generated discussion about the celebration of the unique characteristics of each person and about the stories families tell and retell to celebrate each person's individuality. Students continued the discussion during creative writing class and began brainstorming to create their own stories about themselves. Students were asked to go home and ask family members to think of family stories that describe some special individual quality or characteristic of the student.

While the initial writing, editing, and final drafts of the stories continued in the classrooms, students came to the publishing center and began making their books. To enhance the meaning of the very special stories the students were writing about themselves, the books were designed in the shape of a simple human form with accordion-folded pages for the writing. Although each book's shape was uniform, students were encouraged to embellish their covers with collages that made them uniquely theirs.

Second graders spent the first weeks of the school year making decorative paste papers that would be used to cover their books. Each student first decided which of their paste papers to use and then traced the shape of their book cover boards onto what they considered the most interesting areas of the paste papers. Once they had traced accurately, students cut out the paste paper and glued it onto the cover boards to form the decorative base on which to create their cover collages. A communal scrap box for leftover paste papers was established, and students chose from their classmates' scraps contrasting colors and patterns of paste papers to cut and glue in varying shapes and designs on their covers. Students were encouraged to extend their collage beyond the borders of the covers to create interesting designs and to pay particular attention to the area around the head and face. At the beginning of the year, digital portrait photos were taken of each second grader, and these were printed in 1½-inch circles to represent each student's face on their front book cover.

The classroom teachers gave students long strips of colorful paper divided into four areas with writing lines. Students then transferred their final draft onto these book pages. Then they brought their completed stories to the publishing center and began the book construction. Because it's best to work with small table groups when teaching the steps for folding the pages into an accordion, I first presented a general lesson on the illustration process to the whole class, so that while one table of students was learning the accordion folding and gluing technique, others could work on their illustrations as they waited their turn.

Because most students had filled their pages with writing, only the top and bottom margins were available for illustration, but sometimes students had an extra blank page or half page. The class discussed the difference between decorative illustrations that could be used on the borders and illustrations that retell part of the story and lend themselves to larger spaces. For the decorative illustrations, students looked at examples of repetitive patterns; I encouraged them to make their own either by repeating some shape or design from their covers or by finding something in their stories that could become a decorative element. For example, if a story related something about baseball, the author could make a pattern from a ball and bat. If the student had used circles and squares as design elements in his cover collages, he could repeat those on the inside pages. For larger areas, students were instructed to illustrate a part of the story, to use a picture to show what was happening. If they had time, students could also illustrate the back of their pages. They worked in colored pencils, which contrasted nicely with the colored paper pages of their books and brought some surprising results.

The book construction began with small table groups folding the long sheets of writing paper. Students used tongue depressors or large craft sticks as folding and smoothing tools in place of a bookbinder's bone folder.

Students this age often become very concerned with where their writing is when folding pages; the fact that it frequently disappears from sight or shows up in unexpected places when being folded is often a stumbling block for some students. When told not to worry, that it will all magically be right when the folding is done, these students usually don't believe it until they see it with their own eyes.

Once they had folded the long sheets into an accordion with four pages, the students attached the front and then the back covers and continued or began the illustration process. Some students' stories were longer than others and used more than one long strip, which then needed to be joined in the right order to the others before being attached to the covers. That, however, is the beauty of an accordion book: it can be expanded by simply adding more strips of folded paper.

The finished books stood nicely on their own for display and each book was a wonderful personal statement of the student author/illustrator. As a group, these books emphasized the unique qualities of each individual within the context of the whole class or grade. They served to reinforce the foundation of a curriculum that built outward from the individual to friends and family to an understanding of the larger community.

The Fan Book

The fan book is a variation of the palm leaf book developed by the Egyptians at the beginning of the Bronze Age. These rectangular books have long narrow pages held together by cords or rings through a single hole in one end of the pages, which allows them to spread out like the slats of a fan. This format lends itself to sequencing activities and/or to an illustration on one side and limited text such as short poetry on the other.

The fan book became the ideal solution to a recent fifth-grade project in which students studied the ancient art of Chinese brush painting in their art enrichment class to complement their social studies curriculum, which covers the study of ancient civilizations. Students made their own brush paintings, which were mounted as scrolls. (To take this project a step further, students could read ancient Chinese poetry and use their paintings as inspiration to write their own poems modeled after the examples read in class.)

The paintings and poems were combined to make a class anthology and bound together with the fan book structure, which lent itself nicely to the content and historical context of the book. Photographs of the student paintings were scanned into Photoshop (an art manipulation program) and imported into a QuarkXPress file that was formatted with pages measuring 2 x 7 inches. Each page was printed with a student painting on one side and the corresponding student poem on the back. The pages were then held together at one end with a post and screw through punched holes. This binding allows the pages to spread out like a Chinese fan. Cover boards wrapped in authentic Chinese silk brocade and a silk tassel attached to the post and screw completed this integrated book project that embraced social studies, poetry, and art. Students can easily be a part of this entire production process, from cutting the printed pages to wrapping the cover boards with fabric, and finally, assembling the books.

If desktop publishing hardware and software are not available for your use, there are many ways of publishing student work that are strictly hands-on from beginning to end but still explore the idea of what a book looks like.

The Flag Book

In a another example from the fifth-grade curriculum, students are working on a collaborative project that integrates the book arts with their foreign language study. This project uses a contemporary book format designed by book artist Hedi Kyle, which is called the flag book. The book is constructed with an accordion spine on which flags, or pages, are glued in at least two rows that alternate direction. Because each fold has two sides, when a flag is pasted to the left side of the fold, it will lie down facing in the right direction. Rows of flags that are pasted on to the right side of the fold will lie down facing left. When the book is fully extended, the rows of flags point in opposite or alternating directions to produce a very surprising visual effect. The book can also be read in a more traditional manner by turning the pages when the spine is folded. This allows the reverse side as well as the front of the flags to be used for text or images. This format lends itself very well to an ABC book or a counting book.

Each fifth-grade student is designing his or her own alphabet flag book in either French or Spanish, depending upon which language he or she takes. Work on the text, which includes gathering several Spanish or French words for each letter and writing a sentence that includes one of the words, takes place within the foreign language classroom while students design, illustrate, and construct their books in the publishing center. When the flag books are fully extended, the alphabet letters and illustrations will be visible. When the book pages are turned in a conventional manner, the vocabulary text will appear alongside the illustrated letter flags.

The implementation of this sophisticated publishing project requires considerable time, so it is a long-term project. Students not only learn French or Spanish vocabulary that is further reinforced in the illustration process, but they are also exposed to the vocabulary and techniques of good design principles and bookmaking.

By using a book arts approach to publishing student work, you create many opportunities for enhancing the message the work contains: the way a book functions, how it is bound, the materials used to make it, and even the shape it takes. Books are so much more than words on pages bound between covers. Even within traditional book formats, which often become the best solution for class anthologies and other works by students, the page design and book layout can greatly enhance the content.

The physicality of a book—its look and design, the way it feels in our hands as we turn or unfold or spread the pages to reveal the mysteries held within—can be as much a part of the process of publishing student work as the effort that goes into the written content between the covers. When students are able to participate in all aspects of publishing, whether a book takes traditional form or explores the avenues of book art, students' ownership of the work takes greater hold and often has more lasting value.

Bookmaking Instructions

Accordion Book

Materials
Cardboard cut to size for cover boards
Decorative paper or collage materials for covers
Colored paper cut to size for text pages
Scissors
Glue stick or craft glue

Instructions
1. To form the cover boards, trace and cut a simple human shape from cardboard rectangles approximately 4½" x 9". (See Figure 4–5)
2. Cover the boards with decorative paper or collage materials. Add photo of face for head (optional).
3. Decide on number of pages needed. The width of the pages should be ¼" less than the width of the cover boards. For this four-page accordion book, a 17" x 5½" strip of paper is needed. Lines for writing can be added for young children.
4. Once the writing is complete, make the text pages into an accordion as follows:
   a. Fold the length of the text paper in half once.
   b. Take each end of the folded text paper and fold it back toward the center fold.
5. Attach the wrong sides of the end pages of the text paper to the wrong sides of the front and back covers.

Fan Book

Materials
Cardboard cut to size for cover boards
Decorative paper or fabric for outside covers
Paper for inside covers
Card stock for book pages, cut slightly smaller than the cover boards
Scissors
Hole punch or awl
Pencil
Glue stick or craft glue
Post and screw the same height as the stack of pages for the book (can be found in hardware stores or bookbinding supply sources)
Tassel (optional)

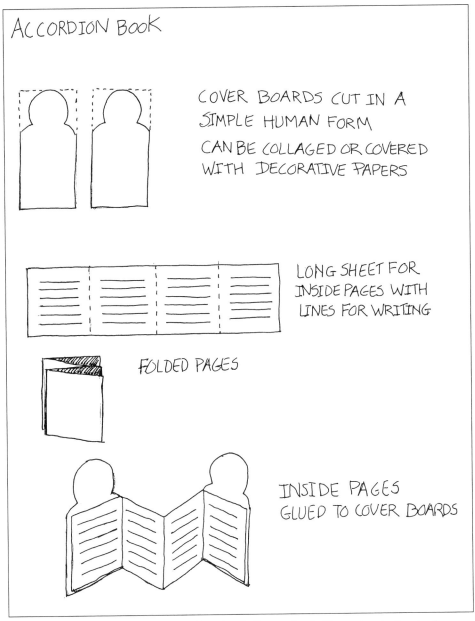

ACCORDION BOOK

COVER BOARDS CUT IN A SIMPLE HUMAN FORM

CAN BE COLLAGED OR COVERED WITH DECORATIVE PAPERS

LONG SHEET FOR INSIDE PAGES WITH LINES FOR WRITING

FOLDED PAGES

INSIDE PAGES GLUED TO COVER BOARDS

Figure 4–5. How to make an accordion book. Pen and ink illustration by Louise Parms.

Instructions

1. Cover boards with decorative paper or fabric and glue endpapers on the inside of the covers. (See Figure 4–6)
2. Use the hole punch to make a hole in the center of one end of a card stock page. Use this page as a template.
3. Place the template over the next page and use a pencil to lightly trace inside the hole to mark the second card.
4. Punch the hole and continue tracing from the template in this manner until all pages are punched. Be sure to always use the first card as the template.
5. Place the template in position on the inside of one cover and trace the hole. If it is too difficult to use the hole punch, use an awl to pierce the covered cardboard and work the hole large enough to accommodate the post and screw. Mark and punch the second cover by using the first cover as a template.
6. Undo the screw and post and assemble the book by placing the post through one cover, then the inside pages, and finally the other cover before attaching the screw to the post.
7. Add tassel if desired.

Flag Book

Materials
Cardboard cut to size for cover boards
Decorative paper to cover boards
Paper for inside covers
Medium-weight paper for the accordion spine
Card stock or blank 3 x 5" index cards for flags
Scissors
Glue stick or craft glue

Instructions

1. Cut cardboard to desired size for covers.
2. Cut decorative paper 1" larger than the cover boards on all sides.
3. Cover the boards with the decorative paper. (See Figure 4–7, p. 67)
4. Calculate the number of flags in each row of your book. To decide the width of your spine, multiply the number of flags per row times two and add an additional 2". The height of the spine should be the same as the height of the cover boards.
5. Fold spine into 1" pleats. Each pleat of the accordion has a left side and a right side forming a mountain peak in the middle.

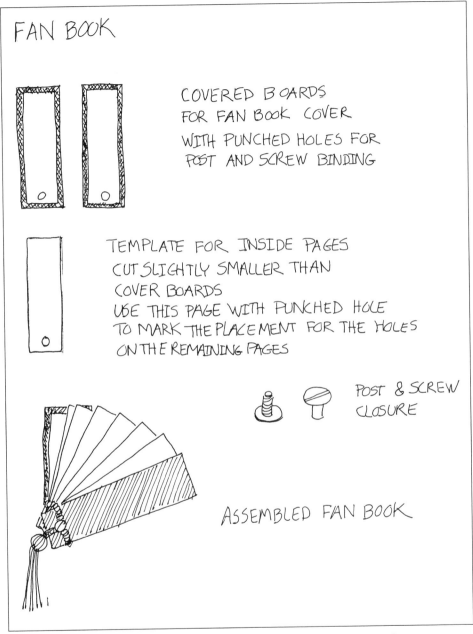

FAN BOOK

COVERED BOARDS
FOR FAN BOOK COVER
WITH PUNCHED HOLES FOR
POST AND SCREW BINDING

TEMPLATE FOR INSIDE PAGES
CUT SLIGHTLY SMALLER THAN
COVER BOARDS
USE THIS PAGE WITH PUNCHED HOLE
TO MARK THE PLACEMENT FOR THE HOLES
ON THE REMAINING PAGES

POST & SCREW
CLOSURE

ASSEMBLED FAN BOOK

Figure 4–6. How to make a fan book. Pen and ink illustration by Louise Parms.

6. Glue the ends of the accordion spine onto the inside of the covered boards along the rear edge.

7. Place the first row of flags (landscape orientation) from left to right across the spine by gluing 1" of the right margin of each flag to the left side of each pleat. Be sure to align the top edge of each flag with the top edge of the spine as you work across.

8. Place the second row of flags approximately ¼" below the first row and work in the opposite direction, right to left. Glue 1" of the left margin of each flag to the right side of each pleat.

9. Continue to alternate direction for each row leaving adequate space between rows for the flags to operate properly when the accordion spine is exercised. Be sure to align the bottom edge of the last row of flags with the bottom edge of the spine.

10. Cut end papers for inside covers ⅛" smaller on all sides than the cover boards and glue in place to finish the book.

––––––––––

No matter how attractive the design or intriguing the shape, a book will not be read unless its stories and poems grab and hold the reader. Powerful stories resound with the student author's voice. As we read or listen to their thoughts and feelings about people and events, our own memories are stirred and relived.

"Sunset on the Lake," a narrative about an everyday happening, is riveting, and as you read it, you will recall and envision your own sunsets. You will be held breathless by Barker's vivid imagery and effective use of metaphors and personification, which seem effortless and natural.

There's one scene that stands out in my mind to this day: "The sun's golden head sank, too. It had been so pretty that I wanted to seize a shovel, jump in the water, and dig the sun out and hang it up in the sky."

After you have read this piece, originally published in *Treasures 3: Stories & Art by Students in Japan & Oregon,* you will be amazed that such superb, powerful writing came from the heart and mind of an eight-year-old. ∎

SUNSET ON THE LAKE

Celeste Barker, 8, W. L. Henry School, Hillsboro, Oregon

If you want to know what the word *beautiful* means, read on. I'm going to tell you about something that you'll wish you could do a couple of minutes after you read this. It started when I was invited to my friend Teresa's house. As Teresa, her mom, and I rode to her house, the car seemed like the slowest turtle in the world. I could hardly wait to get to her house.

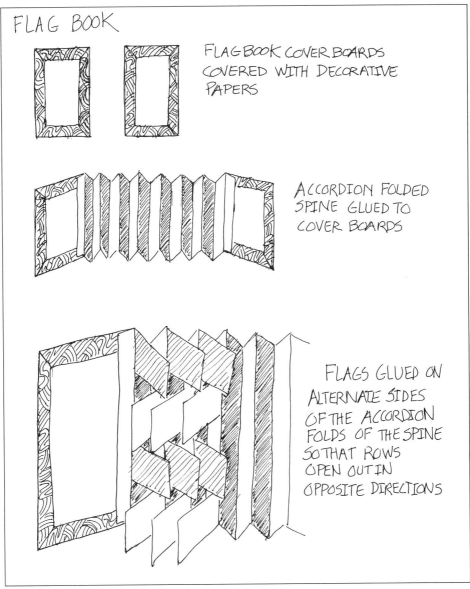

FLAG BOOK

FLAGBOOK COVER BOARDS COVERED WITH DECORATIVE PAPERS

ACCORDION FOLDED SPINE GLUED TO COVER BOARDS

FLAGS GLUED ON ALTERNATE SIDES OF THE ACCORDION FOLDS OF THE SPINE SO THAT ROWS OPEN OUT IN OPPOSITE DIRECTIONS

Figure 4–7. How to make a flag book. Pen and ink illustration by Louise Parms.

When we got there, we played around in her fort. We were swinging on the rope that led to it when we heard a call. "Girls! We're going for a boat ride!"

I was all happiness. A boat ride! What fun! We were actually going to ride in a boat! I changed into my shorts and short-sleeved shirt. Teresa put on her swimsuit. Then we were going out the door and into the car!

The car wasn't a turtle anymore. No. Now it was a five-thousand-pound rhinoceros, going only a fraction of a mile per hour. "Oh!" I thought, "How am I going to contain my joy!"

The car dragged on, and I felt I might die of impatience. But finally, after an eternity of waiting, we arrived at a lake. Teresa's dad unhooked the boat from the car and soon we were in it, floating on the water. The wind was calm, and I could hear birds twittering. Then Teresa's mom turned on the motor full speed, and whoosh, we were flying on the water. Our hair flew out behind our faces, fluttering in the wind.

We saw the sun set like a ball of golden fire, sitting down on the edge of the water as if it were tired. It sent sparkles of gold down the lake—like hands ready to pull up the lake, a blanket, over the golden head that was sinking under the water. The sun had not sunk far, and we could see all the scenery on the opposite shore—tall, proud fir trees, practically hiding the majestic mountains.

Finally the golden sparkles pulled up the covers. The sparkles grew smaller and smaller until they vanished beneath the dark waters. The sun's golden head sank, too. It had been so pretty that I wanted to seize a shovel, jump in the water, and dig the sun out and hang it up in the sky. When the sun yawned, its breath washed away the pink and lavender sky, and left a sprinkling of stars. The stars gradually grew brighter as a deep indigo swept across the heavens.

There are a few moments in my life that I will remember forever, and hold close to my heart. This sunset was a golden treasure—a memory that will never go away.

I had heard a lot about Chapbooks.com from Teachers & Writers Collaborative in New York City (a nonprofit organization where writers and teachers work together to produce materials that will contribute to the teaching of writing), so I wanted to try them out by publishing a schoolwide anthology using their services. I also hoped I would find answers to my questions. Just how good was Chapbooks.com? What was the staff like? How did they treat the customers? Was the publication printing process as fast as they claimed (two-week turnaround time)? In the end, how would the books turn out and what would be the reactions of students, teachers, and parents?

All of those questions were answered to more than my satisfaction. While people and process matter, product still counts, and Chapbooks.com delivered a beautiful volume that students, teachers, and parents at my school still talk about. As one student said in the beginning, "We want a real book," and that's what they got.

Unfortunately, Chapbooks.com was an idea ahead of its time, and went out of business. Sam Swope, a teacher and a writer who worked for Chapbooks.com, offered his perspective. "Even though it was caught up in the Internet bubble and burst, and so was unable to finance itself, Chapbooks.com had a good idea, a powerful one for teachers and students, and one that someone should find a way to make work."

Their static website at <http://www.chapbooks.com> offers insight and information about their past work. In a letter that appears on the home page, Matthew Josefowicz, president and CEO of Chapbooks.com, Inc., writes, "We are proud to have been an important part of the awakening of the possibility and potentials of personal book publishing. We look forward to watching what happens next, and we are terribly sad that Chapbooks.com, Inc., will not be able to be a part of this wonderful phenomenon."

You may be asking, "What's a chapbook?" Historically, chapbooks were small, unassuming books containing poems, ballads, stories, or political and religious tracts. They were an early form of popular publishing and were sold in the streets in seventeenth- and eighteenth-century England and America by itinerant peddlers known as "chapmen." The term has come to mean any small, independently produced book.

Because I feel that the work by Chapbooks.com should be continued, I want to share part of it with you in hopes that you will produce chapbooks yourself using the instructions titled "Publishing Without Chapbooks.com," which are located at the end of this chapter. You can also find these instructions on their website at <http://www.chapbooks.com>. Once you and your students have made your chapbooks, show them to others. In time, with enough interest and action, personal book publishers like Chapbooks.com will offer their services to teachers, students, and families so that they can turn your students' own words and pictures into professional-quality paperback books. It's only a matter of time. In the following revised preface that Sam Swope wrote for his first chapbook, he tells you about the powerful effect of these new books. ■

CHAPBOOKS IN THE CLASSROOM

Sam Swope, Teacher/Writer, New York, New York

This is a new kind of book. Its theme is the tree, and it contains writing, photographs, and drawings by my fifth-grade students, but that isn't what's new. What's new is that this book was printed using the Internet. What's new is that I didn't have to lay the book out. What's new is that it didn't cost a lot of money. What's new is that teachers can now make bookmaking a part of their curriculum.

The value of celebrating and encouraging student writing through publication is obvious. Most teachers have invested serious time at borrowed copy machines, cutting and pasting anthologies. Those collections are wonderful things and students love them, yet the chance to publish student writing in a real book is something else again.

Children know books are powerful, and I've seen the effect chapbooks have on them. In 1995, when I walked into the classroom carrying the first chapbook prototype, a class anthology of stories, my well-behaved students bolted from their seats and mobbed me. The moment they had their hands on those books, they paged through them with shrieks of excitement: "Look, Mr. Swope! I found me!"

Even at such a young age, my students saw that first book in historical terms. They knew it was an important object to keep, and they imagined the day they'd read it to their own children. Because my students happened to be immigrants, copies of our books found their way to relatives in Taiwan, India, and Ecuador. What teacher wouldn't love that? (Of course there was also the kid who proudly took his copy to lunch, got spaghetti all over it, and then abandoned it on the cafeteria floor, but never mind.)

Chapbooks Help Set Higher Standards

Dramatic evidence of the power of these books, and their usefulness for teachers, came the next year when I saw my new students loved reading last year's chapbook so much that my copies quickly became dog-eared. It was obvious to me then that these books are an important ally not only for teaching writing, but reading as well.

Of course, the mere fact that student writing appears in a book doesn't make it good. No child is going to have the patience to read uninspired writing, no matter who wrote it or in what form it appears. But the stories in my students' chapbooks were pretty polished, and that's because chapbooks upped the ante not just for the children, but for me. I wanted my students to look back on these books years from now and be proud, and that meant extra drafts, extra editing, extra cajoling, extra nagging. I found the effort well worth it, though, and unlike the stapled anthologies in my filing cabinet, my students' chapbooks sit on the bookshelf, proud memories of my time with those children.

Publishing with a Purpose

Classroom chapbooks are still in their infancy, but already all sorts of interesting books have been written by students—and teachers, as well. Students in the United States and Singapore collaborated on a book, as did students in Colorado and Alaska. ESL classes have published poems written in their native languages, then translated them into English, and published both versions side by side. Science, history, and religion teachers have published books across the curriculum.

Schools have even created textbooks: primary school students wrote a math workbook full of word problems (answers in the back): middle school honors students wrote *A Beginner's Guide to Poetry*, complete with original poetry; and veteran teachers in Mississippi wrote essays on teaching strategies that are now given to first-year teachers.

For the first time in history, a school can be a publisher, making books that reach out into the community. Students are interviewing senior citizens and writing up their biographies; guides and histories of locales are being written for chambers of commerce; regional cookbooks are compiled for use as fund-raisers.

Events previously reserved for "real" books are now available to anyone. At more and more schools there are book signings, book readings, and publishing parties, often with local newspaper and even television coverage. Chapbooks are now in the permanent collections of school and public libraries. Local bookstores offer them for sale.

The kinds of books teachers and students can, and will, dream up are endless. This is just the beginning. It's an exciting moment in the history of the book.

Students and teachers are publishing every kind of chapbook imaginable. Some are classroom anthologies, while others may involve an entire school or several. Most involve local participation; others go international. You can read chapbooks in English and in other languages. Students in elementary school through the university level are publishing their works in chapbooks. Also, teachers share their ideas and experiences in chapbooks for their peers.

Chapbooks are not solely intended for the classroom, however. Many teacher-publishers involve the community in their publications. Members of the community might participate in their making or teachers might have in mind the community as the book's audience. *If There is a Place,* edited by Stella Reed, is a collection of poems that came from workshops as a part of The Whitney Project's HIV/AIDS education and prevention program. The writing in *Notes from the Field: Gailer Student Experiences in Community Service,* edited by Paul Gustafson, focuses on high school students' reflections on their community service work.

In the following piece, John Kissingford discusses the impact that his students' chapbook project had on the community. He tells how it resulted in meetings that brought teenagers and senior citizens closer together. It was so successful that other schools have implemented similar projects. ■

A LITTLE LIGHT

John Kissingford, Teacher, Montrose High School, Montrose, Colorado

Students and I published *A Little Light: Rural Teenagers Finding Hope*, which uses theater presentations, writing, and discussion to share students' view. This chapbook was a companion to the performance piece we created that semester in the wake of several teen suicides that had touched the lives of my students.

A Little Light showcased the deep and sometimes dark issues that face modern adolescents, as well as their creativity and perseverance. The book was an invitation for readers in the community to be aware of these issues and to celebrate that "light which can shine through adversity." The kids were pleased to see their stuff in print, but the major impact had been on the intended audience: the community.

Sales of the chapbooks, which were a very small part of the fund-raising, went towards financing our tours and buying theatrical equipment that would support the production values of our shows. The real value of selling copies of *A Little Light*, however, was that it increased community participation in and awareness of the work of the VOICES program, which was a process-oriented social issues theater class that I designed and taught. The model for the class was brought to us by the community outreach division of Kaiser Permanente.

We solicited writing about a particular social issue each semester, created theater pieces based on the stories we received, and then performed these pieces in appropriate community venues (usually schools) in order to engender dialogue. Each semester, events in our community would focus my students on a particular social issue, and the VOICES class would be a forum in which to grapple with it: teen suicide, the rift between old and young, school violence, partying, and so on.

VOICES is modeled in large part on the Forum Theater work of Augusto Boal, where the disempowered in a community are encouraged to look at their own stories critically enough to be able to create their own solutions.

The implicit goals of the program included creating real connections between kids, helping them to feel a sense of agency in their world, fomenting powerful conversations within and among different constituents in a community, and addressing the particular social issues a community needs to face.

The communities of Lake City, Colorado, and Ketchikan, Alaska, have experimented with their own versions of such a program. The project has started many great conversations. The semester after *A Little Light*, we worked on the rift between young and old in our community. We matched up my students with senior mentors. That first meeting, seeing teens and senior citizens with their heads earnestly together, was a rare treat. In the more conventional performances we do on violence, prejudice, teen suicide, or substance abuse, the show is debriefed afterward; that is, we open the floor for questions and comments on the play, occasionally moderated by myself or assisted by a panel of adult social service workers. The performers are astonishingly honest during this debriefing, both with younger kids, who admire and emulate their sensitivity, and with adults, who are shocked by the facts of teen life and by the depths of their reflections. The conversations give us hope.

Occasionally, we would encounter powerful negative reactions to our work, usually based in adult denial that these things were happening to kids, that our performances were an accurate representation of our kids' lives. I love to remember the woman who accosted one of our actresses the day after a performance of "Opening Windows." Right there in the supermarket aisle, she read the actress the riot act for playing such a part in such a slanderous play. HER daughter, she insisted, would never have anything to do with what we had portrayed. She stormed off.

Next day, same woman, same actress, same store. The woman approached her with a tearful apology and thanked her over and over. Apparently the woman had gone home and told her daughter about the supermarket encounter, and the daughter had sat her down and told her that every single situation in the play was part of her everyday reality. The woman said that they talked for hours, and was so grateful for her new relationship with her daughter.

The chapbook titled *A Little Light* was another important part of the community dialogue. Most of our theater audience members were teenagers, but hundreds of adults read the book, and dozens told me how amazed they were with the writing, not only the variety and beauty of the prose, but also the depth and power of the subject matter. They, too, were looking at their kids and their neighborhoods differently and starting different kinds of conversations.

The following passage is from a story titled "Overcoming Night" in *A Little Light,* by Diana Le, 18, Montrose High School, Montrose, Colorado. Using carefully chosen words, Le captures a moment with her father—leaving us with an unforgettable snapshot. ■

As a little girl, I could never fall asleep. I always envisioned monsters and demons hovering around. My father came up with a way in which I could sleep. I remember my father's comforting hand gripped tightly around mine. All through the night, our hands dangled like a child's swing between our two beds. One night he accidentally made the mistake of letting go, and the consequence was deafening. His little girl was filled with horror and cried to be sure it was known. He quickly snatched my hand back; silence again. . . .

Even though Chapbooks.com is no longer in business to produce chapbooks for teachers, its staff wants teachers themselves to make their own chapbooks. So its staff members do the next best thing. They tell you and your students how to produce yours. Follow their instructions below (reprinted from their website), and give yourselves a real book. ■

PUBLISHING WITHOUT CHAPBOOKS.COM

From <http://www.chapbooks.com>

We hope that the many people who used or wanted to use Chapbooks.com, Inc., to produce their books are able to do so without us.

Advances in On-Demand Book Printing make it possible for anyone to create their own book, with a little work. Although Chapbooks.com's unique value was to make this as easy and affordable as possible by using advanced Web-based systems, you can still do it without us in a slightly lower-tech way.

There are two parts to creating your own book:

1. creating PDF files of the laid out pages of your book
2. having these PDF files printed and bound by an On-Demand Book Printer

To create PDF files, you'll need to have the full version of Adobe Acrobat, which you can buy at Adobe's online store for about $250.

Installing this software will give you a PDF "printer" called "PDF Writer"—it will appear as a printer choice on your computer whenever you print any document.

Some computers come with PDF Writer already installed. Check to see if you have it already before you buy.

Designing the pages of your book is simpler than it sounds. When you're using on-demand print technology, you don't need to do all those fancy folds and impositions that they taught you about in school when they taught you about books. The printer can do all of that for you.

All you need to do is lay out the individual pages of your book in a word processor like Microsoft Word. We suggest:

1. setting the page size to 5" wide by 7.5" high (in the "File: Print Set Up" menu) and setting the margins to 0.5" all around
2. centering the page numbers at the bottom of the page
3. remembering that odd-numbered pages will be on the right-hand side of the open book and even-numbered pages will be on the left-hand side. Also remember that the first page will have nothing facing it
4. looking at a book on your shelf as a model for the "Front Matter"—title

pages, copyright pages, tables of contents, introductions. Even though these pages may seem unimportant, they help your book feel "real"

5. avoiding using too many fonts. Pick a single font for your body text and another or a variant for the titles and headings

6. creating a front and back cover, and saving these as a separate PDF file from the body of your book. You can either do this as a single page with front, back, and spine all on one sheet, or you can do two pages, front and back, and let the printer "impose" them on a cover sheet and add the spine text

To get your PDF files printed, you can search on the Web or in your local community for an On-Demand or Quick Printer. Key words to look for are:

- "Docutech" (a big, powerful Xerox machine)
- "Print on Demand" or "Books on Demand"
- "Perfect Binding" (this is a type of binding, the same kind Chapbooks.com, Inc., used, not a statement of quality)

Some Quick Printers are more eager than others to do work for individuals (as opposed to for businesses). If you know someone who has a business relationship with a Quick Printer, you might want to ask them for an introduction. Most printers will pay more attention to you if you have a connection to an important client.

The more you can know what you want going in, the easier it is for them to do your work. For example, if you had prepared your PDF files according to the guidelines above, you would say to the printer:

"I want to print [X number] of 5 inches x 7.5 inches perfect-bound books, [Y number] of pages each. I have the pages in one PDF file and the front and back cover in another PDF file."

This tells the printer that he's not going to have to spend a lot of time helping you get your book prepared for printing, which means he'll be able to make some money even if the order is very small. It also helps him give you a price right away, which is important. The biggest headache in printing is waiting for estimates.

Pricing and delivery time can vary widely when you're dealing with individual printers. Some of them might need to charge you a set-up fee to handle such a small order. Others might not. If you're a school, you might be able to negotiate a discount from a local printer, especially if you offer to credit the printer in the book or invite them to the book signing (in a small community). Also, if your school is producing several different books at the same time, you may be able to get a volume discount.

Good Luck!

5

Making a Difference Through Publishing

Entering Unknown Lands

Most of my past student publications have been anthologies showcasing the best of the students' writing and art. Their purpose was primarily to help students improve their writing. With the making of *Treasures 3: Stories & Art by Students in Japan & Oregon*, I began looking toward publications that would make a difference to the readers, society in general, and ultimately, the writers themselves. In such projects designed to make a difference, students' work informs; helps increase appreciation and understanding among people of different cultures; and moves us to take action.

In making *Treasures 3*, my role changed, too. Instead of supervising the production myself, I collaborated with American and Japanese educators. My student editors from various countries also gained an appreciation of their own countries and others as they worked together. During and after publication of *Treasures 3*, I felt like an explorer entering unknown lands. Little did I know what countless teachers and students were doing throughout the world.

However, after reading *Brave New Schools: Challenging Cultural Illiteracy through Global Learning Networks*, by Jim Cummings and Dennis Sayer, I knew. I was inspired by what teachers were accomplishing with international projects to make a difference in people's lives. Jim Cummings described I*EARN (the International Education and Resource Network) and their various undertakings, which had me in awe. For most teachers, I*EARN, a 501(c)3 nonprofit corporation, is an excellent starting point for this exciting new kind of work. A yearly membership fee provides you with many telecommunications tools and advantages, such as:

- full access to all ongoing, online curriculum-based projects

- program support
- a network of both schools and youth service organizations
- a time-saver for teachers—saves having to surf the Internet for project partners
- opportunities to work in any of twenty-nine languages
- a web of structured projects, each designed by participants themselves and each with a teacher-facilitator in: language arts, science, environment, math, humanities, and social studies

For those of you who want to go it alone or with some other organization, I have incorporated advice from I*EARN and my own international projects to guide and help you, too. However, I warn that attempting an endeavor on your own is a formidable task. Please don't consider undertaking such a project unless you already have a working relationship with international organizations, contacts, or possible counterparts.

People commented on *Treasures 3*, wondering why such a great idea had never before been carried out. It was extremely difficult, required a ton of time and work, and was loaded with an endless gauntlet of obstacles and risks. If I knew then what I know now, I might never have supervised the making of *Treasures 3*, but instead, worked on projects with other schools or an organization like I*EARN.

Other Global Telecommunications Networks

You might also investigate other global telecommunications networks, such as the following:

- Global Kids: Global Networking for Kids <http://www.kidlink.org> This is a nonprofit grassroots organization working to help children through the secondary school level be involved in a global dialogue. The work is supported by eighty-one public mailing lists for conferencing, a private network for real-time interactions (like chats), an online art exhibition site, and volunteers living throughout the world.
- The Global Schoolhouse <http://www.gsn.org> This website contains Internet projects of interest to K–12 educators.
- Intercultural E-Mail Classroom Connections (IECC) <http://www.iecc.org> IECC is a free service to help teachers link with partners in other countries and cultures for e-mail classroom pen pal and project exchanges.
- KIDSPHERE <http://hale.ssd.k12.wa.us/friends/kidsphere/html> KIDSPHERE is an Internet-based mailing list that was organized to

stimulate the development of computer networks for children and teachers worldwide. It functions in a manner similar to many of the hundreds of other such mailing lists: providing a forum for the exchange of information; allowing people new to the medium to gain a quick introduction to it; helping to organize joint activities that make use of networking technology; and developing the mechanisms for implementing networks on a large scale.

- Sister Cities International (SCI) <http://www.sister-cities.org>
  SCI is a nonprofit citizen diplomacy network creating and strengthening partnerships between U.S. and international communities in an effort to increase global cooperation at the municipal level, promote cultural understanding, and stimulate economic development.

Starting off with the title for her article, Lisa Jobson gives you a good idea of what I*EARN is all about—action. As you will read, students from around the world work together on projects to bring about change. Jobson paints the big picture of I*EARN and fills it in with details of specific projects. She describes how students collaboratively carry out projects that result in a book, calendar, or magazine. Jobson points out examples where students are working toward helping others and serving particular communities. In this piece, she opens the door and welcomes you to this wonderful community called I*EARN. ∎

I*EARN: EDUCATION IN ACTION

Lisa Jobson, U.S. Outreach/Program Coordinator,
I*EARN-USA, New York, New York

As a global community of over four thousand schools and youth organizations in over ninety countries worldwide, I*EARN supports students worldwide to publish to both local and global communities, providing opportunities to write for a real audience, and apply classroom learning toward making a real difference in the world.

I*EARN <http://www.iearn.org> empowers teachers and young people (K–12) to work together with others around the corner or in different parts of the world at a very low cost through a global telecommunications network. Launched in 1988, I*EARN has fourteen years of experience in the field of educational telecommunications. This experience has demonstrated that learning is greatly enhanced and retained when it is gained through experience and interaction with real people. The common goal of supporting youth to share their voices with a larger audience has prompted many project groups to include, as part of their work, a publication of student work to be shared both within the group and with outside communities.

Projects in I*EARN are designed by participants, all with their own unique goals and outcomes. The common thread that ties together the one hundred or more I*EARN projects happening at any given time is the vision that young people working together can make a real difference in the world, both in their local and global communities. At Erasmus Hall High School in Brooklyn, New York, this takes the form of a magazine called *Inside View*, which has as its goal "expressing the differences and similarities of people around the world by showing their ethnic beauty." At I*EARN schools in South Africa, Zimbabwe, Uganda, Ghana, and Senegal, students and teachers have come together to work on a project seeking to investigate the history of precolonial Africa, in order to develop materials for use in classrooms worldwide. In Canada, a group of students and teachers have begun the Bullying Project, using the power of the Internet to create a virtual space where students can submit poems, stories, plays, songs, drawings, photos, animations, and films related to the issue of bullying.

Whatever the theme or issue that a group is working with, a key element of I*EARN collaboration is that each project produces a final product, which takes the learning out of the classroom and back into the community to parents and school administrators to demonstrate what really can be done with this technology in various curriculum areas.

Students work together using online forums accessible to peers worldwide, carrying out projects as part of a known, sustainable community that continues to work together over time. Students have a space to read and respond to one another's work, so that the process becomes the focus as much as the product itself. Collaborative online conferencing allows for a full project community in multiple locations to take ownership of a project and feel a sense of involvement beyond what traditional submission processes allow. A magazine becomes a reflection of a yearlong discussion rather than a collection of works created in isolation from one another. As with all I*EARN projects, the emphasis is on collaboration, rather than competition for space. Over time, students develop publications that are truly collaborative and interactive, allowing participants to read and respond to one another's writing and also take an active role in determining the content of the publications. By sharing their work with a larger audience, students begin to understand that what they are doing in school is relevant and interesting to others, both locally and globally.

Through participation in I*EARN projects, students develop the habit of getting involved in community issues, thus better equipping them for future civic participation. Among the examples is the Nicaragua Rope Pump Project, in which I*EARN students have raised thousands of dollars to fund the building of wells and the installation of rope pumps in villages in Nicaragua to help people to have clean water sources. With all I*EARN projects, the giving and receiving is reciprocal and

Figure 5–1. "How Children Pay Respect to Adults," colored pencil artwork by Waraporn Montra, 10, Baan Mae Klong Mai School, Umphang District, Tak Province, Thailand. Her artwork first appeared in *The Indigenous Global Art Exchange Calendar 2001*, which is one of the activities of The First Peoples' Project. This project allows indigenous students from around the world to engage in joint projects. Students are involved in writing, art exchanges, and discussions about issues relevant to indigenous students. To find out more about the project, visit the project's website: <http://www.iearn.org.au/fp>.

Karen students such as Waraporn live in small villages along the Thai/Burmese border in Thailand and have their own language and culture. More than two thousand years ago, Karen people lived around the Mongolia Plateau area and moved down toward Tibet because of war. When Tibet was oppressed by China, Karen people moved down along the Yangtze River to Burma (now officially called Myanmar) and along the western border of Thailand.

built in at every level. In the case of the Rope Pump Project, participating students in Nicaragua were able to share their own culture and experiences, and participate meaningfully in discussions. At the same time, young people around the world who had helped provide access to clean water for Nicaraguans found that they could make a difference in the lives of others as part of their education.

This reciprocal model of service and action is built into all I*EARN projects, as students are working with a known community over a period of time, and they may find themselves playing different roles at different points during their involvement in the network. In another example, students participating in "Schools Demining Schools," a project launched by the UN CyberSchoolBus and I*EARN, were learning, discussing, and publishing to raise awareness and funds to try to solve one of the most horrifying problems of our time: land mines. At the same time, these students were able to communicate with the schools designated for de-mining and learned of the experiences of young people who had not previously had a voice on the network.

When students come to understand that what they are doing in school can have real-world applications, and when they see themselves as part of a larger interconnected world, their learning in school takes on new meaning. Our experience has shown that at the youngest of ages, children can have a transformative experience of taking action and effecting change. As Leinz Vales, an I*EARN student in New York City, explains, "You start connecting with things you see on the news once you've got a community of people that can actually work to make a difference." It's our hope that, as access to online technologies grows, schools will increasingly be able to provide young people with experiences of working collaboratively and cross-culturally to effect change with their learning.

In writing this section, I drew on information, ideas, and text contained in the *I*EARN Project Description Booklet 2000–2001,* by Lisa Jobson. ∎

HOW TO START WORKING ON INTERNATIONAL STUDENT PUBLICATION PROJECTS

Chris Weber

Working Relationships Are Key

A key to successful project work is developing effective relationships with involved educators. Establishing close relationships among teachers will help facilitate the difficult task of collaborating on projects across diverse educational systems, time zones, school year schedules, cultural differences, and linguistic obstacles.

With a counterpart, you're not alone, and what a difference that makes. I have kept my faith and enthusiasm for various international projects in large part because of my colleagues on the projects.

Netiquette

Regular, effective communication between the teachers involved is vital to the success of any international project. You and your counterparts will be e-mailing each other on a regular basis, so pay close attention to netiquette. People ask me for specific guidelines. (One example: Don't write using all capital letters, as this is perceived as shouting.) In first communicating with a teacher, I am more formal in my greeting, tone, and language. At the same time, I attempt to write in a friendly voice. Later on, as we get to know each other more, we will establish our own netiquette.

Each person's netiquette is different—some tend to be formal and others casual, so adjust accordingly—be patient and flexible. This lightning-quick technology does not mean you'll get instant responses. Some will answer right away; many in a day or two; and a few take weeks and even need reminders. Personal schedules, circumstances, and communication styles all play a part in response time. Be understanding because there will be times when you won't be as quick to respond as you would like.

However, having just said that, try to respond within a day or two. Otherwise, new mail will rapidly bury the old, you will tend to forget about it or push it aside, and one day you will find yourself stumbling onto that unanswered message. Embarrassed or not, send off a quick response letting the writer know you're still alive. They will understand; just don't make a habit of it.

Choose a Project

Often, it takes time just figuring out what kind of publication endeavor to take on and what would interest you and your students. You gain ideas from others, and this is no exception. Hundreds, perhaps thousands, of such projects abound on the Internet, but you could spend days or weeks searching for them on search engines. There are several I*EARN resources (such as an online newsletter, forums, project description booklet) that will help you find out which of its projects are currently taking place. If you go with another organization, look for resources similar to I*EARN's because you want current information about projects and participants.

Become Involved in a Project

Participate in existing projects before initiating a project of your own. This valuable experience will be a great teacher. You will learn the best use of your and your students' time, your roles, problems and how to solve them, what works, what doesn't, and so on. Identify a project you'd like to work on and find out if the project is still active.

Poll your class first to see if they're interested. Nina Koptyug, an I*EARN teacher, writes, "One of the most important things, for me as a teacher, was making students understand that there was no 'must' about our work." If your class is interested in a project, let your students do what they're drawn to and feel comfortable doing.

Write to the facilitator of the project, introducing yourself and your class/school, and give reasons for your interest in their work.

Figure 5–2. "La caceria," watercolor by Jorge Abel Clacleo, 15, Centro Provincial de Enseñanza Media Nro 3, Patagonia, Argentina. His artwork first appeared in *The Indigenous Global Art Exchange Calendar 2000,* which is one of the activities of The First Peoples' Project.

Suggestions for Successful Project Participation
- Try to create a globally aware classroom/school environment. Students have no idea to and for whom they're writing when they're corresponding via the Internet. It can be a cold, impersonal experience just writing and sending "anonymous" correspondences on the Web. Make the experience richer and more meaningful by giving them connections.

  E-mail messages come to life through photos and maps and a basic understanding of the background and culture of their online peers. You can also foster a connection by having students' photos and artwork added (if appropriate) to a website created for the project.
- Create a system for peer-editing in your class. Preparation and transmission

should be seen as two different tasks. Preparing the message, researching, and creating material to be transmitted are a very important part of the whole process. Students will be writing with real purpose for a very real audience. Create a feedback process where students have the opportunity to comment on each others' work, peer edit, and then revise accordingly.

- Communicate. Even if you can't contribute for weeks, send a note to say so. That way, your partners know that you are still interested in participating.
- Ensure that language is cross-cultural. How much of what is being sent needs explanation or description for an audience from a different culture? Slang or colloquial language needs to be used carefully. Translating student writing into a context that is most universally understandable can open interesting discussions in your classroom.

Starting Your Own Project

Once you have experience participating in projects and have made contacts in I*EARN or other schools or organizations, you can develop your own project. Start with a plan. First, post your idea to individuals who might participate. Get them involved in a discussion and have them help design the project.

Make sure that you understand each other and everyone's ideas at each stage. Paraphrase what other teachers have written, or ask them questions if you're uncertain. Immediately clear up any possible misunderstandings.

From the start, be frank with one another in respectful, tactful ways. All decisions should be mutually agreed upon. International projects require cooperation and ownership by all parties. You will all work hard on the project because it belongs to you and you make the decisions together.

After discussing the project with others, fill out a project idea template similar to the one for I*EARN members (shown below). Of course, feel free to design your own template.

You will find additional related ideas and advice about starting your own project in Chapter 6, Displaying Students' Work on the Internet, and Chapter 7, E-mail Publication Projects.

Project Idea Template
1. Name of project:
2. Brief one-sentence description of project:
3. Full description of project:
4. Age/level of project participants:
5. Timetable for the coming year:
6. Possible project/classroom activities:
7. Expected outcomes/products:

8. Project contribution to others:
9. Project language(s):
10. Curriculum area:
11. Names/e-mail addresses of initial participating groups:
12. Name of facilitator(s):
13. E-mail address of facilitator(s):
14. URL of project webpage (not always necessary if you're facilitating an e-mail exchange):

Suggestions for Successful Project Facilitation

Use Online Forums Whenever Possible   Online forums allow participants to participate at different points in the project, given their own particular school schedule. Because discussions are archived on the forum, new contributors can immediately see the discussion that has happened up to that point, understand who is involved, and know whether the work will be of interest to them. In addition, by using forums, you are enabling participants to participate by e-mail or by way of the Web, on discussion boards hosted on servers around the world, thus keeping cost to a minimum.

Encourage Discussion and Interaction Among Participants   Projects should be collaborative and interactive. As a project facilitator, part of your role, and that of your students, is to facilitate discussion and interaction among participants in your project. Doing so also increases the opportunities for students to receive feedback on their writing, so that the sole responsibility of responding to messages does not fall on you and your students as the project facilitators. Every student who posts a message will receive a response if people commit to responding to two other messages for every one that they post.

Involve Participating Schools and Students in Leadership Roles   Appointing international student editorial boards and facilitators not only provides additional sources of feedback to contributors, but it also helps students to see ways that they can take leadership roles within the project. In some projects, participants may even choose to share the role of compiling project materials into a final publication, thus allowing a variety of classrooms the experience of analyzing and presenting a piece of the project's "final product."

Update Project Information Periodically   Posting updates will help existing participants and will also ensure that new participants entering the project will not be referring to outdated information about the project.

Participate in Another Project   This is a great way to meet other participants and learn about the many different projects initiated by teachers and students throughout

Figure 5–3. Students from the *Cultural Horizons* editorial group at Friaborg High School in Simrishamn, Sweden, review material submitted from schools around the world. Photograph by Cecilia Fröberg.

the world. In this way, your classroom truly becomes a global community member that can draw on the breadth of the network as your classroom develops throughout the year.

Summaries of Ongoing I*EARN Projects with Publications and/or Online Displays

Colouring Our Culture

This project tackles the issues of multiculturalism and refugees through sharing art, writing, and firsthand experiences. Colouring Our Culture provides students and families with the opportunity to participate in an international global art project that crosses cultural and language barriers using student art and the power of the Internet. Students are invited to select from a range of associated topics and themes (suited to their age groups) and to prepare a response in an artistic medium and in writing. A selection of work is exchanged with international schools involved in the project, and students have the opportunity to e-mail their responses directly to the other artists.

The finished work is displayed in a virtual (Web-based) and real exhibition; selected pieces have been used as illustrations in a printed calendar for the year 2000.

Ages: Primary–12
Dates: Ongoing
Language(s): Any
Contact: Jo Tate, Australia <jot@araratcc.vic.edu.au>
Website: <http://www.araratcc.vic.edu.au/users/jot/culture/index.htm>

Kindred: A Family History Project

Participants submit stories and pictures from the oral histories of their families during the twentieth century.

Students should write stories that tell of childhood experiences during the twentieth century, decade by decade. We invite students to explain life in their country for a child during the '20s, '30s, '40s, right up to the '00s. Students may collect their information by interviewing parents, grandparents, neighbors, cousins, aunts, and uncles, or any other person who has an interesting story to tell of life in recent times or in a bygone era.

For many students, the research on the Kindred project has been an opportunity to find out about family members and their lives.

Ages: All
Dates: Ongoing
Language(s): English
Contact: Judy Barr, Australia <judybarr@iearn.org.au>
Website: <http://www.iearn.org.au/kindred>

Joanne Sahhar of Warragul, Australia, described her experiences:

Being involved in the Kindred project through I*EARN has allowed me to really delve deep into the realization of the past, by gaining a vast amount of insight and knowledge as to the powerful and devastating events that have occurred over the years in history, and with it has introduced a variety of rewards, such as being able to discuss such times with other people my age, which are the second generation from those who did experience, and some even survive, such tragic life moments. All my grandparents were greatly affected through the war, and were forced to struggle on in life with their children, and their own life hassles when trying to face each day. The most wonderful thing I have received through this project is discovering that my family was not alone in their "battles," as there were so many other innocent people who were forced to confront experiences equally as treacherous, and in some cases even more devastating.

Judy Barr was similarly affected by what she learned through the Kindred Project. She tells us, "A significant event during the twentieth century was the eastern Europeans' flight from the Soviet Union. Many crossed the border into West Germany. The stories that we have received on this theme included the story of Zdenka Mik, a young girl who was born into a wealthy Czech family in the town of Budweis. Her life was joyful and uncomplicated, and then in the late 1940s her family's story unfolded like a Hollywood movie."

Zdenka Mik's Story
Gita Webb (Zdenka Mik's granddaughter), 16, St. Pauls' Anglican
Grammar School, Warragul, Victoria, Australia

Joseph [Zdenka's father] took a job on the border. It was here that he performed an illegal job, which involved him secretly leading families across the border into West Germany. This was prohibited at the time by the Czech government. Nobody was allowed in or out of the country.

One night, while Joseph was at work, the Mik family received a visit from the KGB police asking after Joseph. They left when Elizabeth explained where he was, but promised to return later that week to question her husband. Joseph returned from work late in the night, and to his terror was welcomed by the story of the visitors that they had received. Without hesitation, Joseph decided that the family would leave the country the following day. Zdenka and Gelinda were woken in the early hours of the morning with their bags packed. Only a few possessions could be taken with them on their journey as all they could take would be a bag that would be light enough to carry on foot easily. . . .

As the family was on foot, it would look suspicious if they were walking around with Zdenka, who was supposed to be at school at the time, so, to cover this up, they borrowed a cart of hay and traveled underneath the straw, hiding from the Russian police. After around two hours, the cart came to a halt. . . .

Finally [they] crossed the border, reaching West Germany. They met up with Gelinda and Elizabeth, who were anxiously waiting in a farmhouse for the safe return of Zdenka. Nervously, the six waited and waited for Joseph to return to them, until after what seemed like hours, they heard the fateful sound of gunshots firing through the silent air, followed by stillness. The air stood motionless as each member firmly held their breaths clutching each other as they hoped and prayed for the safety of their loved one. With that, the door of the farmhouse swung open, and in collapsed Joseph, puffing and panting from the marathon he had just run, to safety.

The Holocaust/Genocide Project (HGP)

Honey Kern, an English teacher from Cold Spring Harbor High School in Cold Spring Harbor, New York, describes this project.

The HGP is a global, theme-based Internet project, with participants from more than sixteen countries.

This interdisciplinary project, encompassing history, language arts, fine arts, music, foreign languages, and critical thinking, enables students, on a global level, to dialogue with their peers, share ideas, conduct research, do common reading of books together online, and access professional authorities and databases about information as it pertains to the Holocaust of World War II, other genocides, and current events. Students and teachers are welcomed and encouraged to use the project's website, <http://www.iearn.org/hgp>, as they research history, literature, art, music, memorial sites, museums, archives, and survivors' testimonies.

We also welcome suggestions for new topics from participants. Students who take part in this project are encouraged to become active in local community/world events in order to understand that respect for human rights is absolutely fundamental to the health and welfare of our planet.

The HGP has a long history of students taking "social actions" to make the world better for all of us. Information about this can be found on our website in the link to the magazine *An End to Intolerance*.

Ages: 12–18, although elementary school students have also participated in the study of conflict resolution and written student book reviews
Dates: Ongoing
Language(s): English, but we welcome translations
Contact: Honey Kern, coordinator, USA <coldspring@iearn.org> or <hkern@iearn.org> or Gideon Goldstein, the HGP mentor in Israel, <gideon@ort.org.il>
Website: <http://www.iearn.org/hgp>

Each year, with an international group of student editors, the students of the HGP publish a global magazine titled *An End to Intolerance* (AETI). Student editors for a past issue of the magazine wrote, "By discussing and making people aware of the Holocaust and other human rights injustices, we are trying to end intolerance and genocide in the world." All annual issues of the magazine can be found on the HGP website.

Honey Kern describes the work of one of the students participating in the HGP:

Jennifer Block began her work on the Holocaust/Genocide Project when she was a freshman in high school. She volunteered to do e-mail correspondence, raise funds for our project magazine via bake sales, and present peer lessons to younger students in our junior high.

Because of her interest and dedication, Jennifer also contributed to our HGP project as a staff writer for *An End to Intolerance*. She was a reporter, then section editor, and moved into the position of senior editor. Her work is still a model for those students who participate today.

An Amazing Experience
Jennifer Block, 18, Cold Spring Harbor High School,
Cold Spring Harbor, New York

The Holocaust/Genocide Project (HGP) is an international online project that focuses on studying and spreading information about world genocides, including the Holocaust. Every year this project publishes an international magazine, *An End to Intolerance,* that is created during the Holocaust/Genocide Project's computer conference. This is my third year working on the HGP and my second year as coeditor-in-chief. Being a part of this project has truly been one of my most amazing experiences throughout high school. I have been given the chance to correspond and share my views with students all over the world, help spread information about the Holocaust to others, and learn about what is being done with this topic in other states, as well as other countries.

I have been brought up with a great awareness of the Holocaust since some of my grandmother's family perished in the death camps. Several times my grandmother has shown me photographs of family members, younger than I am now, who died such cruel deaths. I strongly believe that people must not forget about this time period and the horrors that millions had to go through. I think that everyone needs to know about the Holocaust so that it does not reoccur. I find it hard to believe that some students that I correspond with have barely even heard of the Holocaust.

My participation in the Holocaust/Genocide Project consists of writing e-mail to students and teachers approximately every other day, leading and organizing meetings, writing articles, and editing *An End to Intolerance.* I also have volunteered to help out on interviews for Steven Spielberg's Visual History Project. Steven Spielberg is trying to tape as many Holocaust survivors' stories as possible before the survivors all pass away. I was able to help out with all of the nontechnical parts of the interviews. I was also able to interact and ask my own questions of the survivors both before and after the taping was completed. The survivors showed me by their example that people should never give up hope. Testimonies that I had heard before were just stories, but these were personalized. The survivors taught me about life and how much it means.

During my first year on the project, I mainly corresponded with a Zuni (Native American) elementary school in New Mexico. I later wrote an article about these children, ages six to nine. The main topic I corresponded with them about was prejudice. They sent us their thoughts on prejudice, and we sent back some of ours. They participated in an experiment to show that skin color did not make anyone a better or a worse person. The teacher brought the students a litter of albino mice to compare with the regular mice that they had as pets in the classroom. The children observed that the albino mice behaved just like the other mice, and the only difference was the color of the skin. This activity helped them to accept an albino boy who was in their class. The kids who once teased him began to protect him, and when he was being ridiculed on the playground, the whole class came to his defense. I also corresponded with the Zuni children about love. I saw how much it meant to the children to have someone older to look up to and discuss these brand-new issues and projects with. When I was their age, I barely even knew what prejudice and discrimination meant.

Last year I wrote an article on the Magenta Project. The Magenta Project took place last summer with the goal of informing and educating students about racism. Over three thousand Dutch and South African students took part in an exercise known as "Brown-eyes Blue-eyes," where the students were split up according to the color of their eyes. The brown-eyed students were treated with more respect and given more privileges. The brown-eyed group was given permission to treat the blue-eyed group as inferior. This project allowed both groups to see what prejudice is like firsthand. After this experience, the students discussed what they felt like during the day. Most of them were shocked at what it really felt like to be discriminated against.

Looking back on all that I accomplished and learned, I feel that my work on the Holocaust/Genocide Project was extremely worthwhile. I was able to help others who shared similar interests become involved in the project from both Cold Spring Harbor and various countries around the world. I was given a chance to share my goals, aspirations, and experiences with others. I learned how much hard work goes into preparing and putting together a magazine. Although it took a lot of time and dedication, it was well worth it. When the magazine came back printed and finished, I felt an amazing sense of accomplishment. It was a wonderful honor. Being a part of the Holocaust/Genocide Project is remarkably special and meaningful. It is a memory that I am sure will remain with me forever.

Cultural Horizons

Seth Selleck and Andrew Moseley made a monumental magazine project a reality because they believed so strongly in the idea. They created *Cultural Horizons* (a former I*EARN partner organization). Their persistence, dedication, and hard work won financial supporters and ardent student readers as they did what many thought impossible. They achieved all this because they believed in their dream—one that resulted in one of the best-designed student magazines I have ever seen, paired with superb content.

Despite an eventual lack of funding for the magazine, Seth Selleck wrote, "I believe that the dream and vision of *Cultural Horizons*, a full-color, professionally printed magazine, presenting youths' writing and art from around the world, will live on. The dream we have worked on, together with teachers and students around the world, is too beautiful to die. It lives on in our hearts, and I am sure that one day, someone, somewhere, will pick up a copy of *Cultural Horizons* and find a way to make the dream a reality again."

For information about the status of the *Cultural Horizons* project, or about ordering back copies of *Cultural Horizons*, please write to:

Seth Selleck
Ungdomens Hus
272 80 SIMRISHAMN
SWEDEN
E-mail: info@ungdomenshus.simrishamn.se

A poem and story from *Cultural Horizons* follow, giving you a glimpse into this incredibly beautiful magazine. It's better that I say very little about the poem called "What Is Life?" and let you experience for yourself this exquisite piece. In the story called "Along the Indus," you will spend a day with toiling villagers on the Indus plain in Pakistan. It's more like watching a movie than reading a narrative. Khwaja's sensory details make you see and feel as if you are right there among the Pakistanis. ∎

What Is Life?
Sasa Car, 17, Gimnazija Murska Sobota, Murska Sobota, Slovenia.
Her poem first appeared in *Cultural Horizons: Young Writers Contributing to Global Understanding*, Sixth Issue, September 1999.

Out from the dark we came and into the dark we go.
Like a storm-driven bird at night, we fly out of the nowhere.
For a moment we are seen in the light of the fire, and then
we are gone again into the nowhere.
Life is nothing. Life is all. It is the hand that holds off death.
It is the firefly that shines in the night-time and is black in the morning.
It is the white breath of oxen in the winter. It is the shadow that runs across
the grass and loses itself at sunset. . . .

Along the Indus
Mohammed Ali Farid Khwaja, 19, St. Mary's Academy, Rawalpindi, Pakistan.
This story first appeared in *Cultural Horizons: Young Writers Contributing to Global Understanding*, Fifth Issue, February 1999.

The night ends with the call for prayer; the sound of *azaans* spreads all around like a holy and enchanting spell. This is followed by a refreshing bath in the cold, flowing canal water and by standing up for prayer. With the name of the Almighty, the day begins.

As the sun rises from the fertile, green fields, it sees the men busy with laborious and grueling farming, the women assisting them. The orange and welcoming streaks of sun invite the children to start their merry play and to ramble in the pastures. The cackling of hens and the moos of cows trumpet the beginning of a new day. As the sun gradually grows from a young and nascent orange to a fierce and glowing red, it enjoys the company of the hard-working men. Dressed in *qurta* and *dhoti*, these people work constantly till their white clothes are drenched with sweat and their thick, long moustaches get all wet.

At midday, when the sun gets mighty and cruel, the frenzied environment comes to a sudden halt. It is time for everybody to walk along the winding path beside the canal to their homes. The sun keeps on scorching as the villagers take a peaceful siesta in their small mud-built houses.

A light breeze awakens the villagers and they prepare for a meal of *saag* (spinach), *roti* (bread), and a glass of *lassi* (diluted yogurt). By now, the sun is old and calm; the village again wakes up. Men take their positions in the fields; women get ready to prepare the night's meal; and children occupy the streets. Another couple of hours are spent by the farmers working in the fields with cows and oxen. The canals become the center of attraction for the kids who find it a bastion from the heat. As the sun dies, it sets its eyes for the last time on these fields; green with wheat and gold with mustard.

The village is now lit up by the dim and soothing light of the moon. Euphonious music of flutes fills up the village. The men have a gathering and enjoy the beat of *dhol*, joyfully and victoriously. Tomorrow will be another day, another sun and a new task; and so life in a village on the Indus plain in Pakistan goes on. . . .

6

Displaying Students' Work on the Internet

Your Students and You Can Build Websites

Students and teachers around the world are taking advantage of the Internet to display their writing, photography, and art. Log on, use a search engine, and explore the vast electronic ocean dotted with thousands of student "publication" websites. Some sites contain a few pages, while others have thousands. Students and teachers have constructed websites on every possible subject, with varying levels of interactivity. Setting up websites is becoming easier and more inexpensive—some sites are free.

In this chapter, read about what Richard Barrow and his students have done, learn from them, and then build your own site. It's amazing that he and his students have built from scratch a website of more than a thousand pages. He had no previous knowledge or experience when he began; he has learned along the way. Having gone through the growing pains himself, Barrow is aware of the struggle and challenges in making websites. He shows us how he learned from his mistakes; in turn, we can learn from ours.

Barrow also shares essential, practical advice that you can put to immediate use in building your website. Among the many topics he covers are getting students involved, stages of website construction, design and content, setting up pages, attracting readers to your website, and more. His reader-friendly language is easy to understand.

On a recent visit to Bangkok, Thailand, I had the pleasure of meeting and spending the day with Richard Barrow. He shared with me his tremendous amount of hands-on experience and enthusiasm, which resound in his essay.

CREATING AND BUILDING WEBSITES

**Richard Barrow, Head of Computer Department,
Sriwittayapaknam School, Samut Prakarn, Thailand**

Sriwittayapaknam School in Thailand first started publishing on the Internet back in 1997. It seems such a long time ago now, as so much has happened since then. We didn't really have any master plan as these were the early days for the Internet in Thailand. Not many schools had their own website and a survey we conducted at school showed that only 1 percent of families had Internet access at home. We wanted to create a presence for the school on the Internet, but knew very early on that if we only created the site in the Thai language we wouldn't receive many visitors. Therefore, we started on the road to show people around the world what life in Thailand was like for our students.

Now our site has grown into the largest English-language website in Thailand, receiving thousands of visitors every day. The school has won numerous awards, and foreign journalists and TV crews have often come to the school to interview the students. We now own over twenty domain names such as <http://www.srinai.com>, which between them have thousands of pages and hundreds of pictures. The first site was about the school, but we now publish sites about culture in Thailand, movies, cartoon books, soccer, Scouting—basically, anything that we are interested in.

On My Own

At the start I was on my own. I knew nothing about creating websites. I had very little technical support in English, and none of my teaching colleagues really understood what I was trying to achieve. When you are one of the pioneers, you have to be prepared to make mistakes and then learn from them. So, it was a very slow start, but we did progress as I started to recruit extra help. First the school principal became interested, and she created the school's website in Thai. Then I managed to get some of my keen students, who were good at English, to create their own homepages, where they could tell other people about the pages' creators.

Getting the Students Involved

Once I was confident about my own abilities, I started to involve the students more. At first I would assign them projects to do in their English lessons: writing about themselves and family, holidays, and other cultural things. After the school bought a scanner and then a digital camera, we were able to scan some of the students' artwork and take photographs of their handicraft. The best of these were then put onto the Internet.

Figure 6–1. Thai students working hard on their homepages. Photograph by Richard Barrow.

Later, I let the students produce their own homepages during their computer lessons. At first these were only a basic page with a photo of the student and a brief introduction about themselves and their family. Then, as I became more ambitious, I let the students with a higher ability in English create their own miniwebsites. These were made by using a set formula: "Introduction," "My Family," "My School," "My Holidays," "My Diary," and "My Thailand." So, every student had the same six-page website, but it was up to them to create their own style. You can see an example of this at <http://www.thaistudents.com/class61>. A small group of students helped us with the rapidly growing number of school websites. But, as they became more proficient, they started to create their own sites. These started small at first but quickly blossomed as they started to become popular with visitors from all around the world. Two good examples of these sites are <http://www.ThailandPictures.com> and <http://www.LenFree.com>.

Benefits

The students have benefited greatly from this experience. The Internet is an easy medium for them to express themselves. It is similar to publishing a book, though obviously we are the publishers and can write what we like. The students love it when they get positive feedback, when people write in their guest book or send them an e-mail. It is also an excellent opportunity for them to use English in real-life situations. All of the students who have homepages have their own e-mail account at thaistudents.com. They often receive letters from students around the world. Some of them are just asking questions about life in Thailand. But others are looking for pen friends. The students get a lot of self-satisfaction when they write a letter in English asking questions and then receive a prompt reply. It shows them that they have managed to communicate successfully in the English language. It also shows them that they are not the only people that have difficulty with English. Even native English speakers can't spell!

Building Your Own Website

Before you create your first website, you should first ask yourself the question "Who will my visitors be?" Adults? Children? Parents? Strangers? You will also need to clearly set out your aims and your motives for starting the site. Our school site is probably different from the average site on the Web. We knew very early on that we wouldn't have many of the students' parents visiting. So, the main section was aimed at students and teachers from abroad who wanted to know what it is like to go to a school in Thailand. We created a "virtual tour" of the school so that people could wander around visiting the classrooms, kitchen, Buddha shrine, and the snack shop. They could even go onto the roof for views of the surrounding area. To this we added pages about special ceremonies at school (such as *Wai Kru*, where the students pay respects to their teachers) and festivals (such as *Ashana Puja*, where the students go to the local temple to make an offering to the monks). We also put in art galleries for the students' work and made links to their homepages.

Stages of Constructing a Website

Once you have the idea and you have worked out your aims, you can then start making your website. First, you will need to collect together all of the information you will need and some illustrations, too. We often get people asking us questions about the different fruits in Thailand. So I asked one of my students to put together a mini-website on this subject. He did his research by visiting a bookshop to find a book about fruits in Thailand that had the names in both Thai and English. He then bought a CD–ROM that had hundreds of royalty-free pictures of Thailand. He was lucky, but he could have used one of our digital cameras to take his own pictures.

Design and Content

Once this student had gathered all of his materials, he started planning his website. He had to think about the layout and how many pages he would produce. When creating a website, you have to be careful and not have too many graphics or pictures on one page as it will take time for it to download. Generally, people surfing the Internet are impatient, and they will leave your website if it takes a long time to load. There has to be a careful mix of text and pictures. Text will always appear first, so give them something to read while they are waiting for the pictures to load.

Next, he used a graphics program such as Adobe Photoshop to create banners, titles, and a background image. There are now many different graphic programs on the market that are specifically aimed at people who want to create websites. These often come with a library of ideas and ready-made banners that are easy to adapt. Our students find Ulead PhotoImpact an easy program to use. You can also buy CD-ROMs that have thousands of graphics that you can use. For example, a flashing "new" sign clearly shows people which pages were recently added. If you search for webmaster resources on the Internet, you will find sites where you can download graphics like these for free.

Setting up Pages

Now you are ready to start creating your first website. There are quite a few different website creators on the market. Probably one of the most successful programs is Microsoft FrontPage. This is a WYSIWYG (what you see is what you get) program. Basically, you can create your page in much the same way as you use a word processor. With a click of a button you can also see the HTML script. This is the language of the Internet, and to the uninitiated it probably looks like Greek. I know some schools that teach students to make websites by typing in the HTML language. But if you are a beginner, or someone who doesn't want to learn a new language, then using a WYSIWYG program is your best option.

At school, we use the latest edition of Adobe PageMill as this is very easy to use and has many extra features if you need them. We found that if the students could already use a word processing program, then they could use PageMill with little further instruction. In fact, the students were ready to put pages onto the Internet after only a few lessons. But the more pages and images you add, the more complicated it becomes. So the rule we have is, always start with a simple plan. Let the website grow as you yourself grow with experience and knowledge.

Challenges and Difficulties

We made a lot of mistakes in the early days, but we learned from these. Internet publishing is not like book publishing. If you make a mistake, you can correct it the next time you update that page and upload it onto the Internet. If you are lucky, no one spotted the mistake.

The "Footsteps on the Beach" website <http://www.thaistudents.com/thebeach> about the movie *The Beach* demanded a lot of effort from us, but we were comforted by the fact that so many people were visiting. The site had over five thousand visitors every day from more than 120 different countries around the world. Due to the different time zones, people were visiting our site every hour of the day and night. People were coming back two or three times a day looking for new information, which spurred us on to keep giving them something new.

With a normal publication like a magazine or newspaper, you have one deadline for each edition. We had as many deadlines as there are minutes in a twenty-four-hour period.

Other websites that we have created were less demanding. A few years back we put a website together about Scouting in Thailand <http://www.ThaiScouting.com> as there was no information on the Internet on this subject. We took more care in putting these pages together as we didn't have any daily deadlines. But, once it was finished, we didn't have to do any updates. We could move on to concentrate on other sites.

Collaborative Internet Projects

Not all of our projects have been confined between the school walls. After the popularity of our *The Beach* website, we realized we had thousands of Leonardo DiCaprio fans visiting us every day. So we decided to create a website for them called "Leo Fans Only!" <http://www.LeoFans.com>. Obviously, we didn't know much about Leonardo other than the fact that he was in *Titanic*, so the site is a collaborative effort of people from all around the world. Through the use of message boards and chat rooms the Leo fans now run the website with little input from us. They post the latest news and pictures and basically provide something new for visitors that come every day.

On a few occasions, we have linked up with schools in different countries to share our cultures. The students exchange letters and artwork and we publish the results on the Internet.

Costs

A website can cost anything you like. It is actually possible to do one for free. If you know HTML, you can use Notepad to create your page. You can download free graphics from the Internet. You can use a host provider such as geocities.com or tripod.com, who will let you store your website on their hard disks for free. Once your website is finished, you can download a free version of an FTP (file transfer protocol) program that lets you upload all of your website files onto the Internet. It is even possible to have a free Internet connection these days. Total cost: zero.

However, if you are more serious about creating a presence on the Internet, then you will need to pay some money. You will need software programs to make the webpages (such as Adobe PageMill and Microsoft FrontPage) and graphics programs (such as Adobe Photoshop and Ulead PhotoImpact) to make titles and banners. You will also need an FTP program (such as Ace FTP or WS_FTP) in order to upload your Web files onto the Internet.

Next you will need a host server (a place to store your pages on the Internet that lets people have twenty-four-hour access) and a domain name (the address on the Internet where people can find you). Places like tripod.com give you ten megabytes or more of hard disk space for your websites. These are okay, but they have two disadvantages: you must have their advertisements on your pages, which is what makes the service free, and the website address is often long and difficult to remember. We have a site at tripod.com that has this address: <http://members.tripod.com/~sriwit>.

If you don't want the advertisements, then you have to pay a monthly fee of anything from $15 upward. The more features and hard disk space you want, the more you will have to pay. But the Web space belongs to you and if you decide to put your own ads on the site, then the revenue belongs to you, too. You will also need to buy a domain name for this site. Just about everyone seems to have their own "dot-com" names, and if you want to be taken seriously, then you will need to buy (or more correctly, rent) a domain name. These cost $15 to $35 per year. We bought <www.paknam.com> in order to help promote our city and province. If someone already owns a domain name that you want, you can offer to buy it from them. But be warned, some names sell from $5,000 up to over a million dollars.

If you don't mind the ads at tripod.com or geocities.com, there is something you can do about the long address for free. You can get redirectionals that point to places on the Internet. For example, if you type <http://come.to/thebeach> it automatically goes to our "Beach" website at <http://www.thaistudents.com/thebeach>. But you have to be quick, as it is first come, first served. You discover things like this as you spend more time on the Web.

Advice for Interested Teachers

When you come to create your first website, keep it simple to start with, and don't try to get too ambitious too soon. The Internet has some limitations compared to a book. The pages do load slowly so you have to think carefully about how much you put on one page. Get the students to write about things that interest them. That way it won't seem like hard work to them. Be prepared to learn from your mistakes. Surf the Internet a lot to see what other people are doing. The Internet is the best textbook for learning about websites.

How to Get Readers to Your Website

That old notion "build it and they will come" doesn't really work on the Internet. There must be millions of websites out there by now, and your site is just a drop in the ocean. If you are doing a website about your school, then you already have a captured audience. But what if you are doing a site about something different? Let's take the example of our website for the movie *The Beach*. We started it in the very early days, even before the filmmakers arrived in Thailand. We had no competition at that time, and so there was only one place on the Internet to find information about *The Beach*. By the time the movie came out, over a year later, we were well established, with more than 360 pages and 600 pictures. All of the other websites on *The Beach* paled in comparison. But still, even if you have a good site, people can't find you unless you do some promotion.

There are some professional businesses that, for a fee, will help promote your site. But, if you have the time and patience, you can do this yourself by visiting some of the popular search engines such as yahoo.com, excite.com, and altavista.com and submitting your site. After a couple of weeks your site should be on their databases. For our *The Beach* site, we also posted information about the site on message boards attached to firmly established Leonardo DiCaprio fan sites.

But I think our best promoter was word of mouth. We were providing something that no one else had, and word quickly spread on the grapevine. Before the filmmakers arrived in Thailand, we were only receiving half a dozen visitors per day. This quickly shot up to three hundred the very next day and then five hundred and then after a few days the numbers were in the thousands. As the word started to spread farther, newspaper journalists started contacting the school, which gave us even further promotion.

Thai Students Online: Looking Forward

The school website at <http://www.sriwittayapaknam.ac.th> became so popular with foreign students doing a project about Thailand that we decided to branch out and produce a more in-depth website about life in Thailand. That is why we started Thai Students Online at <http://www.thaistudents.com>. The school website then focused more on school life and the Thai Students site on the culture of Thailand. We set up a section called Project Thailand and invited students from around the world to send us their questions. We also linked to other websites around Thailand made by Thai students and schools.

It is difficult to predict the future, as we have surpassed all of our expectations. But one thing is for sure—growth. The school now has well over a thousand pages on the Internet. Some of the websites that the school or students started have become so well established that we decided to provide them with their own home on the Internet; <http://www.thailandlife.com> and <http://www.thailandguidebook.com> are wonderful examples. The students and teachers are even running shops in our own Thai cybermarket.

7

E-mail Publication Projects

Publishing with Students, an E-mail Project

In a very real sense, writing *Publishing with Students* has been an enormous, international e-mail publication project involving hundreds of participants, who combined, have thousands of years of experience. Using e-mail, I have been able to contact so many talented teachers from around the world in a short time period. Such an endeavor would have taken so much longer via regular mail. In fact, it probably would have been impossible. At my desk in Portland, Oregon, I have communicated and worked with some teachers who were writing their first published piece to those who were nationally known educators. What a thrilling trip it has been, filled with delight and discovery!

Looking into the future of student publications, I see e-mail projects playing a tremendous role. By participating in them, students will come to know and better understand their peers in other states and countries. Readers around the world will hear their voices. What a tremendous forum for increasing global understanding.

Teachers everywhere are tapping into the technology of the Internet and producing e-mail-driven publications. Anna Citrino, a teacher at Singapore American School, has written this chapter about her e-mail projects that involved two schools in the U.S. along with her own school in Singapore. From her work, you can glean information and begin formulating plans for your own project.

What's most impressive is the thoroughness with which Citrino covers every aspect. Whether she's writing about establishing and maintaining communications and relationships or ways to save time, Citrino provides pertinent details, one after the other. Her extensive lists identify the key points. The provided student samples answer your questions. After reading her piece, readers will have the advice, guidelines, and information they need.

One might think of communicating via e-mail as cold and impersonal, especially since you will rarely have the chance to talk face-to-face with the other person. Citrino is aware of this and engages her students in activities that bring them closer together. For example, the students begin by introducing themselves and including their recent photos. Because they can see each others' faces, their partners are alive and real. The need for camaraderie among the teachers is vital, and Citrino tells how she develops strong working relationships with her peers.

In closing, she writes, "I read comment after comment in the end-of-the-year evaluations describing how the students have come to like writing poetry when they didn't care for it before. These are the kinds of moments that give me hope for the future, that allow a person to see the meaning and value of doing an online exchange. Everywhere there are opportunities to open a dialogue. There is time. Invite someone in."

I can't help but stop and think that throughout her chapter, Citrino has invited you in. ∎

GOING WILD, AN ONLINE EXCHANGE OF NATURE WRITING: A MODEL FOR E-MAIL PUBLICATION PROJECTS

Anna Citrino, Seventh-Grade Reading, Language Arts, and Social Studies Teacher, Singapore American School, Singapore

Purpose and Intentions of Project

Interested middle school students at Singapore American School in Singapore, Sierra Vista Middle School in Arizona, and Sumrall Junior High in Sumrall, Mississippi, participated in an online exchange. The project's purpose was to encourage students' exploration of nature. Additionally, we hoped to create a forum for students to explore, develop, and use their writing abilities as a way of communicating their experience with nature among themselves as well as with wider audiences outside the school.

As a middle school teacher, I wanted the exchange not only to help build a strong foundation for students' writing, but also to provide a context that better enabled students to reaffirm connections with the natural world where they live and to find ways to reflect its value. One of the schools in our exchange, in Singapore, is located in a large urban area, while the other two, in Mississippi and Arizona, are located in smaller, more rural and suburban areas. We felt we could learn from each others' observations and perspectives resulting from our diverse locations and help each other come to value the natural world around us a bit more because of it.

Oftentimes, people's attempts to raise consciousness about ecological issues have involved presenting others with facts. This project differed in that its goal was to get students exploring the natural world, both on their own and in conjunction with their science and art classes, over an extended period of time, and then to use these observations and impressions to transform their reflections into poetry or prose that incorporated both fact and feeling.

Establishing and Maintaining Communication and Relationships

Finding willing and committed participants in an online exchange isn't particularly difficult if you already are connected to a network of teachers who have e-mail. One simply needs to conceive of the project and send out a message inviting all those who would be interested to respond.

Three teacher participants is a workable number for a project. It is small enough to allow a person to manage to communicate with the other classes and still feel a sense of intimacy, but big enough that in case one of the participants drops out or finds himself unable to participate fully during the exchange, the project can still continue with those who are available. Having done several online conferences over the years, it has been my experience that all participants of the project will not be able to participate equally at all times, even if the teachers are all committed, responsible, reliable individuals. Teachers cannot always predict ahead of time exactly where the demands or other outside opportunities of the school year will take them, and it's best to allow for flexibility in the way the project is set up. Having three teachers or classrooms allows for this flexibility.

Another part of setting up the project is to tell others at your school what you are doing. Inform your administrator about your proposed exchange, the scope of your plan and its purpose. Keeping administrators informed about the exchange helps them not only to understand what you are doing and its value, but can also sometimes lead to financial support. It is also helpful to communicate your plans to other teammates you collaborate with so they will know what you are doing and how it might affect or influence them.

Keep a flexible mind-set at the start of the project. The project should be carefully thought out and planned if it is going to get off to a smooth start, and if you want all involved to experience success with the purpose you've set out.

Getting Going—Components of the Project

There are several practical things teachers can do to begin:

1. Clearly define what it is, its purpose, and the reason why you want to do the exchange.
2. Define what teachers will do and what students will do (roles).
3. Define what will actually be exchanged in the project.
4. Describe the topic(s) for the exchange, the format of the pieces, and where they will be located in the computer's files.
5. Determine guidelines for students' responses to each other.
6. Create a timeline of what will happen, or what pieces will be sent when.
7. Determine budget expenditures.

Writing out this information clearly at the onset of the project allows time for participants to discuss online what they think will work or what needs to be changed, ask any questions, and make any adjustments in the schedule or overall conception of the project before getting students involved. This part of setting up the exchange is simplified if one teacher conceptualizes the project and writes out the plan for others who have expressed possible interest. This way teachers will know what they are getting into before they commit to the project and will be less likely to back out part way through.

Once participants agree to the plan, place it in the conference folder, a file set aside on your computer (in your e-mail or word processing program), or on a web-page on the Internet (if that's where you will carry on your online communication) for later reference. Being able to review the original agreement can help the project keep its focus over time.

Keeping Communication Flowing

Once the project is set up and moving along, it's important to keep communication going, not only among the students in their exchange of writing or responding to each other, but also between the organizers. We chose to organize our project by creating one common folder at our conference site. The teachers in my conference carried on their conference through Bread Net. Teachers participating in our conference gathered students' various writing pieces and then copied and pasted all the messages into one message sent to a conference folder we had on Bread Net so other teachers could read them.

Once the message arrived at the various teachers' computers, the information was disseminated either by printing hard copies for students or by forwarding the writing or responses to the students' home e-mail accounts. The same thing was done for students' responses to each others' work.

To keep communication flowing between you and student participants, you may want to e-mail notes to students, reminding them when to send their pieces or responses or simply encouraging them to keep writing. Without the constant flow of conversation, students' energy can get pulled in other directions.

Beyond passing on information to students, I tried to get them to feel the value of what they were doing. I aimed to establish a sense of a community of writers sharing their work and to convey my belief in the importance of the work they were doing. To help create this atmosphere in the conference, I wrote various other kinds of e-mail notes to students, including comments from other writers about their writing process, excerpts from other writers' pieces, and ideas for writing. I also sent them some of my own pieces on the topics they were writing on, poems, essays, or quotes from writers—all in an attempt to make the conference a more vital experience with a human touch.

Though e-mail conversation with participants definitely helps keep enthusiasm for the conference going and helps make it more alive, it can also take considerable time. You will have to judge for yourself how much of this you can feasibly consider. If possible, you might want to consider setting up your conference folder so that you can post messages to a group of students all at one time. You can save yourself lots of time in copying messages this way. Also, if students have the ability to communicate directly to each other via a website, you could cut down on the response time to students' pieces, as well as broaden and heighten the dynamics.

Making Adjustments

As the endeavor moves along, you'll find adjustments you will want and need to make. Several weeks into ours, we decided to cut back on the frequency of sending original pieces because it all became too much for both students and teachers to try to send pieces, read them, and then respond while carrying on the regular curriculum during the week. We all breathed a sigh of relief when we allowed ourselves more time: one week to send an original piece and the following week to respond. With the lag time of getting everything ready to send online, this worked much better for us.

We made other adjustments as well. We included guest professional writers in our conference the second time we did the same exchange, and it took us time to get everyone in sync. Not everyone was familiar with how the software and folders worked or generally how things were set up. Sometimes one school is on vacation or involved in a big project and has less time to spend than another. Sometimes emergencies happen. Support each other through these difficulties as much as you can and you'll be surprised what difficulties you can surmount. Things are not going to go smoothly all the time—that you can plan on. Keep open communication about what's going on with each other. Ask questions.

As organizers, continue throughout the project to communicate with each other to clarify your situations, needs, and expectations. Review your timeline every now and then; tell each other what you have in mind, what you want to do, what you think you're planning to do according to the project guideline. Allow for adjustments. Flexibility is an essential ingredient to a successful exchange. Things will go more smoothly if you work together as water does, bending around the rocks and obstacles you encounter.

Guest Participants

One of the steps we took to get the guest writers on board and in sync with the exchange was to outline their duties clearly.

First, get the guests set up on your exchange by telling them where the exchange will be located and any directions they need to locate things once they link up to it. Second, before they decide to work with you, clarify the amount and type of commitment they'd be involving themselves in.

It is important for teachers and guests participating in the exchange to decide if you want your guest participants to respond to drafts as they are submitted or only to pieces being submitted for final revisions before the book. Making this decision will help everyone better decide how much attention to give to the students' pieces and how to manage their time on the exchange. In our project, we simply asked the guest writers to respond to student work sincerely, honestly, and with concrete thoughts, reactions, and suggestions that demonstrate sensitivity toward the students' efforts.

Introductions and Photos

A final thing you might consider in setting up your project is including photos and short introductions of the participants. Photos can make the exchange more tangible for students, and the introductions can stimulate interest and enthusiasm for the exchange. I remember my students rushing to the computer to see the photos of the other participating students. They were equally eager to see how they looked in the photos of themselves that we sent to students at the other locations. Artwork that students make in response to or in collaboration with other student writers is another way to bolster dragging spirits in the midst of a long exchange. If you have access to a digital camera, it is rather easy to send jpeg photos to the classrooms in the other locations. If these are not available to you, you can always take prints or slides and have them scanned in.

Initial Steps

To get your project off the ground, you'll need to do the following:

1. Gather names of students who want to participate in the project. Make a letter that outlines the exchange and its timeline. Explain in it how things will go during the exchange. Give it to students who want to participate.
2. Write up a letter that asks for parent and student permission to use their work in any article, book chapter, etc., that you or your coteachers may want to write.
3. Make introductions. Have students write a brief description of themselves and the place they live, focusing on a particular, significant aspect of that place. The piece should be about five to ten lines. Send them out the following week. Online project coordinators (teachers) could help students generate questions they want to ask of students in the other locations, if they like.
4. After introductions are first sent out, begin the exchange for week one. Remind the students on the first day of the week what the prompt (the topic for the week) is. Give them a week to write their piece and hand it in. Send the pieces in one bunch to the other teachers participating in the exchange.
5. Notify online guests, if you are using them, that the exchange is beginning.
6. Share with other teachers examples of suggested ideas for prose and poetry pieces/forms that could be used during the exchange as models, or as a springboard for discussion.

Benefits

Much of the work many teachers do in the classroom is developed and carried out in isolation. Participating in an online exchange, however, develops a kind of unique collaboration that can bridge great differences in space and cultures, diminishing the isolation. It can enable teachers to build a support system outside of the immediate classroom context, extend classroom boundaries, and build new dreams for what is possible with one's own students. Though at the start you may not know the teachers you work with on an exchange, you may find you grow into friends who support each other, not merely as co-collaborators on the exchange, but as individuals with a respect for each others' unique achievements.

One of the benefits of students responding to each other in this kind of online exchange is the many responses students receive from their distant cowriters, as well as the guest authors. These serve as encouragement to keep writing. For some students it became a turning point in their awareness of their potential to contribute something creative, necessary, and positive to the world. In addition, it helped students discover how they could define and shape a sense of themselves that they were previously unaware of. One of these students, Lennie Waite, explains:

> Throughout the writing exchange I learned a lot. I learned about picking topics to write about, and how to picture a place in nature and then write about it. I began to get better at writing and eventually the words would write themselves instead of me having to sit there for a long time and think about what to write.

The poem below, by Leslie Wolverton from Sumrall, Mississippi, is followed by a response from Jessica Widel, in Singapore. This example from the exchange demonstrates the kind of effort students took to describe a particular location in precise terms and the type of encouragement students in different locations were able to give. The poem shows a clear attempt to shape an idea carefully. Though the responder's comments are stated in general terms, she does give reasons for why she liked the poem and offers an example to support her opinion. These kinds of responses encourage writers to continue writing, aiming to make their observations and word choices precise. Additionally, responders learn to look more carefully at what makes a piece work well as they formulate their comments, thus reinforcing these qualities as they write their own pieces.

Mississippi Weather
Leslie Wolverton, 14, Sumrall Attendance Center, Lamar
County School District, Sumrall, Mississippi

WINTER
The brown grass crunches under my feet.
The cold, crisp winds blast at my face
and tousle my hair.
Wildlife is scarce.
Animals have gone to their homes and rest,
waiting for the cold to pass.
Ice collects on the leaves of the trees,
where dew once rested.

SPRING
Light April showers moisten the woods,
bringing fresh new life to what once was barren.

Seedlings that laid dormant over the chilling winter,
sprout from the soil beneath me.
Birds, freshly rested from a winter's nap,
flutter from branch to branch and chirp softly.

SUMMER
The bright sun warms my wet skin as it shines down upon me.
I dive into the river and flow with the strong current of the waters.
Wildlife is abundant and stirs in the forests.
I cast my ambassador reel into the lake.
I race my four-wheeler through the woods,
as the small branches whip at my arms and legs.

FALL
The crisp smell of burning leaves lingers in the air.
I inhale the cool air and feel it enter my lungs.
Falling leaves of crimson, orange, gold and bronze
fall to the ground, covering the dying grass below.

Response to: Leslie Wolverton
Place: Mississippi
Title of Piece: Mississippi Weather
Date: January 23, 1998
Responder: Jessica Widel, Singapore

Leslie,

I read your poem and really enjoyed it. I liked your use of words, and how you made the reader feel like they were there in each season. I like how you expressed your thoughts and interpreted them into words. I really liked your creative use of words in each season, and how you took details and elaborated them to make them something beautiful. I especially liked the sentence: "The cold, crisp winds blast at my face and tousle my hair . . ."

I really liked your use of words and how you made the scene come alive. Overall, I enjoyed reading and responding to your poem.

Teacher Rewards

Those of us coordinating the project or serving as guest authors trust and respect each other. We support the work each person has done and the decisions we have individually made during the project. We see each other as learners as well as teachers or writers, and have grown confident in each others' commitment not only to the exchange but also to each other as individuals. Through all our changes and emergency situations, we've stuck by each other, bent as needed, and supported each other. Our exchange has continued to be enriched as a result.

One of the best rewards of the project is watching students' skill as poets develop and reading the quality of what they create, as in the following student example.

> **Coral**
> Peter Frost, 12,
> Singapore American School, Singapore
>
> Long lines cut into the sandy ocean floor
> Antlers of all colors
> Sprout like weeds
> From rocks and grit
> Colorful furrows walk down the dunes,
> Red, green, and blue,
> Absorb the waves of light
> From gently lapping waves,
> Build their ramparts up and up
> To create a rainbow chamber,
> Entrapping and imprisoning
> the molecules of water
> Making a home
> For the workers who built them
> Wave-scraping apartments
> For microscopic organisms
> The tiniest of ocean folk
> Colored mosaics of life
> with brightly hued walls;
> The open dance floors of crabs,
> These strange figures,
> Cast in a water mold
> And hewn from the sea itself
> Masterpieces of art created
> By artists of the smallest sort

The guest writers' responses—extended commentary on students' pieces—were invaluable. As outside experts, their comments validated students' writing in a unique way that peers and teachers could not.

Online Challenges and Difficulties—How to Overcome Them

One of the central challenges of the exchange is simply keeping up with it. Before and during the exchange, lots of discussion occurs between the teachers and guest writers, as well as with students, concerning what we are doing, in addition to the actual exchange of the work itself. The three of us who were the teacher coordinators in the exchange have done it twice. We love the kind of energy and motivation it brings to our students and the way it gets them to take a prolonged look at the natural world, reflect on its value, and express their connection to it through their writing. We have decided, however, that if we do the exchange again, we plan to reduce the number of weeks in order to keep up the momentum without wearing ourselves out.

In Singapore the exchange took about an hour and a half of my time each night until the first half of the second quarter of the exchange, when we were only sending revisions of pieces to each other. Teachers spent a lot of classroom energy and time on the exchange, as well as the time it took to get pieces up online. At all of the schools, teachers had to work with students to revise their work to get it ready to put into the chapbook we were creating to accompany the online work. This work took considerable time.

Ways to Save Time

1. Consider creating a webpage using one of the free webpage sites available on the Internet. Then post student work and comments there instead of e-mailing individual messages. This could save hours of e-mailing time. We chose not to do this because not all students had access to the Internet.

2. If you are doing the exchange on a website, rotate the monitoring of the work posted among the teacher coordinators.

3. Check the site only a set number of times during the week. The teachers would decide how often to check the site. This method makes it more difficult to respond immediately to participants' concerns, but if everyone accepts the restrictions, it can work.

4. Reduce the length of the project. Participants will be more willing to expend the extra energy an exchange commonly takes if it lasts only five or six weeks instead of nine weeks or longer.

5. Consider narrowing the focus of the exchange. Concentrate only on poetry, for example, rather than opening the exchange up to a variety of genres. Another way would be to write on fewer topics.

6. Involve fewer schools or less students.

7. If you are creating a chapbook as the culmination of the project, divide up responsibilities so that one of the participants produces the book while a different teacher spearheads the exchange itself. A third person, if you have one, might work on managing the artwork (if any) for the book.

Saving Time on the Culminating Activity

Many online exchange participants create a chapbook of their writing at the end of the project. However, this part of the exchange can be extremely time consuming. Here are some ideas for culminating activities that don't involve producing a book.

- Post the work on a school webpage.
- Host a public reading or several readings for other classes.
- Enlist the support and help of other teachers at your school. For example, talk with the journalism teacher and invite students who work for the school newspaper or morning school TV broadcast to do a piece about your exchange. (Even before the culminating activity, you can certainly involve other teachers in the various aspects of the exchange as appropriate.)
- Decide that the exchange itself and some sort of online final reflection will suffice.

What you do depends on your purpose and goals for the exchange.

Not Being Able to Meet in Person

Another significant challenge to an online exchange is the inability to just sit down together mull things over with the other coordinators, guest authors, and exchange partners in the same place at the same time. Since this opportunity is unavailable, coordinators need to frequently check in with each other online and ask how things are coming along, and to review deadlines, due dates, and other phases of the project. While it might seem to you that things are clear because you all agreed to a particular plan at the start of the year, it doesn't necessarily mean everyone remembers that plan once you get going. The particular circumstances one teaches in and the demands of the school year as it progresses can cause things to change, making it worth your time to talk to each other about what's coming up.

At the start, put a copy of your timeline, role descriptions, and formats for carrying out the exchange in your conference folder where everyone can refer to it. This can help prevent confusion. It's a good idea to view these as working documents rather than as an inflexible, unalterable contract. It is difficult to anticipate everything that one might encounter before the exchange, and it only makes sense to agree to alter and improve aspects of it as you work.

Use a Specific Format for Submissions

A smaller challenge in the project, though a helpful one to hurdle, is to get students to submit pieces online in a particular format. At the start of the project, I gave students a letter with a visual example of the format to use for work they would be sending online. An accompanying suggestion encouraged them to keep a copy of all their work on a disk or on their hard drive—for future reference and in case they wanted to use that piece to revise for publication. I also requested that students spell check their pieces before sending them online. The format for sending original pieces was as follows:

From: (your name)
Place: (country you are writing from)
Title of Piece:
Date:

Format for sending responses was as follows:

To: (name of author)
Place: (state or country person is located)
Title of Piece Responding to:
Date:
Responder: (your name and state or country)

Another tip is to request that all teachers in the exchange separate their students' responses from their writing pieces; they should also separate responses that go to one school from the responses that go to another, and then send these as separate files. If you do this, the teacher receiving the file won't have to sort through twenty or more messages to find the ones for her students. It simply saves time and makes things move along more smoothly.

To reduce problems, ask students to place the copy of the piece they are e-mailing directly into the e-mail message itself. Do not send them as attachments unless everyone participating in the exchange shares the same type of computer operating system, has compatible word processing programs, or has appropriate software translators. Otherwise, participants will not be able to read the pieces and they will have to be resent inside the e-mail message anyway. Some of the formatting can be lost this way, but if the writer saves the document in the word processing program as a rich text file, the formatting can be preserved when it is either placed in the e-mail message or sent as an attachment.

Routines

Typical routines for the exchange vary from site to site and from the start of the exchange to the end. Each of us carried out the exchange in a slightly different manner. In two of the classrooms, the exchange was part of the classroom work for all students in a particular class. Teachers in these classrooms worked with students on their drafts, giving them examples and guiding them through revision. In the third classroom, the exchange was carried out as an extension of the work students had done on nature writing in a previous quarter.

If several weeks went by without a student at my own site getting a response to his or her piece, I asked teachers at the other sites to find a student to respond to his or her work. I tried to keep a general eye on who was getting the most responses at the other sites and who was not. If I noticed some students at the other sites were not getting responses, I matched them with students at my site and asked my students to write a response. Since it was difficult to keep up with who was or wasn't getting responses at the other school sites, I relied on teachers there to keep an eye on their own situations and to notify me if someone fell through the cracks.

Websites

In a number of ways it would be simpler to carry on the exchange through a webpage created specifically for it. On a webpage, messages can be sent directly from a student to a common site so that the teacher does not have to copy each message for each student and forward it separately. A webpage allows all students to access the site and read each other's pieces and comments all in one common place.

However, a webpage is really only an option if all the students in your exchange have Internet access and software like Netscape or Internet Explorer, which allows you to get on the Web. You would also need to be able to provide students with the time to get on the Web and send their messages at school if they do not have access at home. Students with home computers could write their messages on a disk, bring it to school, and paste the message into a message board on the webpage. If you choose to do this, students will need to make sure the files they create at home are compatible with the computers at school or the information on their disks will be inaccessible. Macintoshes can often convert files from IBM-compatible computers, but the reverse is not always true. If we had chosen to do our conference on a webpage, we teachers would still have needed to link up in a separate website location or through e-mail where students wouldn't have access, in order to carry on the business and personal discussions related to the exchange.

Roles and Duties of Teachers: Working Together, Making Decisions

I took on the role of initiator and coordinator of the exchange, proposing structure for the exchange itself and roles for participants. Once the exchange was underway, my role was to keep it focused and rolling, anticipating possible questions and concerns as best I could. Everyone participating in the exchange agreed to the basic structure, helped refine it as we went, and worked to keep their part of the exchange going. If we saw a need for change, we brought up our concern or question in the conference folder. We chose to keep only one folder for the conference so that everything could be read by all teachers and guest writers, and so that all revisions and concerns were openly made and discussed. This process worked for us, and even helped develop our mutual respect.

Student Responsibilities, Roles, and Involvement

The students' general responsibility in an exchange is to send their writing to other student participants and to respond to others' pieces. At the outset, students who had chosen to participate in the project via e-mail were given a letter that they could later refer to. This letter explained their role and responsibilities and essentially guided the students through what they would do in the project. Students also received online reminders.

Necessary Equipment

This exchange can be carried on with a minimum of equipment—one computer with a modem and a word processing program in each classroom and/or at home—though, of course, the more computers available to students, the easier it will be to carry out. We used both IBM-compatible and Macintosh computers.

If you want to send photos or other visual documents to each other, which I highly recommend as a way to keep the interest in the project moving along, be sure that you send them in a file format that the other teachers' computers can translate. It should be some kind of picture format, such as Netscape or the Picture Viewer program that many newer computers have.

It's important that all people involved in the project have a basic understanding of word processing and how to send and receive e-mail. For teachers and participating online guests, it's also important that they know how to either access the webpage you've made for the project, or use the telecommunications software and network that you've selected for the project.

The Possibilities

Possibilities abound. It would be fun to connect students for a real-time exchange on our topic, perhaps utilizing the technology that allows telephone calls or live camera through the computer. Considering the time difference between locations, this is potentially problematic but not impossible.

Another extension to the exchange I'd like to make if I had more time to work on it would be to ask the previous year's students to comment on the current students' work. This could be done through a webpage or on a shared folder on the intranet at a particular school site, and could help further instill the importance of the writing they are doing and its value to the community at large.

At my particular school site, I have worked at making links between the nature writing that students have done for the exchange and the work students are doing in other disciplines. The art students at our school, for example, selected several of the students' poems to turn into calligraphy pieces with illustrations modeled after those used in children's books. These were then displayed in the foyer of the main office of the school, on bulletin boards, and in classrooms. In addition, students in the art classes made masks on the themes of earth, air, water, and fire.

As you can see, there are many possibilities for teachers and students. It's best, though, to start small with something you feel is manageable and possible, extending from there as you get a sense of what will work in your particular environment and what you are able to commit yourself to.

Explorations, Creations, and Results

I continue to do online exchanges because I believe in the power of the written word to change the world. What students learn through participating in an exchange is more than writing skills, though they certainly gain those as well. Many of the students in our exchange chose to write poetry. As Lucille Clifton said at a recent writing workshop I attended, "As long as one person in the world is writing a poem, the world is a more human place." This is the other value of doing such an exchange. What happens during an exchange can help to humanize the world. Students have the opportunity to share their ideas with an interested audience of peers over an extended period of time. The exchange gives them a context in which they can grow toward understanding the value and power of well-crafted words spoken with honesty and heart. The exchange also provides a forum for open dialogue across cultures, age levels, and the biases of appearances, socioeconomic status, and intelligence. At the same time, the students are communicating about their particular places, ideas, values, and experiences—inviting outsiders into their worlds and creating new ways to connect and make meaning.

While doing an exchange, a teacher does not necessarily know which seeds she is sowing will grow. She simply plants the seeds. Then she waters them all. Some will grow. Cory Nguyen has been one of those students during the exchange this past year. Cory is in love with writing poetry. He asks to read his poems for classes or for a school assembly anytime he has the opportunity. He writes pieces about nature to show me even after the exchange has finished and tells me he is working on a poetry book.

I watch Cory calmly read a new piece he has written to the class. I meet with a student from the previous year's exchange at lunch to discuss how she might publish her pieces. A parent stops me in the hall to tell me how her son has read many times over the book we published from the exchange last year and how she received a poem from him that he wrote for his grandmother who recently died. I watch as students read their poems to the applause of bookstore audiences of fifty and assemblies of eight hundred. I read comment after comment in the end-of-the-year evaluations describing how the students have come to like writing poetry when they didn't care for it before. These are the kinds of moments that give me hope for the future, that allow a person to see the meaning and value of doing an online exchange. Everywhere there are opportunities to open a dialogue. There is time. Invite someone in.

8

The Inquiry Approach and Publishing

Inquiry Linked with Publication

What is real inquiry? How can students and a network of schools learn about and practice it? What does inquiry have to do with publication? And how can publication help launch the inquiry process? These are a few questions that Mark Wagler answers.

At the outset, he lays out potential activities that later turn into realities as Wagler takes you on a tour through a typical year in the making of the inquiry-based publication titled *Great Blue*. You glimpse students performing at annual fundraisers and gathering at yearly conferences. In the fall, you sit in on his lessons, where students are examining student models from previous *Great Blue* issues. Knowledge gained from this analysis will be used in planning and implementing their upcoming inquiry projects. He describes his students investigating questions they raise in all subject areas, and you're with them—asking questions, gathering data, analyzing it, and drawing conclusions. In the spring, you work side by side with a group of teachers who are putting together the latest issue. There's one word to describe both this literary journey and *Great Blue*—phenomenal!

COMMUNITIES OF INQUIRY: A YEAR IN THE LIFE OF *GREAT BLUE*

Mark Wagler, Fourth/Fifth-Grade Teacher, Randall School, Madison, Wisconsin

Imagine students working on long-term investigations based on their own questions, reflecting all areas of the curriculum. Conjure up classrooms of students working on multiple projects: here a survey, there an experiment, data everywhere. Picture kids doing interviews in the community, puzzling over algebra, or analyzing media.

Fancy those children working together, reporting on research, brainstorming strategies, drafting and peer editing articles. Suppose they could publish what they've learned in a journal distributed to many hundreds of students and adult educators. Contemplate the pride kids will feel after all their hard work. Dream of the vast potential of student wonder and performance.

And open your eyes to *Great Blue*.

Heron Network classrooms in the Madison, Wisconsin, area organize much of their curriculum around *Great Blue: A Journal of Student Inquiry*. As school begins, students in grades one through six begin reading articles from past journals, looking for ideas—especially questions and procedures—for their own inquiry projects. In late fall or early winter, they gather at the Memorial Union of the University of Wisconsin for an annual student conference; here students first experience the larger community of the Heron Network, as they meet hundreds of other students engaged in long-term investigations.

In late winter, students perform music, humor, dance, and drama at the annual *Great Blue* Variety Show, raising funds to cover publishing costs of our journal. By spring break, students will have completed their projects and written an article for publication. Before school is out, each author receives a copy of the new journal. In between these events are the day-to-day structures necessary for supporting student inquiry and holding the network together.

Perennial Inquiry

Inquiry is trumpeted nowadays as a key standard in all curricular areas. Much that is labeled inquiry or problem solving in contemporary theory and practice, however, has a cookbook flavor. There is little time in American pedagogy for real student questions, even less for the laborious processes of students carrying out extended investigations in an attempt to answer these flickers of wonder. Our schools are more geared to producing train clerks, consumers, patriots, and dilettantes than to educating mathematicians, artists, activists, and scientists.

Real inquiry, in school and out, has a narrative quality, the feel of students struggling to make sense of the world. Like creative adults, students need room to make mistakes, time to explore detours, support for the odyssey. Most important, they need a chance to follow their own curiosity and passion, and the opportunity to work on extended projects that make a difference to them and the world.

What does inquiry feel like in one Heron classroom? Enter Room 202 at Randall School in the fall of 1999 and observe the fourth and fifth graders. Over time you will see that our entire curriculum is intended to support student inquiry. On the second day of school, I hand out individual copies of the major text we will use all year, the 1999 issue of *Great Blue*. Students take turns reading paragraphs out loud from the articles written by students in Room 202, fourteen of whom have returned as fifth graders. The authors are reminded their hard work led to success. I challenge them, also, to begin imagining projects for this second year. The new fourth graders see a model of what they will be able to do.

As we read, I ask them, "What is the question she asked?" "What procedures did he use?" "What data did she collect?" "What conclusion did he reach?" "What help did she get in her project?" Soon they are able to answer more complex questions such as, "Do the data support his conclusion?" "If you did a similar project this year, what could you do to improve it?" I show older issues of our journals and remind them of the lineage of our work—each year Heron students build on what has been accomplished before. Next we expand the image of our community of inquiry by reading articles from other classrooms.

In the early months, my primary focus is helping students develop work habits and skills that will sustain extended investigations. Instead of worksheets that go home each week, students keep all their work in notebooks (one for each of the five *Great Blue* sections); they will use their notes midyear for writing a series of essays. Writing fluency is critical: students who have difficulty recording observations, reflections, and procedures usually cannot work for long on an independent project. Writing keeps them on task, allows me to quickly monitor their work, and gives them notes for reports and articles. We begin every day with journal writing, when students are most capable of writing at length, followed by journal reading aloud, which gives students practice in speaking to the whole class, a crucial skill in an inquiry-based curriculum.

I guide their first inquiry projects, breaking them down into daily tasks. For example, each student chooses an outdoor environment near their home, typically a backyard, that they will regularly observe throughout the year. At first I specify what they are to observe and record about their "place in nature," with assignments to map vegetation, list weather features, record what they notice with individual senses, note details of species, draw or measure individual items, or report what they find in the soil. Then I eventually permit them to take notes on whatever they observe. I provide similar guidance for ethnographic and reading projects.

One way of supporting "I Wonder" projects—extended science investigations based on student questions—is by initially limiting the range of our inquiries. While textbook science is a mile wide and an inch deep, university and commercial labs have a much narrower focus. This semester, my students are limited to researching relationships in our "Living Machine," an elaborate series of containers connected by flowing water, which models biological habitats, hydrology, water chemistry, and certain aspects of geology. For the fourth graders, I model the inquiry process for them by developing several group questions: together we set up procedures and collect data. Meanwhile, fifth graders begin research on nutrients and plants, habitats of fish and snails, and worm composting. Fifth graders who have trouble finding a question or getting materials must either read related articles in past issues of *I Wonder* or *Great Blue*, or participate in the group research. By semester break, all students will have reported on their research at lab meetings, and will have written an essay on "Living Machines" that incorporates observations, student research, and class discussions.

Some of our exploratory projects in December will become *Great Blue* articles in April. Students have recently finished writing a five-page essay on family foodways, based on a long series of homework assignments where they interviewed family members about gardening, mealtime traditions, and special recipes for holidays and other celebrations. They have just begun another essay, a portrait of themselves as a reader, which will pull together their independent reading during the fall with reflections on what they have learned already and what more they hope to accomplish as readers.

Observe two fourth-grade girls in December. Every opportunity they get, they're in our lab area, working with daphnia. Because they want to know how many young these small crustaceans have, they need to isolate single mature daphnia in individual containers, then check regularly for tiny offspring. They're currently keeping the little critters in individual test tubes in algae solutions. They are struggling to understand why big daphnia sometimes die without offspring. Are the containers too small? Do they run out of food? Are the daphnia dying of old age? At the same time, they also struggle with understanding research processes: asking questions that can be answered, collecting sufficient data, and analyzing the data.

"It Figures!" projects are now emerging. The sixteen of twenty-four students who have chosen to be in the algebra group are groping for mathematical questions that are easy enough for them to get their minds around but difficult enough to warrant several months of investigation. This is the stage, when they are trying out and sometimes switching questions, in which they most often read articles from past issues of *It Figures!* and *Great Blue*, getting a feel for what is possible, and sometimes, queries they can build on. Our good fortune this year is having a student's father, a professor of mathematics, visit us once a week to introduce topics that can be developed into extended explorations.

Check us out in early February. Students have finished two more essays: an autobiography and an account of how their "place-in-nature" has changed with the seasons. Our class has made a quick video introducing us to other classrooms in the Heron Network; at our student conference we saw the videos other students made and attended workshops that modeled the inquiry process. Two mature fifth graders have already completed "I Wonder" projects, one on variables of algae growth, the other an extension on last year's project on how fast snails move. Within a week, five of the students will be doing apprenticeships outside of school for up to one day a week.

Figure 8–1. Up close in a schoolyard prairie: Inquiry begins and ends with wonder, moving from questions about the world to taking delight in it. Photograph by Becky Cook.

Our pace has picked up. At the moment, students are giving extra focus to their biggest independent undertaking of the year, their "Great Blue" project. Because *Great Blue* will be read by at least several thousand readers, it prompts students to do their best research and writing. Students have just written at least ten questions in each of our five curricular areas. Now they conference with me to identify one question that meets these criteria: interesting enough to work on for a month and a half, complex enough to generate lots of information, and answerable with our resources.

The Questions

Inquiry begins with curiosity, wonder, questions. Other years questions about nature have been the most popular. This year students are especially interested in cultural questions. Throughout the fall, students did ethnographic fieldwork in their families and neighborhoods. Several students want to take these explorations further. In January we began reading Joy Hakim's *All the People*, about American history since World War II. Several students want to dig deeper. Research prompted by the following questions, leading to "Kid-to-Kid" articles, will depend primarily on observations and interviews:

- What are the important stories about my ancestors?
- What foods do people of my culture use for healing?
- What are some important food traditions in Mexico?
- How has African American music changed from 1950 to 2000?
- How is the culture of American kids different from the culture of Norwegian kids?
- What is the culture of my ancestors?
- How have fads changed from the '50s to the present?
- What happened in World War II in Asia and the Pacific?

Other students want to read about culture for their "Great Blue" project. Expecting them to do more than present facts, I ask them to evaluate the books as media. Several students want to look at other media and other perspectives. Their questions spark investigations resulting in "Critics & Fanatics" articles.

Communities of Inquiry

Midwinter, inquiry erupts everywhere in our curriculum. The room is abuzz with kids working on complex projects.

We work in and investigate community, which serves as both context and content of our studies. Local natural communities are the focus of our science curriculum. Not only do students individually examine their outdoor places in nature, but our classroom "Living Machine" is constructed as a model of wetland and upland habitats. Nearby cultural environments are similarly the primary locus of our social studies curriculum, which is grounded in ethnography. Our inquiries are active, present-tense, hands-on—not regurgitations of past research recorded in libraries. Metaphorically, even our investigations into reading and mathematics are local, since students usually attend to their indigenous problem solving and reflections, instead of the more distant conclusions of experts.

For their "Great Blue" projects, students observe their own artistic processes, evaluate books in our library, test classmates' football throwing, and taste perceptions, and survey teachers about fads. They also interview ad writers, talk to family members about Mexican foods and African American music, and reflect on patterns of their own cultural experience. Each article develops out of such local probing and nearby support.

Of all structures in our classroom that support inquiry, the most important is multiaging. Second-year students come back with questions and skills for carrying out projects. They know some of the language and process of doing inquiry, and have developed sufficient writing fluency to easily record data and reflections as they work. While my first-year students often struggle—inquiry projects take a lot of effort!— they are supported by observing and working with the fifth graders. Seeing other students engrossed in the day-to-day minutiae of research, and hearing them enthralled as they report both intentions and results, does far more to engage the fourth graders than anything I could say about the delights of inquiry. Without this peer modeling, and the spiraling effect of returning students grasping at more complex questions and procedures, our investigations would be fewer and simpler.

This year, although students have the option of working with a single partner, all do their "Great Blue" projects by themselves. Still, students support each other in other ways. They are sources of information, subjects for tests, providers of materials, editors of rough drafts, and problem solvers. When a student this year is stumped trying to find World War II veterans to interview, two others suggest their own grandfathers. When a fourth grader struggles with drawing people, a fifth grader demonstrates her strategies. Several students compare lists of prime numbers.

Periodically I ask students to give project updates at class meetings. These reports help students keep track of their progress. Meanwhile, the curiosity of the listeners provides encouragement. When someone is stuck, the rest of us brainstorm solutions. Near the end of the process, as students begin reading sections of their articles to the whole class, we offer suggestions for completing aspects of the research or for clarifying the exposition. If the story is not clear to us, who have seen the research in all its stages, it's not likely to make sense to a larger community of readers.

Take another look at our classroom, this time in early March. Every day we have one or more "Great Blue" work times. To make sure everyone is on task, we follow a few simple rituals. "If you can start working without talking to anyone, get your notebook and begin." Typically half of the students begin working quietly. "If you have a big problem, put your name on the list on the board. If you are not able to work on your project while you are waiting, read some *Great Blue* articles." At this point I give permission to go to the library, suggest someone to call on the phone, and answer other short questions. Next I consult individually with students whose names are on the board. Socratic dialogue is what I aim for as I help them answer their own problems. Students who have already finished their research are writing a draft of their article, creating figures (drawings, graphs, maps) to illustrate it, or working on peer editing.

Around the edges are other people we rely on. Our librarian helps students select books, the computer teacher provides time for typing drafts and helps students with graphs, teachers for ESL and emotionally disturbed students help with drafts of articles, community members respond to telephone inquiries, an architect mentor helps his apprentice with an article on floor plans, and a grandparent volunteer comes in regularly to work with several students who need extra support. Most important are the parents. Not only do they volunteer in class during work time and type articles, they are behind the scenes at every stage as they help their child identify a question; help locate books, interviewees, and materials; read and edit drafts; and give lots of encouragement. Real problem solving takes extraordinary effort and support.

Teachers as Publishers

The Heron Network students know is ephemeral, because every year more than half the students are new. The other Heron Network is a band of teachers who love working together, year after year. The curriculum in Room 202 would be impossible without this collaboration. Heron teachers know each other in several contexts. A few were originally student teachers with other Herons. Some of us are close friends. Most of us participated in one or more Heron Institutes, where we developed our capacities for inquiry science. Recently most of us were members of the three-semester Kid-to-Kid Video Exchange Project, where we received training in video production, made videos with our students documenting local culture, and with our classrooms viewed the videos received from other classrooms.

What we provide for each other, as we collaborate in pedagogical inquiry, is support for a style of teaching outside the mainstream. Via meetings, e-mail, telephone, and occasional social gatherings, we communicate our deep passion for student inquiry. When one of us has a problem, the others usually understand. Our most intensive time together comes each spring when we lay out *Great Blue*.

March this year brings a flurry of messages on our listserv as we arrange layout days, discuss how many copies to print, and collaborate on securing additional printing funds. Beginning March 29, we work four nights in a computer lab at the University of Wisconsin. We remind each other how to use Adobe PageMaker to lay out text and graphics, scan images, proofread, choose artwork for cover pages, compose our introduction and afterword for teachers, and order out for Chinese. Along the way we chuckle over articles from other classrooms and tell stories of student struggles and achievement. On April 12 we put the journal to bed.

Our publishing process has changed considerably. What began as two teachers assisted by one parent has evolved after twelve journals into ten to twelve teachers assisted by various community partners who work with us on our projects. Staff at the Wisconsin Teacher Enhancement in Biology program at the university laid out five of the earlier journals, after teachers had completed editorial work. For several years these staffers also coordinated an all-day conference at which student

127

authors gave presentations (speeches and displays) in the morning and worked in university science labs in the afternoon.

We have experimented, at times, with students helping in the editorial process. One year, for example, students from one school came to another school to spend a whole day editing manuscripts, which were then returned to the authors for final rewrites. We've also tried to get drafts of articles on our website for other students to read and edit.

A time crunch has limited their role to in-class peer editing. Many of our students are not ready to sustain a long project before second semester. At the other end, we used to be satisfied to receive the journals several days before school is out; now we want to have them for at least a month so that we can read the articles. This year my class began their projects in the end of January. First drafts of articles were peer edited by other students, with final drafts due on March 17. Graphs and drawings were due a week later. This gave me two weeks to work with several stragglers, get articles typed (a few students and parents helped out the slow typists), edit all articles, help with difficult graphs, and scan images.

Heron teachers have become very clear in our expectations of each other. First, we agree to arrive at the initial session with all articles on a disk (edited by the teacher), all figures scanned, and articles and figures labeled in code and grouped in folders. This year, a few teachers apologized for not being finished; as usual, the rest of us were gracious. Our other agreement is to come to as many layout sessions as we can. Teachers who have less time usually explain their circumstances (e.g., out-of-town guests, a national math conference). This year, almost every teacher came to three or four work sessions. Heron teachers who are not publishing articles in a given year are not expected to do layout, but usually one or more volunteers anyway. We make most decisions collaboratively. This year one teacher volunteered to write the afterword, a second to approach our funding sources, and a third to coordinate the budget and work with the printer.

Each year one or two teachers take the responsibility to be "the editor." That person sets up a system, oversees our progress, and knows who is working on what and what still needs to be done. Typically we have one or more short meetings each evening to coordinate our work. The editor also takes responsibility for working out the quirks of our layout programs (formerly QuarkXPress, now Adobe PageMaker) and prepares the overall format. We often have volunteers with considerable computer expertise, including the manager of a public access Internet site, a former Heron teacher who now creates Web-based courses for the university, and a student who works in a university computer lab and will have his own Heron classroom next year.

It takes a lot of work, but it gets a little easier each year. Publishing our journal ourselves builds our team spirit. We develop confidence not only in publishing, but also in our teaching strategies. As we work together, we talk about changes for next year—in our publishing procedures and in our teaching. We are doing much more than making a journal; we are nurturing an ongoing community of inquiry.

Eureka!

On April 26 each student gets their own copy of the 2000 issue of *Great Blue* (online version at <http://danenet.wicip.org/heron>). The class is intensely quiet. Each student first searches for their own article. Next they slowly flip through the pages of other articles. I hear laughter and banter, and see proud faces. The next day well-known people in the community come to Randall classrooms to read from their favorite books. We give these readers—the superintendent of Madison schools, an assistant superintendent, and the president of the school board—copies of *Great Blue* signed by each student at their article. For the rest of the school year, this new issue is the most-read text in our classroom. Students take it home overnight to show their parents; their families purchase extra copies for grandparents; and students begin autographing their articles for each other.

In late May five students from another Heron classroom write letters to five of my students, describing what they enjoyed in the articles we published in *Great Blue* and telling my students what we would discover in the articles they wrote. One letter, to one of my Mexican American students, is especially poignant: "You wrote about Cinco de Mayo and Mexican independence. We don't have independence yet in Kosovo, where I come from."

Room 202 will finish other important work after we put *Great Blue* to bed, most notably, essays about community service projects and a twenty-eight-page booklet about our biweekly "Mornings in the Marsh" that we made for our Learning Circle in the International Education and Resource Network.

But the real climax to the school year came earlier, on the day students flipped through the pages of our journal and completed one long journey of inquiry. Now multiply our experience times the number of Heron classrooms to get the full impact of a *Great Blue* year.

9

Publishing Models

Learn from These Two Programs

This chapter showcases two educational programs where large numbers of students are being published. The Communication Arts Center (CAC) in Clarkston High School, Michigan, and the Students at the Center (SAC) in New Orleans, Louisiana, are devoted to getting their students published. Their programs show you that it's possible for the majority of students in every school to be published, whether it's in a classroom publication, a contest, or an outside publication. Moreover, you realize why we need to consider giving our students this opportunity—not only for their good but for the good of us all.

I was astounded when I first learned about this program and just how many students were getting their work published. Along with in-school publications and publication projects, students at the Communication Arts Center (CAC) submit their works to contests and publications with great success.

Dick Swartout and Linda Denstaedt share the secrets of their success. They candidly discuss their early failures and how they questioned their teaching strategies that led them along the dramatic shift from teacher to writer. In so doing, Swartout, Denstaedt, and other teachers sought to develop a community of writers living the writerly life. Key questions about their plan, which could be asked by many teachers, are thoughtfully discussed. They lay out their program and approaches clearly and also let the reader know that they are building writers.

Writing and publishing are intertwined in real life and at the CAC. In their writing-for-publication component of their curriculum, you learn about a host of strategies and activities that teachers use for guiding students along the submission process. The "Do's and Don'ts for Submitting Writing" list has one great tip after another. Photocopy it and post it in your classroom.

It's fitting that student writers share their reflections about writing, publishing, and the CAC. Tom Wisniewski, a senior, wrote a poem and a piece about writing for the public that left me in awe. When the public doubts or condemns public education, have them read writing by students like Wisniewski. Read and appreciate his work and him. Then picture in your mind dozens of other students like him being nurtured by dedicated, skilled teachers, and you will have an idea of the CAC. ■

DEVELOPING WRITERS AND WRITING LIVES: PUTTING THEORY INTO PRACTICE

Dick Swartout, Communication Arts Center Facilitator, Clarkston High School, and Linda Denstaedt, National Board Certified Teacher, Communication Arts Center Facilitator, and Director of Writing Proficiency K–12, Clarkston Community Schools, Clarkston, Michigan

The Communication Arts Center is the heart of Clarkston High School's writing community. Its mission is to develop writers and writing lives, but it has also created a vision of quality teaching and learning. The Center staff uses four core beliefs to build this program: decision making is based on the importance of community, choice, conversation, and publication outside the school. This community consists of both staff and students who see themselves as writers and who live a writerly life.

In the first four years of this program, over three hundred students and staff members have been published or recognized in local, state, national, and international writing competitions. It's a great beginning, but the Communication Arts Center is a place that is defining itself as it defines both student and staff learning.

Making the Shift from Teacher to Writer

Teaching was not always so thoughtful or innovative for us. For much of our teaching careers, a combined sixty-five years, we taught writing from the teacher's perspective. We thought creating good student writers was as easy as having students complete the teacher's assignments. After all, we knew what was best for our students. We provided the readings, topics, length, and variety of the exercises and even outlines: there was no room for student opinion or choice. We hate to say we failed miserably. Instead, let us say, we developed writers with adequate technical skills, and, on occasion, writers who managed to find their own voices and write with conviction despite our best intentions.

So, what changed us? We learned to step outside ourselves, to objectively judge our successes and failures as writing teachers. We questioned our methods. But most important, we became writers. Stephen Dunning, educator and author of *Getting the Knack: 20 Poetry Exercises 20*, was an early influence. He introduced us to the belief that being teachers and writers simultaneously would change our instruction dramatically. If we were to teach writing as writers, then it followed that students must learn to write as if they were writers. Thus, we came to believe in community.

As believers in community, we did not abandon our curriculum. We still wanted students to write well in a variety of forms and styles. We wanted to read quality literature with the class, exposing students to the literary canon as well as to multicultural writers and emerging contemporary voices. We wanted to prepare students for the reality of standardized tests. Building a community of staff and student writers became more powerful than following a curriculum: our work defined teaching and learning in a new way.

Creating a Community of Writers

The Communication Arts Center (CAC) did not emerge overnight. The first hurdle was illustrating the power of authentic learning. Assistant Superintendent Dave Reshcke supported Linda Denstaedt as she piloted the program. In the fall of 1996, she shared a 10 x 15–foot room with another innovative program called Earth Vision, which did primary research on the ecology of our community. The room was crowded with six computers, a teacher's desk, bookshelves, two filing cabinets, eight rectangular student tables, and twenty computer chairs. She wanted to replicate the sense of community and independence she experienced when she studied at Vermont Studio Center with Stephen Dunn and Robert Pinsky.

With a room, financial support, and one hour a day, she went in search of colleagues. Dick Swartout and Claire Needham Layman were her first connections. The conversation was to the point: "I want to change the way we teach and the way students learn. Are you in?" From there, the questions have been endless and the answers have changed our colleagues, our students, our school, and us.

In the two pilot years, over 150 students were published or recognized in writing competitions around the state, four staff members were published, and the Center was recognized by Michigan Education Association, which selected it for the television commercial series called "Public Education Works." In addition, we defined the essential parts of the program:

1. authentic writing audiences—competitions and publishing opportunities beyond the school

2. Teachers as Writers—a bimonthly group of staff who write, work in response groups, and talk about writing as writers

3. training in teaching practices essential to a writing community—a writing workshop environment

4. collaborative lesson design—strategies to enable students and staff to learn simultaneously in the same classroom.

Learning Together in a New Setting

The Communication Arts Center is situated on the main hallway next to the Media Center. It is a large room filled with technology: twenty-six computers, a digital film editing station, a scanner, and a thirty-inch monitor for televised shows, videos, or broadcasts from the in-house television studio. Like the eight other computer labs in the building, the CAC has unlimited Internet access and the latest software. It is furnished with six round tables and chairs, bookcases, and storage cabinets to facilitate small-group conversation.

During the six-hour day, the CAC is facilitated by three English teachers who are also published writers. They are responsible for teacher training, whole- and small-group instruction, individual conferencing, and collaborative lesson design. The week is divided into three parts. Mondays and Tuesdays, students leave content and English classrooms to work on self-initiated projects. Wednesdays and Thursdays, staff members bring their students to participate in collaborative lessons designed and taught with CAC facilitators. Fridays, CAC facilitators plan upcoming units and workshops and meet with individual teachers to discuss a lesson design or teaching practices.

The Defining Questions

Question 1: How Do You Create This Sense of Community in a Traditional High School Setting?

A community grows where writers live and work. Therefore, when we converse, instruct, or model writing, the CAC facilitators work from the perspective of real writers living writerly lives.

First, we shared our own writing with students—not just the final pieces, but the rough drafts as well. We modeled our lives as struggling writers. We kept a writer's notebook, we apprenticed to writers that we admired, and we sought publication and were published. And we asked them to join us and do the same.

We learned quickly that trust was the primary ingredient in developing a community, so we forged personal bonds with each of our students. We preferred to listen more than we talked. We negotiated learning goals respecting their decisions as writers, and, at the same time, we encouraged them to experiment and stretch themselves. We did not focus on the product, but, instead, focused on the writer. We asked students to engage in a writing life that extended beyond completing an assignment, the classroom, and the year they had us as teacher. This raised a new problem.

Question 2: How Would We Meet the Needs of This Growing Group of Students Who Had Committed to "a Writerly Life"?

First, we listened to the voices of our most talented writers who came to us with writing lives. Geoff Denstaedt, a senior and four-year CAC visitor, began writing in elementary school. He had been published in middle school; during high school he has been published ten times and recognized in nine competitions. He writes poetry and screenplays, filming and digitally editing his work. He writes:

> Since age ten, I've learned to see the everyday poems that sneak up on you. "The world is a poem," my mother said, plunking a ripe cantaloupe or tucking the corner of a bed sheet. So I kept a writer's notebook and found the simplest things often rendered the best poems. Writing poems or screenplays meant capturing the cinematic moment and using point of view and detail to advantage.
>
> But it is more than that, and the CAC helped me learn to study, play, and talk to other writers as part of my process. I've learned to craft my writing by studying the world of poetry and filmmaking and by listening to visiting writers and filmmakers who critiqued my work or directed my learning. For me, writing is about revision—the new direction that a reading, experiment, or conference can provide.
>
> Galway Kinnell's poems have influenced me, but his wisdom expresses my gratitude: "When I found the world of poets, I realized I was not so odd after all." So I can say, when I found the CAC in ninth grade, I realized I had a community in which to feel accepted and learn.

Talking to our students helped us understand that a writer needs time: regular, predictable time, self-directed time, time to talk, time to play and experiment, time to study, time to read, to throw out, to start again, to revisit, and to revise. So we asked: How could we give students the gift of time? We answered that question with four approaches:

1. Independent student work: On Monday and Tuesday, individual students leave their "home" classrooms to visit the CAC. This program differs from a typical pullout program in that students leave a writing workshop environment to attend the CAC, so all students are working on writing. The work students bring to the CAC can be an extension of classroom expectations or advanced self-initiated work. Such visits are coordinated with the

CAC staff and the cooperating English or content teacher. Students are excused and the self-initiated project replaces any classroom assignments. This enables the cooperating English teachers to enjoy a reduced class load, aiding them in one-to-one interaction with their remaining students. Some cooperating English teachers require that all students confer with a CAC staff member or other student writers in the CAC as a routine part of the writing process. This emphasizes the importance of intent with an eye on audience. A writer may be his own first audience, but writing is usually intended for a larger audience than the self or the teacher. In the CAC, students can work independently, conference with the facilitator or other students, read, or join a writer response group.

2. Hands-on Training Model: On Wednesday and Thursday, English teachers or content teachers collaborate with CAC facilitators in a hands-on training model. This training enables workshop environments to flourish. It is built on the belief that learning is social transaction and that a learner constructs knowledge through both spoken and written language. Therefore, creating a classroom culture of study and talk is essential. This type of classroom requires extended periods of time for students to self-initiate projects, talk through their work with peers and teachers, and work through confusions to apply their learning to a written product. CAC facilitators collaborate in the following ways:
   - model instructional strategies
   - coteach with staff during a training unit
   - conference with students or deliver minilessons
   - assess student performances to instruct staff in designing lessons to meet student needs

3. Collaborative lesson designs: On Friday, teachers and CAC facilitators collaborate on lesson designs or discuss instructional strategies to improve student performance. These sessions are conversational discussions assessing student performance, determining lesson goals, and designing activities to cultivate students' growth and their ability to recognize and use their writing strengths to produce quality projects.

4. Author visitations: Each year the CAC staff identifies authors and genres to promote. These authors work in a small-group setting with interested students. Students elect to attend a two-hour workshop in which they generate new writing or critique their work with the author. Students study the writing of the visiting author prior to the visit. In our first four years, we have had visits from four poets, three short story writers, two documentary filmmakers, and one songwriter. Next year we plan to work with writing in multiple genres and are planning a visit by Tom Romano and a cartoonist.

Question 3: How Important Is Student Ownership and How Can It Be Accomplished?

Ownership, a feeling generated in the student by the work itself, shifts writing out of the assignment mind-set. The shift affects the writer, the product, and the classroom. Therefore, it should be at the core of a teacher's decisions. We believe the student should have the power to make decisions about the writing; after all, it is her piece. Choice is the driving force. Choice doesn't mean "free-for-all." It simply means the power to choose and control the learning and writing decisions.

So how does a teacher instruct when a writer controls the decisions? What if the writer says, "I like it this way"? Well, that is exactly what happens if the focus of the work is on getting finished or getting a grade. For us, the focus is on learning and playing. So the writer who comes to the CAC knows they will go through a series of experiments. The writer will work through semipredictable, individualized steps based on personal learning goals, genre, and skill level. Essentially, the four-part rhythm goes something like this:

1. Find something interesting. We ask: "Why are you interested in this piece?" We suggest that students should not use work they love so much they cannot imagine changing it. We also suggest that students number and keep track of their drafts since they may wish to return to an earlier draft when they are done experimenting.

2. Set a learning goal. We ask: "So what do you want to learn?" Usually this is related to craft, such as first-person point of view or use of concrete detail. At this point, the CAC facilitator recommends an author and often a specific poem, story, screenplay, or essay to study. Students read the work, and we discuss it.

3. Experiment with the writing. We recommend saying, "Try this strategy and see what happens." This work is truly experimental and has a "maybe, maybe not" approach. The student writer applies a crafting strategy learned by apprenticing a professional writer. This work can lead to radical revision for some students, while others may simply add to the current draft. We accept that it may create effective writing or it may not. But the work is valuable even if the experimental writing is abandoned.

4. Conference on the new work. This conference usually begins with the vague question: "So, what do you think?" Developing a writer's sense of what works is at the center of this question. The conversation begins with the writer's opinion, not the teacher's.

A student will return to the writing several times. He may do steps 2–4 up to four or five times. Each time, the work is initiated by the writer or negotiated by the teacher. If the teacher believes the writer would benefit from learning to handle dialogue, they will negotiate a dialogue experiment. Once a student has agreed, the experiment must be done. However, if the student chooses to abandon dialogue in a later draft, that decision is acceptable. We believe the experiments have value because they build writerly skills and strategies. The product is secondary. This work is always done with regular conversation and respect for the student's opinion. It encourages a student to make decisions, since the experiments generate new work; eventually, cutting and shaping occurs. It requires the teacher to approach the work as study and play rather than with a mind-set of "correctness." In our experience, a piece of writing rarely stays the same or even close to the same. Plus, student writing gets progressively better.

For us, writing is about building the writer, not the product. Helping students build self-talk strategies is the practiced agenda of the conference. Lucy Calkins in *The Art of Teaching Writing* (1994) quotes Don Murray:

> In his important article "Teaching the Other Self: The Writer's First Reader," Don Murray (1982) likens writing to a conversation between two workers muttering to each other at the bench. "The self speaks, the other self listens and considers. The self proposes, the other self considers. The self makes, the other self evaluates. The two selves collaborate." (p. 165)

It is this collaborative self-talk we encourage. It builds ownership and writerly instincts that emerge again and again.

Question 4: How Important Is Publishing?

The answer is obvious—very important. Why publish? Publishing causes students to see their work as valuable. It creates ownership and pride. It creates a real audience and an authentic purpose for the work. We function under the belief that you're not a writer if you haven't collected a rejection slip. Sending work out is the last step in the writing process, and as writers, we want to get our voices heard in the world. As a result, many teachers require that all students submit work to competitions or publications throughout the year. Winning is not the goal. Sending is.

Published student work provides a tangible standard of success. Students who wish to be recognized by Detroit Free Press Writing Awards can look at the work of the forty-two winners from Clarkston. Teachers examine published student writing as models, discussing strategies the authors used that distinguished the pieces. Beginning writers are always encouraged when they know the name of a student who has previously won; success seems more possible.

We can show students how a single poem fared in five different competitions, which emphasizes the notion that readers have a subjective view. This enables us to talk about audience. Writing that remains personal with hidden meanings is really intended for a small audience—possibly self and friends or family. When a writer intends the work for a larger audience, the writer must consider issues of clarity as well as the taste and skill level of the reader. Being a mainstream writer who writes for a general public is different from being a literary writer who writes for an audience of other writers within the context of a literary tradition. We ask our students to write beyond the personal level, choosing the type of reader for which their work is intended.

Publication for a competition means revising with an eye on the competition's format and rules. Student writers see this work as a learning opportunity. Lisa Hopcian, a sophomore, spent months working on her short story "Philodendron," which received an honorable mention in the Detroit Free Press Writing Awards. She says, "It seems I am never done experimenting with different strategies. I'm always willing to open new doors and discover different aspects of my work. Motivation to revise is tough for a teenager, but it is a big part of being a good writer." Lindsay Tigue, who also received an honorable mention in short story in the Detroit Free Press Writing Awards, says, "Atmosphere [at CAC] is crucial. There are usually a couple of teachers to give you advice when you need it. Also, peer advice is readily available." Finally, Rachel Arndt, who received an award of commendation in poetry as a ninth grader, says, "Entering the Detroit Free Press Writing Awards and being recognized was a wonderful experience. Working steadily on my poems every day in the CAC, looking back, seeing what I could revise, conferencing with the teachers available, helped me become a more aware writer. With the goal of publication, I came to realize the desirable and undesirable things in my pieces and develop a more mature voice. Conferences helped me talk to an adult writer like a writer."

One of the barometers of the success of our writing program is the Detroit Free Press Writing Awards, which draws entries from the seven counties of southeast Michigan. In the contest results just published, our student writers made up 10 percent of the four hundred recognized writers from over four thousand entries.

Another avenue of success is in our own publications. We published two magazines this spring: a school literary magazine, *To the Openhanded,* and a collection of ninth-grade poems, *Testing the Waters.* Publishing can take many avenues, such as:

- Classroom publication: Simply publishing in the classroom widens the audience beyond the teacher. That is the number-one and best reason to do it. Students will not develop a sense of ownership if the writing is only for an assignment. Plus, writing that will be read by others is taken more seriously. Publishing also requires students to meet a publishing standard in formatting and editing.

- School literary magazines: We recommend a magazine juried by staff and students with a clearly stated rubric. Juried magazines will raise the level of writing in the school and set a standard for future writers.
- Contests: Compile a list of local, state, and national contests. Once you begin looking, it will be easy to find dozens for high school writers. Contests provide a deadline as well as a predictable audience. Plus, competitions offer opportunities for a wide range of interests and abilities. Some offer monetary prizes, but most competitions honor a student's efforts with letters and certificates of achievement.
- Publications: Compile a list of local, state, and national publications. Include the standard for publication for each. Preparing a manuscript for an outside publisher is an important learning experience. It encourages students to format and edit to an industry standard.
- Once you begin looking, it will be easy to find dozens of high school publishing opportunities and competitions. Most competitions come in the mail addressed to the department chair or language arts coordinator. Teachers can also use *The Market Guide for Young Writers* as a resource.

Preparing work for a competition is a learning experience in itself. Each competition will come with specific formatting and submission guidelines. We publish a list of competitions at the beginning of the year. The list includes the categories, general submission requirements, and the deadline date. The teacher then uses these dates to determine revision and formatting workshop blocks to be inserted in the instructional calendar. Writing for publication is an essential and required part of the 9–12 curriculum in all classes.

While individual classroom teachers deserve great credit for encouraging and preparing their students, the Communication Arts Center serves as the central clearinghouse for contests and publications. Also, it is the CAC teachers who serve as mentor writers for those students who seek publication and competition. Specific contest formatting expectations are distributed in the month prior to a competition. All writing goes through a revision workshop and is edited and proofed before being placed in a student portfolio. The portfolio enables students to build a body of work. This work begins in September of their ninth-grade year and continues until June of their senior year. As a result, work written in May of the sophomore year can be submitted to a competition with a March deadline in the junior year.

Most of the department members require a portfolio conference as part of the semester final. Students prepare for this portfolio conference by compiling and reflecting on their work. Although students maintain the portfolio in a variety of formats, they usually save their work on the school's computer network. January and February are big submission months, so many teachers run revision and submission workshops as part of their portfolio exams. As a result, it is an easy process to reformat the portfolio pieces to a particular competition's format. It's helpful for students to consider some basic formatting guidelines.

Do's & Don'ts for Submitting Writing

DO edit your work carefully. Get help from an adult editor or peer editor to proof your final copy.

DON'T rely on the computer for proofing. It will not catch errors in homonym usage and other words spelled correctly but used incorrectly.

DO read the category descriptors carefully. Be sure your work fits the definition provided. Follow the rules. First cuts are often determined by errors in following contest directions.

DON'T send writing that doesn't fit the call for submissions. An essay can't be considered a short story just because you send it under that category. If they want three to five poems, don't send just one.

DO complete any application or authenticity form and include it with the submission. Work must be original.

DON'T send collaborative work.

Of course, DON'T send work plagiarized from other writers.

DO read the formatting instructions twice and then double-check the final copy before you put it in the envelope.

DON'T expect that all competitions have the same formatting instructions.

DO read the deadline rules carefully. Some competitions state "postmarked by" and others state "received by." Postmarks count. Be sure to have the post office hand stamp the postmark if you mail your work on the last day.

DON'T wait until the last minute to prepare a piece. Most competitions will gladly accept work immediately. Look at the submission period and submit early rather than late.

DO call the contest if you are confused about any instructions or rules. People are happy to talk to student writers.

DON'T underline your title or put it in quotation marks.

A Senior's View: The Demands of Writing for the Public

Tom Wisniewski is a senior who has been published five times and recognized in eight competitions. He has been a regular visitor to the CAC all four years. In ninth grade, he began to take writing seriously, leaving his English class most Mondays to work on self-initiated projects. Although Tom considers himself a poet, he has also written essays and experimented with short fiction. He is currently studying how to invent a story, which gave him a powerful opening line for the following prose poem:

Seeing
Tom Wisniewski, 17
Clarkston High School, Clarkston, Michigan

When I was twelve, my father died. Not in the literal sense—his heart kept beating and every morning he opened his eyes—but he died, all right. It wasn't a sudden death. Not like a thud or a gunshot, more like the slow decay of a ripe apple or the way an oak tree loses its leaves in the fall. Seeing him one Saturday morning, I noticed his hands, worn and wrinkled, and his eyes, a pale foggy gray. The room smelled of newsprint and coffee, and I knew there was nothing left. Later that night, I found his camera tucked behind a few boxes in the basement, the lens shattered. For years, my father's camera had been his center, his salvation. On windless summer nights, he drove his old pickup down dirt roads, chasing glorious sunsets. He framed the barn behind the oak trees, a silhouette of a horse, and the sylvan lake across the mountains. Early in the morning, when mist had settled on the ground, he rose. A broad smile crossed his face, and he stole away to the darkroom. Until crows crossed the red sun, he worked and worked, developing his heart. But love was such a small thing those days, and from the kitchen, my mother called his name. "David, David," she said, as if the repetition might summon him to practical matters. My father, of course, never heard those words. Not even when she packed up, leaving behind remnants of clothes, lilac perfume, leather sandals. Not even when she shattered his lenses one by one. He sat at the table, hands covering his face. This is not seeing. This is not seeing.

Reflecting on his last high school poem and his writing life, Tom writes:

Virginia Woolf claims a writer needs a room of one's own. For me, this room is the CAC. There, I write without the distractions of home, place, and people. I love going to the center because it is removed from the rest of the high school, yet full of interesting and engaging young writers. I see the CAC as a sanctuary from the moribund school halls where people sleepwalk, sleeptalk, sleep–go to class. Writing is a lonely process, and although I find the necessary solitude there, I also find good company when I'm looking for it. For that reason alone, I've spent almost all of my lunches in the CAC revising, talking about writing and literature, or just shooting the breeze with my friends and fellow writers.

Mrs. Denstaedt, my writing mentor, has never laid down an ultimatum, demanding that I must submit my writing. However, she has been a consistently resolute teacher who encourages me to publish my work. As a result, I write for myself, but also for the contests. True, contests have always been a goal—an external goal—but

I'd be lying if I said they didn't inspire me to work at a higher, more sophisticated level. A change in audience means a change in the quality of writing, and so I've come to the belief that superficial motivation isn't always so bad. Writing for the public demands personal evaluation and constant self-assessment. It makes you responsible for your writing alone; it gives you something to work for beyond the audience of your English class; and it broadens your world.

The poem "Seeing" came from my notebook. The issue of seeing was probably planted into my subconscious when our class "nurtured" our seeds early in the fall. Mrs. Denstaedt's seed was "being seen," and I later incorporated the same idea into a fast-write. Later in the year, when I began work on a short story about a boy with a Chinese mother, I wrote: "When I was twelve, my father died." From there, I invented line by line, writing about what I know (photography), but also fictionalizing the father. Ultimately, seeing became a thread that illuminated the meaning of my poem.

However, "Seeing" was not pure invention; it also came from the close study of a published author. While working in the CAC one day, Mrs. Denstaedt introduced me to Robert Haas, one master of the prose poem. I apprenticed "Duck Blind," mainly playing with syntax and diction. I noticed his use of many simple sentences punctuated with the occasional longer, more lyrical line, gave his poetry a very musical quality. I paid attention to his diction and later replaced words like "silver" with "sylvan" for the more unusual, melodic quality. I varied my sentences, using fragments, lists, and compound constructions. I also chose repetition in the mother's repeated calling of the father's name, which reverberates in the poem's final repetition—"This is not seeing. This is not seeing." These final sentences bring the poem full circle and allow the reader to understand the father as a lost, frail man. The effect is dramatic and powerful.

In the end, I think freedom in writing comes when the writer is willing to let go of reality's inhibitions. Writer's block is a nonissue when you write about whatever comes to mind. My advice? Let the line take you, rather than trying to shape and coerce it. Listen to the character's dialogue. Follow the connotations, the surprises, and the Freudian slips. Revise later.

Building a Community

A single decision can create ripples that change an entire school district. That is what happened when Clarkston High School's English Department decided to emphasize student publication and authentic writing experiences for real writers. Over the last few years, more and more students have come to think of their English teachers as writers because our department lives as a community of writers. Students and staff have learned the language of writerly conversation, and we expect that conversation will be maintained in writer's notebooks, response groups, literature circles, genre studies, and workshop classrooms. Teachers as Writers groups are popping up in elementary buildings. First and second graders are sending their work to competitions and winning. New teachers are invited to join the ongoing conversation about writing and teaching and to keep a writer's notebook, share their writing with their students, and develop teaching practices that seek authentic audiences.

These days we are "doing the discipline," and this attitude propels us into other authentic projects. This spring the CAC organized a K–12 Teacher as Researcher group led by Dr. Laura Roop in conjunction with the University of Michigan and the National Writing Project at the Oakland Intermediate Schools District. This work will provide us with another entry into authentic work as real writers. As researchers, we will become better observers and assessors of our teaching, and we will ask students to join the conversation as we study together. As researchers, we will seek audiences to publish our findings, and we will expand our writing opportunities, engaging in scholarly, research-based writing as well as poetry, fiction, essay, and screenplay. As researchers, we hope to attract the interest of teachers outside our department, extending our growing community.

In an epigraph to his *New and Selected Poems*, Stephen Dunn quotes Vincent van Gogh: "The best way to know life is to love many things." We have discovered that living life as real writers encourages you to love many things. These days we are just enjoying the ride.

Jim Randels is a natural-born storyteller, and what a wonderful story he has to tell! Under his guidance, students have collaborated with city organizations on many projects, including publication of *Our Voice*, the citywide teen newspaper. As students develop their writing, they strive to write and serve their local communities at the same time, which is part of the "call and response" system that Randels describes. This service-oriented approach to writing makes so much sense and has such far-reaching impact that one wonders why more teachers and students aren't involved in similar programs.

Four of the Students at the Center's publications show how these teenagers write about important issues. In the introduction to *Murdering Addictions, Weaving Nests*, you become part of a circle of students discussing drugs and violence. The student author's insight and resolve bring hope to a deadly situation. Randels calls upon Adrinda Kelly, another student, for assistance in discussing the books *Resistance* and *Writing with the Whole Village*, which honor the students' ancestors and the past.

Their intense, powerful writing focuses on very real topics that affect their lives. In each line, you feel how deeply Randels and his students are invested in their work. And you applaud them. ∎

CALL AND RESPONSE: PUBLISHING IN THE STUDENTS AT THE CENTER PROGRAM

Jim Randels, Teacher and Codirector, Students at the Center,
New Orleans Public Schools, New Orleans, Louisiana

Stories have many complicated origins. In New Orleans, where we live at the end of the continent's most powerful river and stand in a stream of culture that flows from many sources, we know this well. In the gumbos we cook, the jazz we celebrate, the buildings that house our living and dead, and even the color of our skin, we know that the pathways to the present are intricate, long, and deserving of careful consideration.

The tale of book publishing in the Students at the Center program is no exception. Here we offer a couple of strands of this tale. Forgive us if we indulge in too many winding paths; or if you find our story follows too straight a path, contact me at <jimrandelssac@earthlink.net>, or in New Orleans at McDonogh #35 Senior High School, or Frederick Douglass High School (see Appendix F for their addresses) for fuller and other versions of the story.

The Process

The process at the heart of the SAC approach insists that students avoid simply following formulas of writing. Instead, they learn formulas and adapt those to their own writing. They begin to see themselves as people who draw upon a variety of resources to solve problems in writing and create meaning, rather than as people who simply follow directions and rules. They read widely and discuss fully to prepare for writing. They work in a setting that keeps the class size small enough and the curriculum flexible enough that they can explore the relationship between their experiences and the texts and events they study. And finally, they work in the context of community groups, neighborhood organizations, and school issues.

Call and Response

Placing students in the SAC context for in-depth skill development; interactive learning; and meaningful, curriculum-based community collaborations makes possible the "call and response" that enriches SAC publication projects. This concept of call and response, of the relationships among numerous elements merging to create quality writing, is fundamental to SAC publishing projects. It happens as students discover connections among course material and activities; receive inspiration to preserve the stories of ancestors, friends, family, and self; and earn recognition as powerful resources for community organizations. In the classroom, students learn the ways the texts we read, the material we write, and the issues we discuss speak to one another.

As the students study historical events, understand the limitations of commercial media, and engage themselves in school, family, and community issues, they begin to want to preserve untold stories. They develop a sense of mission, a calling, in their writing projects. The students' constant attention to revision and the connection among all elements of coursework lead to high-quality thinking and writing. This quality, in turn, causes community organizations, educational groups, and social service agencies to call upon SAC students to collaborate with them on writing projects.

Call and response is thick in the air of New Orleans, as thick as the humid summer air that hugs us every second. We hear it in African drumming, gospel music, blues, and jazz. We know it in the river, whose currents and floods majestically refuse to obey human control in their drive to the Gulf of Mexico. We understand it in our public schools, which have followed a long arc from segregation by race to a legal, barely perceptible integration that now segregates schools by the value students and their parents place on education, creating from an earlier overt racism, a subtle, more powerful system of injustice. We consciously develop call and response as a way of learning and working in our SAC classes.

Responding to the Calls: SAC Publications

The Call of Community Organizations: Teen Sexuality *and* Murdering Addictions, Weaving Nests

Service is not the only way SAC students contribute to needs that community organizations identify. SAC publications often originate in response to requests for student writing on particular topics and for special events.

Two chapbooks, *Teen Sexuality* and *Murdering Addictions, Weaving Nests,* originated in response to requests for policy essays by teens on four key issues. The Institute of Women and Ethnic Studies, a New Orleans–based nonprofit organization specializing in women's health and adolescent media advocacy issues, sponsored four statewide writing contests. The contests sought teen perspectives on four key issues and offered prizes of $600 and a free trip to New York to the four winners. The topics for these contests were:

- discussing strategies to prevent teen pregnancy
- explaining whether or not sex education in schools interferes with or enhances parental relationships with children

- analyzing the role media plays in youth violence
- exploring drug and alcohol use and abuse

GaBrilla Ballard's Introduction to the book *Murdering Addictions, Weaving Nests* describes how the need for such a book arises from teen and classroom experience.

A six-year-old is fatally beaten. A young woman decides that her fist against another's face is the answer. A deal gone badly claims the life of yet another member of our family, our community. We are here to create a picture, to tell a story.

In a circle, we sit and contemplate visions of violence and drugs in our community. I can tell by the contorted looks on the faces of the students that those visions aren't pleasant ones. After minutes of contemplation, we exchange words. I slouch heavily in my chair; one hand rests on my jaw. The other twists my coiled hair, waiting my turn, holding on to the images of bruised brown bodies in my mind.

One young man then speaks of his excitement when a fight is going on. He explains how the students run to see whose face is on the other side of the fist, then scatter like red fire ants when the echo of gunshots ring out. "We run with astonished looks on our faces hoping that we can add more flame to the fire, so we can leave the scene feeling fully entertained."

These actions result from countless witnessing of such atrocities. Acts of violence not only do something to the human body; they do things to the human spirit. Instead of finding ways to stop an altercation, we numb ourselves, figuring if it is not our problem personally, then it isn't our problem at all. But we at SAC, through small student writing sessions and dialogue, realize that it is everyone's problem.

Natasha, shy and soft-spoken, ducks behind her cocoa-colored hands and refuses to come closer into the group. Instead she creates images from her pain that give us a clearer understanding of her silence. Such images are indicative of our community's current situation. She makes others who read and identify with her work say, "Yes, I understand."

On the other side of the circle, Bruce and Glenda throw words at each other. Bruce ducks Glenda's verbal bullets with determined energy, that is eventually channeled to writing pieces that provoke thought and inspire. His readers must turn around and look at what's going on, not just here in New Orleans, but everywhere. *Murdering Addictions, Weaving Nests* is a collection of our thoughts, stories, and poems that express our desires to study the problem and ultimately solve it. It is also a testament to the strong spirits, sophisticated thinking, and nourishing hope that arise when our young people dig deep within themselves, face difficult subjects, and write through them.

When students think deeply about and "write through" issues that confront them, they not only begin healing themselves but also offer important insights to adults. Organizations and school systems that support such work improve young people's lives and begin to define educational accountability in ways that extend beyond simple test scores.

The Call of Ancestors: Resistance *and* Writing with the Whole Village *(SAC Student Adrinda Kelly, coauthor)*

The sense of learning, as something that occurs not just for the individual, infuses SAC work in other ways. SAC students express this communal sense of learning through our desire to understand the historical context out of which our education and writing grows. The books *Resistance* and *Writing with the Whole Village* reflect the respect we have for our elders. Most SAC students develop an understanding that we must not only write about our own experiences but also preserve stories of our elders and ancestors. The students receive assistance in and inspiration for this work from books we read, historical societies, and our own experience of the ways outsiders can distort or even neglect someone else's stories.

Resistance—a collection of SAC writings inspired by the largest slave revolt in the Louisiana area—represents an extension of the important work of the African American History Alliance of Louisiana (AAHAL). This grassroots organization has resurrected a neglected chapter in local history. AAHAL's research into public records of the time reveals that slave revolts happened almost continuously in this area during the period of enslavement. The large revolt of 1811 involved more than five hundred freedom fighters and even received press coverage in Europe. AAHAL presents a lecture and slide show on the revolt, provides tours of the areas where the revolt took place, and publishes a book about the revolt, *On to New Orleans*.

Resistance was developed through the educational resources that AAHAL provided. When exposed to this information, many students feel obliged to study these neglected and stolen ancestors and take lessons from them that they can apply to their lives today. The student writing in *Resistance* employs a variety of strategies. Danielle Joseph and Cabriolle Brooks create scenes from the sketchy details in *On to New Orleans* about Gustave, a young boy who was the favorite slave of Master Trepagnier. Trepagnier promised Gustave his freedom when he turned twenty-one. But when Gustave reached twenty-one, the slave master broke this promise. Gustave became one of the revolutionaries of 1811 and participated in killing Trepagnier as part of the efforts to liberate enslaved Africans. Other writers, such as Lesley Quezergue and Adrinda Kelly, explore the ways Christianity was distorted to become both an active and a passive tool of oppression. Michal Gray examines the ways revolutions have changed since 1811, noting that cultural revolutions, such as the Harlem Renaissance, adapt liberation tactics to meet the times in which they live.

Throughout *Resistance,* the students honor their ancestors. As we do this, we begin to think in more complex, sophisticated ways about our current situations. One essay that reflects this thinking is my title essay for the collection. In it, I imagine the situation in which my ancestors lived but also see those circumstances as part of a continuum that leads directly to the racism that my peers and I still experience. About halfway through the essay, I stop to ponder the decision to flee the plantation, join marooned colonies, and become a freedom fighter.

> Understand that here, in New Orleans, enslaved people sought refuge in swamps before they would endure another day of dependence and say thank you for the sustenance their bloody hands had provided. Imagine the same hands that cherished a black woman's hips made bloody in the sugar cane fields of master's enterprise. Imagine having to mend those hands, to cradle the broken fingers that made your children, restoring them with your tears and your care. A cycle of brokenness begins that is bitter to the spirit, and it becomes easy to consider death and murder in the connotations of freedom.
>
> And when the day came to pillage and plunder like some great avenger, black men again slashed the sultry air with blinding smiles as beautiful as they were deadly. To be a woman then and have bloody hands sear your hips in a painless lovemaking! To know that this child of insurrection would be your own, no longer having to share your breasts with the greedy pink babies your womb did not remember. This was the reward, and it steeled your soul from remorse. Enough to kill and be judged and know that your babies would own themselves.

After recounting details of the actual revolution, my analysis moves to a meditation on the liberating value of my studying this history. I sense a direct connection between the inspiration that enslaved Africans took from earlier revolutionaries to the importance that studying these past heroes has for my peers and me.

"And in the end there was death for all who had resisted. White men claimed a victory for slavery, and slaves again encased themselves in the costume of bondage. But underneath their rags something pulsated and trembled in memory of their brethren. Slaves did not forget Charles Deslonde and his attempt to liberate them. Uprisings sprang up across the nation and whites grew worried because they knew that the 'change' sung about in Negro spirituals was imminent. The education of black students was structured to negate African history, instilling a psychological void that manifests itself in total assimilation into white culture, surrendering blacks to white domination . . . again."

Almost two centuries later, it is easy for me to distance myself from slavery and the people who endured it. However, slaves did not merely endure oppression. They resisted bondage in uprisings like the 1811 revolt, culminating with the Civil War.

I don't know African American history beyond the textbook pantomime of the "kind white master," but I do know this: Charles Deslonde, Nat Turner, and others like them mobilized these words into action:

> No chains to bear, no scourge we fear;
> We conquer, or we perish here.
> We conquer, or we perish here.

There is no need for me to be ashamed. Slavery was not a passive institution, and mine is not a race of domesticated animals.

Writing with the Whole Village paints an even broader stroke of the living principle of *Sankofa*, the West African concept and Adinkra symbol that means "learning from the past in order to understand the present and prepare for the future." SAC students offer this book as an illustration of studying the past in order to understand the future. The book also pays homage to a wide array of community organizations with whom SAC students work. One section collects essays and book reviews rooted in archaeology, anthropology, and history internships. Another chronicles the twice-monthly book discussion series students conduct with elders at Community Book Center. The final section offers SAC student writing based on their trip to New Mexico, during which they performed a play they wrote about the 1811 slave revolt. In all of this work, collaborating organizations and students feel compelled to study and honor their past.

Building Frameworks for Future Publications

In the summer of 2000, six SAC students from four schools joined the two SAC project codirectors to produce a website design document through funding from Xavier University's Division of Education. The website's theme, local heroes in struggles for social justice, attempts to define heroes in less traditional, less simplistic ways. It also emerges from the SAC emphasis on honoring elders and ancestors. The unique feature of the website will be its heavy inclusion of student reflective, creative, and analytical writing inspired by the local heroes they research.

Three of the students will spend half a day during their senior year completing an internship in youth media productions. Using some of the grant award SAC received from the Open Society Institute, these students will be trained in radio, video, and journalism under the tutelage of locally based and internationally renowned writer and publisher Kalamu ya Salaam.

During the 2000–01 school year, they will share their expertise in media production with students at the eight SAC sites. They will work with SAC codirectors, teachers, and students to produce websites, plays, radio, video, print journalism, and books related primarily to the local heroes website.

Using modern technology, community resources, and SAC student writing, they will lead the expansion of SAC publishing into multiple media. Their work will represent the progressive development of SAC work as students take the lead in producing publications to honor the often neglected voices of ancestors and teenagers.

10

Publishing Is for Teachers, Too

A Blessing in Disguise

I failed to get my first manuscript published, which turned out to be a blessing in disguise. If I couldn't get my own work published, then I promised myself that I would help students publish their work. As student work after work was published, I felt fulfilled seeing my students do what I had been unable to do.

Also, rejection was a valuable teacher. I learned how to handle disappointment and keep things in perspective, which I shared with my students. I empathized with students who undertook the challenges and risks of submitting their writing because I had been there, too. Thus, my teaching methods grew more practical and realistic. I couldn't have taught writing as effectively or published with my students had I not tried myself.

While you can submit your work in journals or magazines, it's not necessary. Display your writing on a website—yours or someone else's. Or self-publish your own work in a simple book that is photocopied and then stapled together. It will make a tremendous difference to your students and you. Just write and publish!

Reading this essay by Ada and Campoy is almost like attending one of their workshops, where you walk away uplifted and recharged. Their passion and enthusiasm for teachers and their writing and self-publishing flows throughout this piece; it is contagious. They give you the advice you need because they *know* and have *heard* from teachers themselves just how difficult writing is for many of them.

Ada and Campoy also know we often don't know where to begin, so they include a detailed list of the types of books teachers have written and self-published. It contains descriptions and commentary about each type of book: autobiographical, childhood experiences, about one's name, and more. Also included are superb examples to show you the wonderful books that other teachers are making. As you go over this list, your own ideas will surface and shout, "Write and turn us into books!"

After finishing their essay, you will seriously consider writing and publishing a book about yourself or someone in your life. Those of you who do will change yourselves and your students forever. You won't settle for making one book. No, you will be hooked for life. ∎

Teachers as Authors: Unveiling the Author Within

Alma Flor Ada, Author, and F. Isabel Campoy, Author, San Francisco, California

If we are concerned with having our students conceive of themselves as writers, it will be important that they can see the process evolve in front of their eyes, that they see their teachers also as authors.

Along the many years we have been involved with education, we have witnessed with pain how many times teachers feel uncomfortable about their own abilities to express themselves in writing. Teachers who feel passionately about issues of social justice and equality, who have valuable opinions about educational practices, do not find it easy to write a letter to an editor or to write an article expressing their views. Excellent teaching ideas go by unheard and unknown because the excellent teachers who devise them do not feel at ease writing a methodology book.

To be able to write what one thinks, feels, imagines, dreams is extremely liberating and powerful. And many times, it is less dependent on possessing a particular set of skills than it is in having the confidence and the desire to try.

We offer our courses for teachers on "Unveiling the Author Within" not only because more empowered teachers can better empower their students, but also because classroom authorship makes imminent sense for children and also offers the possibility to facilitate a much more meaningful home/school interaction.

Children live in two distinct worlds: home and school. Unless these two worlds understand, respect, and celebrate each other, children will feel torn between the two, and may feel compelled to make unnecessary choices that may disrupt their inner peace, make them feel disloyal to their family and community, or, in some cases, internalize shame about their own parents. Children should not have to take sides between home and school, but rather see them both harmoniously integrated in their lives.

One of the major discrepancies between the home and school culture may be, precisely, related to habits concerning literacy. While the school may emphasize the book culture, the home perhaps shares wisdom in a different way. If the school is going to emphasize the value of books, then it is the school's responsibility to see that the families and community of its students are fully represented in those books, so that the books do not serve an exclusionary purpose, but rather an inclusive one. It is the school's responsibility to see that books don't come between children and parents, but rather are another vehicle to foster their interaction.

A strong process of classroom authorship can indeed facilitate that the community becomes the focus of books written and published in the class, that each family is portrayed, and that the accumulated wisdom of the parents and relatives is recognized.

An added benefit of teachers writing: When the teacher engages in a process of writing personal books about herself, her family, her aspirations, or life experiences, she has the opportunity of sharing them with the parents of her students. In doing so, she is relating to the parents from a human perspective, and at a level of equality. Many language-minority parents, or parents who are economically disadvantaged, feel intimidated by the school, because their own school experiences may be lacking, or may have been unsuccessful. They may look at the teacher with a great deal of respect, but also from a distance.

Teachers who have accepted the invitation to write about themselves, their name, their families, their life experiences, have opened up a very different route of communication with the parents. They have allowed a bridge of equality to be built. We all have names, we all have relatives and friends. In everyone's life there has been someone who was a model, an inspiration, someone to be remembered with kindness and appreciation. At this human level there are no false distinctions between the teacher and the parents.

Those teachers who have discussed with their students the process of their writing have given them very empowering models. As they told the children that ideas were not always easy to formulate, that they struggled to express their feelings just right, or that words were sometimes elusive, they will be freeing the children for their own experimentation, and giving them the self-assurance to try once again.

The teachers who have made copies of their books and sent them to the homes have not only developed new connections with the parents, but also, many times, encouraged them to become writers as well.

The teachers who have visited each others' classrooms as authors, showing and reading their own books and answering children's questions about the authorship process, have felt deeply enriched by the experience.

Authorship carries a tremendous expectation in society. Many authors are respected and honored, celebrated, and highly regarded; consequently it is logical that new authors would feel they "don't belong in the group." What we would like to share with you is the pride and ownership of teachers' voices. Teachers with sometimes thirty years of experience in the classroom, write and publish their first book with the testimony of who they are and where they came from, voicing the pride of their histories and setting the example of pride in their roots for their students and the families of their students.

How to begin? One word at a time, is our advice. Do what you ask your students to do. Buy a mirror, look at yourself, and tell the image you see in the mirror that there are many stories behind those eyes that need to be told through your voice. We all have a personal story. We all have experienced situations, encountered people, learned lessons that we need to share. Start there. And don't stop.

Types of Books Teachers Have Written and Self-Published

Autobiographical Books

Autobiographical books can take many forms. They can focus on one childhood anecdote, present a panorama of one's whole life, or describe a person who is part of one's life. By choosing to write about her life, the teacher provides the message that she is willing to truly share of herself as a person. Additionally these types of books provide an excellent model for children's own writing.

Often parents feel overwhelmed by the social distance between themselves and the teacher. Autobiographical books demystify the teacher as a remote authority figure. Instead, he or she will become an accessible human being. This will help overcome any resistance to communicating with the teacher on the part of the parents. These books can also make it easier for parents to share information about themselves with their children.

Childhood Experiences   Experiences from the teacher's childhood let children know that teachers were once children, just like them.

About One's Name   There is an interesting story behind almost everyone's name. In *¿Por qué me llamo Yolanda? (Why My Name Is Yolanda)* by Yolanda P. Villalobos (El Paso School District, 1992), the author tells a compelling story of a lonely World War II soldier, her own father, and explains how she came to be named Yolanda. *Y los mariachis siguieron tocando (The Mariachis Kept on Playing)*, by Roberto V. Belis (El Paso School District, 1992), is a romantic and tragic story, masterfully written, that explains the author's nickname, "Guerito."

Relationship to Other Family Members   Family members are very significant in the life of the young child. By sharing their experiences and feelings toward their own families, teachers are inviting children to recognize and analyze how they relate to others, and the role others play in their lives. *Mi abuelita y el abrigo rojo que me regaló (My Grandmother and the Red Coat She Gave Me)*, by María Teresa Campa

(Los Angeles Unified School District, 1992), recalls a childhood experience, the gift of a red coat. The author describes her grandmother and the profound influence this small, silent but powerful woman had on her life. The refrain, "My grandmother loved me and I loved my grandma very much then" provides continuity throughout the text, which is illustrated with striking, authentic black-and-white photographs.

The Process of Becoming   A powerful message teachers can share with children is that life is a process of becoming. By sharing with the students how the teachers themselves have grown or learned something, they offer the hope that the children may also someday transform a life that is currently oppressive or limiting. For example, *I Was Not Always a Teacher,* by Judy Houston (Houston Independent School District, 1991), traces the author's work experiences as a teenager (waitress in a pizza parlor, cashier in a gas station, and farm worker) and how she eventually became a teacher. The brevity of the text, the author's own attractive line drawings, and the story's humor make this text appealing to children of all ages.

Adult Experiences   The students' interest in the teachers' lives is not limited to the past. They will also enjoy knowing what happens in their teachers' lives today.

The Immigrant Experience   The last decades of the twentieth century saw a significant wave of immigration to the United States. There is a mistaken but widespread notion that immigrants take away jobs from native-born citizens and contribute to the depletion of the economy. Instead, in terms of economic productivity as well as in many other ways, immigrants have been and continue to be a source of strength for the United States.

Immigrants are special individuals because it takes a great dose of courage and resilience to be willing to abandon one's own land and settle in a foreign country. As a self-selected group, immigrants are not necessarily typical of their country of origin, but share with other immigrants the special traits of perseverance and commitment to succeed. Statistically, immigrants give more to the country where they settle than what they receive. But despite the great contributions that immigrants make to society, the immigrant experience is very difficult for the individuals involved. And children are no exception.

Adults tend to believe that children are adaptable, that they easily forget, and that their suffering is short-lived. In reality, what happens is that children don't know how to verbalize what they feel, and too often, when they try, there is no one ready to listen. Immigrant parents have much to cope with, and in the struggle to make a living and survive the language and cultural differences, they may not be able to listen sufficiently to what their children are experiencing.

If the teacher himself has experienced immigration, or if he is the son or grandchild of immigrants, he will be able to share his own experience or that of his family. In doing so, he may be offering a very valuable gift to his students and their families—the invitation to reflect upon their own lives. This is the first step in beginning to heal the wounds of uprootedness.

In *Ni de aquí ni de allá (Neither from Here nor There)*, by Lorena G. Barbosa (El Paso School District, 1992), the teacher/author courageously recounts her own immigration experience at the age of eleven, after the death of her father. She writes of the painful change from being an outstanding student to being a newcomer who can't speak the language and is scorned for not being able to perform adequately.

Biographical Books

People are a fascinating subject. Just as it is possible to write about oneself, one can write about others. Sometimes these categories overlap. For example, Terry Campa's *My Grandmother and the Red Coat She Gave Me* could have been easily considered as belonging to either an autobiographical or a biographical category.

Relatives: Our Parents and Grandparents   For many of us, some of the most important beings in our life are, unquestionably, our parents. In traditional cultures, such as the Hispanic or Latino culture, where the ties with the extended family can be as close as those of the immediate family, grandparents play a very important role.

Valeria Andriola uses the form of a letter to tell her story, *Nonna Carissima (Beloved Grandmother)* (University of San Francisco, 1992). Each paragraph of the letter occupies a page, illustrated with a photograph. As her grandmother's life unfolds, her love for her granddaughter becomes evident. To make the book even more striking, Valeria pasted each page on cardboard and laminated it. The use of lace paper doilies on the inner pages, and of real lace, rhinestones, and fake pearls on the outside cover, are also expressions of how much her grandmother means to the author, and of the author's willingness to honor this connection.

Relatives: Our Own Children   The relationship to their children is perhaps the most precious experience that parents can have. It is not surprising that many teachers choose to write about their own children. A special book in this regard is *El mundo a través de los ojos de Cecilia (The World Through Cecilia's Eyes)*, written by a teacher in the El Paso Independent School District, 1992. "How does it feel to walk?" Cecilia asks, sitting in her wheelchair. And the author, her mother, can only answer, "I do not know. I've never thought about walking. I just do it." Cecilia answers, "If I could walk, I'd be a ballerina." The dialogue in the text, based on real-life dialogue with her daughter, reiterates Cecilia's longing to walk, to run, to dance. The author concludes with the realization that although Cecilia can't walk, she dances, runs, flies with her mind, and in her heart. Illustrated by a combination of computer graphics, line drawings by the author's talented niece, and color photographs of Cecilia, this book touches the heart of all readers.

Relatives: Our Significant Other   By sharing life intimately with another person, we get to know others in great depth. And our partners—their actions, their thoughts, their dreams—can become the subject of powerful descriptions. *Montañas (Mountains)*, by María V. Rubert (El Paso School District, 1992), uses mountains as a metaphor. The mountains of their native Puerto Rico, the mountains her husband has seen on his trips, and the mountains that surround their adopted city of El Paso are the recurrent themes of this book. As the author writes about her husband's intense love for mountains, she lets us appreciate her deep regard for this man with whom she has shared thirty-five years of climbing the mountains of life. This striking book is illustrated with photographs pasted on colored construction paper as well as with collages that combine the author's own color drawings with glossy illustrations cut out from magazines.

Students   There is of course no limit to the people who could be the subject of a biographical book. It could be particularly significant for a teacher to write books about the children in his or her class.

Books about Animals and Nature

Animals and nature can provide a diversity of topics. Sometimes books can be written from an unusual perspective. *Soy dueño de los Acosta. Libro por Bogart. Fotos por Familia Acosta (I'm the Owner of the Acostas. Book by Bogart. Pictures by the Acosta Family)*, by Herlinda Acosta (El Paso Independent School District, 1992), provides one such example. The author of the book writes the captions that accompany this photo album in the first person, as if written by their dog, Bogart, who "owns" the family. The wonderful humor of the captions is complemented by the bright colors of the posterboard used to frame the photographs. The pages are held together by a ribbon and further secured by clothespins enlivened by glue-on dog biscuits.

ABC Books

ABC books can offer a structure for any topic. Not only can they be used for categories such as birds, animals, plants, and cultural festivities, but also family members, family experiences, and even family values.

Counting Books

Similar to ABC books, counting books offer a structure that can be helpful for first-time or reluctant writers. *Contemos con los niños* (*Let's Count with the Children*), by Patricia G. Ramos (El Paso Independent School District, 1992), is a counting book that begins with *one* teacher and *two* languages, and concludes with *twelve* children, the full number of students in this bilingual classroom. While the elements counted in the book are all things that can be found in most classrooms, they have been presented with ingenuity (the number eleven is depicted by the shape of small arms when two students are raising their hands to ask a question or offer an answer) and with true poetic sensitivity (the number three is illustrated with drawings of fall, winter, and spring, the seasons that the class has seen passing by their window).

Fantasy

For this category there are no limits. Teachers should feel free to create any story they wish, with real-life characters or with animals, toys, or any other fantastic types of characters.

The story can approximate real life or go beyond the boundaries of realism. By freeing her own imagination, the teacher will be better prepared to allow the children's imagination to flow as well.

Our History, Our Lives

All children need and deserve ample literature in their home language as well as in the majority language of the country in which they live. They need literature that depicts their reality, their communities, their history, and their daily lives, and also stimulates their imagination. Teachers who know and work with these children can be creating the literature that is lacking. But even if a teacher does not want to embark on the long road to becoming a published author, the richness of media in this technological age makes it very feasible to produce multiple copies of any handmade book. For those who do not wish to think in technological terms, all that is needed is paper and pen.

Whether printed on the computer, illustrated with photos scanned into the computer, or made by hand, you could produce your first book today. You can decorate it with fabrics, with lace, with stickers, magazine cut-outs, dried leaves and flowers, photographs, or anything meaningful and available to you. The joy of the process and the liberating experience will be a great gift to yourself, your family and friends, and, if you are a teacher, your students.

Caretakers as Authors

Adults who care for children benefit in more ways than just the academic progress they see in their children when they become authors. They will become protagonists of their lives as they become the protagonists of their books.

Benefits of Self-Published Books

Self-publishing books, in the classroom or school, brings about multiple benefits. Self-published books will:

- build bridges between home and school by increasing mutual knowledge of each other, in the process of sharing life experiences and personal reflections
- invite self-reflection
- lead to deeper living
- bring out the artist, the creator hidden in each of us
- build self-esteem
- foster reading, vocabulary building, and literacy in general
- promote the validation of life experiences and our history
- facilitate understanding of others, bridging cultural differences
- empower us, as protagonists of our own books, to look at our lives from the perspective of a primary character, not just a secondary one
- contribute to create a print-rich environment in our schools and classrooms and in the homes of our students
- provide an opportunity for children and their parents to engage in meaningful, lasting experiences
- become valued treasures to be kept as reminders of important moments of our lives and to preserve memories throughout time
- be beautiful and valuable presents

Making books can motivate us to—

Remember
Reflect
Dream
Be authors, artists, creators
Be whatever we may want to be.

Revising can be a pain in the neck. Just when you think you're finished with a piece, you're back revising it again. But this is what writing is—rewriting, rewriting, rewriting. Is it easy? No! It's a struggle that requires all of my persistence and determination. Ken Schultz wrote *Ken Schultz's Fishing Encyclopedia: World-wide Angling Guide,* which weighs more than nine and a half pounds, is 1,916 pages long, and is composed of more than a million and a half words. After four years of working on it, he was asked, "And what was the most fun part of the project?" "'Fun' was a word that didn't come up too often," Schultz said. "'Bayer aspirin' came up a lot."

"On Revision," by Eric A. Kimmel, will take away your headaches and anxiety about revision. In a down-to-earth, inviting way, he tells you exactly how he revises and how he feels about revising. Kimmel, an award-winning children's book author, takes you through his approach and shares his practical tricks-of-the-trade. Use them yourself and then pass them on to your students and colleagues.

Following his advice, you will take full advantage of the wonderful opportunity that revision gives us—the chance to shape and strengthen our writing to the point where we want to share it with a larger audience. Then, as Kimmel says, when your piece is published, you will wish that you could continue to revise. ■

ON REVISION

Eric A. Kimmel, Author and Professor Emeritus of Education, Portland State University, Portland, Oregon

Let's be honest. Nobody likes to revise. I've been writing professionally for over thirty years. Yet I still breathe a long sigh, fix myself another cup of coffee, make a sandwich, check to see if I have any e-mail, feed the cat, walk the dog—anything to delay having to sit down and start rewriting.

But the truth is that good writing is largely rewriting. Some of my best work doesn't begin to emerge until I finish my third, seventh, tenth, or even twentieth revision. It's similar to a child starting school. That first day is filled with bright hopes and brilliant potential. Yet those hopes and potential will remain unrealized without the hard work that goes with learning.

Revision is the hard work of writing that turns potential into achievement. Think of revision as a sculptor approaching a stone. The sculptor envisions the figure inside. To bring it out, he must chip away the extra material, smooth and polish the stone until it achieves its final form. It is slow, laborious work. Yet without it, the sculptor's vision will remain only a dream.

Revision is part of the writing process, and possibly the most important part. Through revising, we have the opportunity to rethink what we've written. We discover alternatives that we may not have realized existed when we wrote our first draft. Characters deepen as we come to know them better. Opportunities emerge to make our writing much more interesting and exciting than it was in the first draft. These are opportunities we might never have discovered had we not continued to revise.

Here is how I approach revision. You might wish to try my method for yourself. However, always remember that every writer is different. The only "correct" way is the one that works for you.

When I write a first draft, I go very quickly from beginning to end. I don't worry about grammar, spelling, punctuation. All that matters is getting my first version down on paper so that I have something to work with. I do the actual writing on my computer, but I don't revise on the computer. I print out my first draft. I need to hold the paper in my hand and write my notes and corrections on it with a pen.

I generally let the first draft sit for several days. That way it seems fresh and new when I begin revising. I approach revision with the same concentration I bring to writing the first draft. Revision isn't something I want to rush through. I know I must give it the time and thought it requires. I may stall a bit before I begin revising, in the same way that an athlete pauses to take a deep breath before entering an important competition. But once I start the work, my concentration is total. I don't like to be disturbed, so I do my best to make sure I am not. Don't answer the phone. Let the doorbell ring. Close the door to the room I'm working in. Sometimes it helps to find a "hideout." I often work in the neighborhood library. I don't tell anybody where I'm going, and I don't promise to be back at any certain time. In other words, I'm carving out my own mental space. When I'm revising, I'm off the planet.

It is important to approach revision with the same excitement with which you began your first draft. It is often said that writing is a process of discovery. Each revision carries you further along the journey. You know in your heart if you're done. If you're not, then keep working. It's done when it's done, and not before. How do you know? Read it aloud to yourself. You'll start feeling that sense of joy and pride hearing words you've written come together in just the right way.

Reading aloud is the activity that helps me most. When I begin to revise, I read my first draft aloud to myself, or have someone else read it to me while I make notes on a copy in my hand. Hearing a piece read aloud alerts us to its flaws in a way silent reading never can. We get a sense of what doesn't sound right or feel right. We begin to better understand what isn't working. The challenge is to identify sections that don't work and think of ways to correct them. This is the challenge facing every writer. Revision is like working on a puzzle. A solution to the problem exists. Our task is to find it.

Beginning writers have no idea how many times a professional writer rewrites and revises. All my books are written and rewritten at least seven to ten times, sometimes as many as fifteen or twenty. Good writing doesn't happen in a few minutes. It requires far more time and effort than most people realize. As I work on each successive draft, I discover more things that I really like, and fewer and fewer that I want to change or improve. When I reach the point where I can truly say there is nothing that I wish to change, the story is ready to be sent to an editor.

Working with an editor is like working with a coach. You are not necessarily the best judge of your own work, any more than parents are the best judges of their child's athletic ability. A good editor helps by pointing out areas in the writing that need to be rethought. She indicates inconsistencies, identifies missing information, points out places where the story lags or rushes by too quickly. She calls our attention to episodes that may be in questionable taste. A good editor never tells a writer what to do. She asks questions, identifies problems. It's the writer's job to consider these issues and come up with solutions.

One example of this process in action is a book I recently finished writing, called *Robin Hook, Pirate Hunter*. It was a fanciful tale about a group of children, much like Peter Pan's Lost Boys, who fight wicked Captain Thatch and his pirates. The final scene had the kids, armed with swords, pistols, and cannons, slugging it out with the buccaneers. That bothered my editor. She didn't like the idea of armed children gleefully engaging in violence. She asked me to consider changing it.

I admit that I was not initially receptive to the suggestion. I've always loved pirate tales. The point of doing a pirate story, as I saw it, is to have that scene where cannonballs whistle overhead, cutlasses slash, and the scuppers flow with blood. My editor did not order me to make the change. She kept telling me that the scene really made her feel uncomfortable. In the end, we compromised. I kept the final battle, but I had my crew achieve the victory with the help of ink-squirting squids and friendly porpoises. The cannons fired hornet's nests. There was lots of noise, but no one, not even the pirates, was actually injured.

I wasn't completely happy with the changes. I felt my editor was being wimpy and that I had unnecessarily gone along with her.

Then came the incident in Columbine High School.

My editor's instincts were correct. Given these times, a children's picture book filled with illustrations of kids armed to the teeth would have been dead on arrival.

A good editor whose judgment you trust can be the most valuable partner a writer can have. I don't necessarily follow all my editor's suggestions. However, I always consider them carefully. When disagreements arise, we discuss them. Sometimes I convince my editor I'm right. Sometimes she convinces me. In the discussion I frequently discover things about my work, good and bad, that I might never have realized on my own. An editor is a partner, not an adversary. After all, we're both working toward the same goal—making the work as good as it can be at this point in time.

I use the phrase "at this point in time" because I never consider any of my writing to be completely finished. Even published work can always be improved. Often, when reading aloud to audiences, I'll make changes in the text as I go along. I'll often reread a published story I wrote several years ago and wish I could have it back for another revision.

Sounds crazy, doesn't it? At first we avoid revising; then, when we no longer can, we wish we could. We ought to cherish having the opportunity to make revisions. Writers are fortunate in that regard. How many athletes would give anything for the chance to play a crucial game over again?

Writers get as many replays as they want. So keep revising. The ability to revise is our gift and our strength.

Afterword
Above the Clouds and in My Blood

What Keeps Me Publishing

After meeting a publication deadline, teachers are drained to the point of exhaustion. Some teachers, including me, listen to our minds and bodies and ask just how long we can continue publishing student work year after year. While it's a worthwhile endeavor, teachers need to and usually find ways to give themselves the energy to continue. For every teacher, the reenergizing process is different.

Nearly every year, I trek in Asia. Among the mountains, I am reborn living a simple life, one step at a time. With each day, I shed stress and anxiety, leaving my daily routine far behind me. There, in those mountains, I come in touch with my own humanity. For a brief time, I soak in the beauty of another land's peoples, landscape, and culture. I am lost in that world.

Students often ask upon my return if I thought of teaching or school. They are surprised to learn that very seldom, if at all, did I think of the classroom, assessments, or staff meetings. After all, the primary purpose of traveling is to have fun, immerse yourself in a new adventure, and not worry about your everyday toils. Already, I am looking forward to future treks in: Nepal, Zanskar (a region in northern India), Tibet, Bhutan, and South America.

Travel for your own sake and your students'. When you come back to your classroom, you will bring a whole new self with you—one the kids and you will appreciate and enjoy.

Walk with me now as I tell you about a recent adventure in Nepal, and you will see what keeps me publishing.

*"The din of the dusty world and the locked-in-ness of human habitations
are what human nature habitually abhors; while, on the contrary,
haze, mist, and the haunting spirits of the mountains
are what human nature seeks, and yet can rarely find."*
—Kuo Hsi (eleventh century)

I went to Nepal because of its mountains and fell in love with its people. This girl near the village of Birethanti located at 3,600 feet (1,097 m) in the Annapurna Sanctuary, Nepal, sought my help for her injured foot. It was a chilly December morning, and she was dressed in thin cotton, typical of many Nepalese children, but unlike the trekkers, who are layered in high-tech, cutting-edge trekking clothes. Photograph by Chris Weber.

Rinzin Sherpa's headlamp, like cat's eyes, dances in the cold black night as he descends to high camp to retrieve my hiking boots, which might turn out later to be lifesaving. In the distance, I gaze peacefully at the massive wall of mountains rising majestically above the Lhotse Shar Glacier. Sitting on a ledge at more than 17,000 feet high in the Himalayas, I take full advantage of this rest and breathe deeply of the thin air. My mind and body drink the air and rest completely.

I have been in the Everest region for over two weeks now, and in the morning I will attempt to summit Island Peak (Imja Tse) on my first climb ever. I think that the toughest part is over. After all, Rinzin says that the climb is going to be easy. I have no idea what lies ahead, only the mountain towering above me into the heavens. Just as so many student publications could never begin if I were aware of what was to come, my ignorance of the difficulty and my grand visions push me forward.

Into the night upon that mountain, Rinzin and I continue our climb. Sometimes we are scrambling up and over boulders on all fours. The *clink, clink* of our ice axes biting rock rings into the deep and silent night. Other times we are hugging an extremely narrow path of treacherous loose gravel and rocks.

I can still hear it, even now, the first time it happened: I kick a rock and it falls off into the dark void. I stop and listen, waiting to hear it land. No anticipated thud.

Vegetable seller in the town of Mugling, a bus stop between Kathmandu and Pokara, Nepal. Photograph by Chris Weber.

Girl washing dishes on a cold morning, village of Banthanti, situated at 8,740 feet (2,664 m), Annapurna Sanctuary, Nepal. She had a soft smile and a sweet disposition. Photograph by Chris Weber.

Silence. I know then and there just how high I am and the scent of danger so close. I cannot afford a misstep—it might be my last.

Darkness cloaks the danger as I fight off the fear, trying to focus on each step. Life is very simple: breathe deeply and step, breathe deeply and step. I make sure that I have three-point contact with rock or earth before I take the next step or make the next handhold. It is agonizingly slow work; we are crawling up toward the ridge top, which seems to inch away each time I look up at it.

Finally, dawn breaks and I see we are on the south ridge, at an elevation of approximately 19,024 feet (5,800 m). Sheer drops of thousands of feet fall on either side of us. The wind begins to pick up, and I hope and pray that it won't gust at high speeds. The climb is tough enough without wind complicating it.

A jumble of rocks and boulders forms a narrow, twisted staircase just ahead and above. "I might die today," I think to myself. Friends, family, school, and *Publishing with Students* seem light-years away, as I wonder just how I got myself into this struggle. Yet there is a mountain waiting, and I can talk to myself all day long, but it will do me no good nor get me any farther. Emotions and thoughts whirl, but slowly, I quiet my mind.

The climb cannot afford any more reflection on my part, so I push on. I focus totally on looking ahead, *never down*.

At times, icy fear drains what little energy I have. I am near the end of an exhausting trek, just recovering from altitude sickness, having had no sleep the night before; after summiting, I will have at least a ten-hour walk to Chhukung village. I am climbing on empty, on my willpower, and Rinzin's encouragement.

After an eternity I edge around a rock wall onto a rock "bridge." Halfway across it, the rocks are covered with snow and ice, a frozen white carpet leading onto the upper portions of the mountain. This is no time for celebrating. Rinzin and I take a moment to sit and rest on this bridge barely three feet wide. I want to superglue myself to it because three- to four-thousand-foot sheer drops await me on both sides. I slowly and very cautiously kneel down, getting a firm grip, while I hold the camera over the abyss and snap a photo with an outstretched hand. For a moment, I entertain a crazy notion, but I decide that there's no way I will lean over and get the photo I want from these dizzying, frightening heights.

Frozen, ice-blue lakes dot the glacier below. I am small and insignificant; with a strong gust of wind, I'll be blown into the land of rock and ice far, far, far below.

Himalayan giants surround us. In the east, Makalu (27,806 ft/8,475 m) and Baruntse (25,329 ft/7,720 m) tower over minor peaks. To the south, the beautiful shape of Ama Dablam (22,495 ft/6,856 m) crowns the Chhukung Valley. Above and beyond to the north lie Nuptse (25,851 ft/7,879 m), Lhotse (27,892 ft/8,501 m), and Lhotse Shar (27,505 ft/8,383 m). Yet, there is little time to enjoy the company of these noble mountains.

Rinzin helps me put on my seat harness and crampons. I know so little about the equipment and feel really stupid but grateful for his patience and assistance. Frequently I rub his hands with mine because his are prone to frostbite and are beginning to get numb. (Rinzin had gotten frostbite on another climb, and since then, his hands grow cold more quickly.) We are ready, and once off the bridge and onto the classic icy ridge, I am dancing in paradise, proud and elated. I'm relieved to be on "safer" ground surrounded by a snowy glacier and so proud to do what I just did, conquering my fear, taking me higher than I dreamed. I breathe more easily, and for the first time in hours, I just enjoy the view—open skies and majestic, towering mountains.

I know that we have a ways to go and that crampon work is not easy. I follow Rinzin up the gentle, undulating ridge with a gradual ascent. After the night climb, cramponing up a relatively easy ridge with the sun out in blue, cloudless skies is almost like a summer day's stroll, or as if Christmas has come early.

Off the ridge, we head northwest toward the summit. About thirty minutes later, we face a bergschrund. A ten-foot high ice wall (the uphill edge of the bergschrund) is separated from the downhill lip of the bergschrund by a narrow, deep crevasse. It extends in both directions as far as I can see. An *interesting* problem. I watch Rinzin effortlessly go up and over the wall. I take a couple of breaths and then kick my left boot straight into the ice wall, pushing the front crampon points into the ice. Then I slam the ice ax with my right hand into the hard snow above my shoulder. I front-point with my right boot and follow by slamming the other ax with my left hand into higher ground. There I am hugging the cold wall, not exactly knowing what to do next. I take more breaths and then go through the process again and again until I struggle over the top to join Rinzin.

Between us and the base of the summit lies a wicked field of *nieve penitentes* (Spanish for "penitent snow"). Everywhere foot-high, cone-shaped columns of rock-hard snow stand between the hollows; it is like stumbling on a bed of nails with boots of nails. My legs are turning to Jell-o. I slow to a stop every step or so, wanting so badly to just lie down and rest. My ankles burn with every step I take. Rinzin keeps yelling at me to continue on. I have nothing left in me but my resolve to go as far as I can.

I drag one boot and then the next, inhaling and blowing, inhaling and blowing air. At this altitude of over 19,000 feet, there is less than half the oxygen found at sea level. Almost gasping, I quickly suck in all the oxygen I can and exhale, panting and puffing. My legs are gone; it is all I can do just to put one foot in front of the other. I do not know how I do it, but finally we reach the base of the summit ridge.

I pause to gaze up at a snow/ice couloir—a steep wall of snow and ice some 492 feet high (150 m) with a 50° pitch—too high and difficult for me. If climbing that near vertical wall of snow and ice wasn't enough, the couloir is covered with *nieve penitentes*. In other words, thousands of ice daggers jut straight out from the couloir erasing any faint hopes I had of summiting. I ask Renzin how long it might take him to climb the couloir. Rinzin tells me that it would take him an hour and a half to climb the couloir. If I got back my strength, I might be able to do it in two or three hours, but we don't have the time. We have to descend to high camp, take down the tents and pack up all our gear and equipment, and then walk back to Chhukung, many miles away. Just not enough time for a summit attempt.

I collapse in the snow telling Rinzin, "I am happy here." He tries to get me to climb higher to possibly summit, but my voice and the look of contentment on my face tell him this is as high as we will climb on this trip, some 19,516 feet (5,950 m)—the highest I have ever been. I am so tired and glad to just sit and rest. I decline to stand with axes raised over my head for a photo; I am exhausted, so I just sit and smile for the camera. Let the photos tell the truth. Climbing mountains is a struggle, requiring all of the will and energy you have and then some. . . .

Photograph of Chris near the summit of Island Peak (Imja Tse) 20,305 feet (6,189 m), Everest Region, Nepal. Photograph by Rinzin Sherpa.

Up on the mountains, we test ourselves, discover who we are and what we are capable of doing.

I must go back to the mountains as surely as I must breathe.

Trekking in the mountains is my passion; it's in my blood. Like publishing, treks are never-ending journeys with challenging highs and lows. Trekking renews and reenergizes my body and spirit, in much the same way creating beautiful student publications energizes.

Contact me (*chriscarlweber@earthlink.net*) if you want to learn more about treks in Nepal that I am going to co-lead. Perhaps one day we'll be standing together above the clouds.

As you may know, climbing a mountain means little unless you get down safely. E-mail me and I'll send you the rest of my Island Peak story.

Appendix A

Giving Voice to Your Students' Dreams

Arun Narayan Toké, Executive Editor,
Skipping Stones: A Multicultural Children's Magazine, Eugene, Oregon

So, you want to see your students published! At *Skipping Stones*, we receive over one hundred submissions each month, on the average. Yet we are able to publish only about one out of ten. And most other magazines do not devote as much space to children's creations as we do at *Skipping Stones*. Clearly, it would be unrealistic to expect to see all your students' names in print. However, there are things that you can do to make your students' creations stand out in the crowd!

Do Your Homework: Know Thy Publisher!

Each magazine has a reason, a purpose for which it exists. For example, at *Skipping Stones*, our purpose is to encourage multicultural awareness, nature appreciation, social responsibility, and international understanding. *New Moon*, as another example, is a magazine for girls and their dreams. Similarly, most magazines have specific editorial goals. Therefore, it is better to first get to know the magazines where your students hope to publish their work. To simply send your students' creations indiscriminately may mean many rejections and eventual discouragement.

Perhaps, the best way might be to have students write to one or more publishers to request their guidelines for submissions, editorial philosophy, and upcoming themes or editorial calendar. This would be a great exercise in letter writing for your

Figure A–1. "Tenderness," the cover photo for *Skipping Stones*, Volume 3, No. 4, Eugene, Oregon. Copyright © 1991–92. Photograph by Vasilyev Kostya, 14, Photo Club of Sevastopol, Sevastopol, Ukraine.

students! They might also request a sample copy and information about any contests sponsored by the magazine. Always include an SASE (self-addressed stamped envelope) when requesting free information. That's one of the many unwritten golden rules.

Does your school or library subscribe to some of these magazines? You might ask your students to bring to the class a magazine or two that they receive or love to read at home. Soon you will have a handful of possibilities. As your class looks through some of these prospective publications and their submission guidelines, it will be more obvious which magazines are your best bets. You might look for things like types of articles, ages of authors, and format of writings (e.g., poems, stories). How many youth submissions are published in each issue? What's the editorial slant? Select a few magazines that seem to be open to receiving the genre of writing that your students are good at creating.

Quality Counts!

Choose a few exceptional pieces to send, rather than all the classroom assignments generated by students. Often, we get large, bulky envelopes from teachers containing fifteen or twenty-five poems, stories, or essays—a lot of extra work for the editors! This does not mean that all the burden should rest on your shoulders. Let students themselves be the judges. They can work in small groups of three to five to select one or two writings that they feel good about sending. Chances are that editors would probably like them as well.

What makes an A+ submission? Revisions hold the key to getting a good piece of writing ready for sending. To revise a good piece of writing so that it is almost ready for publication, students might use one or more of the following steps:

- Self criticism: What do students *like* or *not like* about their own writing? They might read it out loud at home to their siblings or parents, or to themselves, and revise until they are satisfied.
- Students could read their creations to the class for a peer review. A student whose work is being reviewed should always feel encouraged. Working in pairs or circling up in small groups is sometimes more comfortable for students.
- Once the students are satisfied with their work, you might help with grammar, spelling, and so on. Make sure that the typing is done reasonably well, or that the students have used a legible font.

The Art of Packaging: The Cover Letter

After a few polished pieces have been selected for submissions, the next important step is a thorough checkup for things like legible return address and age/grade of the author.

Help your students prepare a good cover letter to introduce themselves. It may even be better if the teacher sends the submission package with an introduction letter for the student creators. A few sentences about each student to highlight their cultural and/or socioeconomic background, scholastic aptitude, unique experiences, and any volunteer projects that they have been part of are very helpful. Editors also like to know ages and/or grade levels of authors. Cover letters should be about three or four paragraphs, not to exceed one double-spaced typewritten page.

Make sure that both school and home address and telephone are included as school is out during summer and winter breaks. Sometimes submissions are not processed for several months, and by then, the student might have already moved on to another grade, or, perhaps, to a different school. So it is always a good idea to add the student's home address and telephone in the cover letter.

Editors love to see attractive artwork and photographs to illustrate articles. You might include good photocopies of any available illustrations or photos. If you do send the originals, it is highly recommended that you include a large return envelope with adequate postage.

If the publication's guidelines require a parental/school release form, make sure to include it.

Often, your student's work could fit into a specific department, column, or page of the magazine. For example, *Skipping Stones* has regular spaces like Letters to the Editor, Poetry Page, What's On Your Mind?, NEWS (north, east, west, and south) and Taking Action, and Dear Hanna. These offer creative exchange of ideas and an open dialogue. If your student's creation is geared toward such regular spaces in a magazine, chances are good that it will get accepted.

It is fine to send simultaneous submissions to two or three different magazines at the same time, but you must indicate so in your cover letter. And it is good practice to let other editors know when a piece has been accepted by a different magazine.

Creating Your Own Class/School Publication

If you can't find an appropriate avenue to publish your students' work through established media, you might just start your own publication. We have seen several superb student-published newsletters, magazines, and other periodicals. Yearbooks and class magazines are equally great to get students motivated to write and illustrate. Encouraging pen pal letters or e-mails is yet another way to get the juices flowing in your budding young authors.

The Wait and Handling Acceptance or Rejection

In the *Bhagavad Gita* (the famous Hindu book about how to conduct one's life), Lord Krishna tells Arjuna, the great warrior, to do his duty and not to worry about the fruits of his actions. This teaching also applies equally well to aspiring young authors. Once the submissions have been mailed out, the ball is in the editors' hands.

Keep on writing and sending your creations to prospective publications, even to the same ones again. But it is not wise to hold your breath and wait for an acceptance letter. You will hear from the editors when they make their decision.

If you do not hear from the editors within three to four months, it is a good idea to send a letter (with an SASE) to find out the status of your submission. It seems to expedite the process. For their convenience, you might even include a duplicate copy of your submission along with your letter of inquiry.

A letter of acceptance is what you wait for, but sometimes it might take a year before you see your story in print. As a contributor, do expect to get a complimentary copy of the magazine. Some publications might even pay a small honorarium in addition. In rare instances, you might receive a letter from the managing editor notifying you that your poem or story (even though it was previously accepted for publication) will not run for one reason or another.

If and when you get a rejection letter—even an impersonal form letter—remember that it does not necessarily reflect upon the quality of your work. Rejection letters may not elaborate on the reasons that led to an unfavorable decision. But even if your work is excellent, it might not be accepted for reasons such as, did not fit the theme being planned, too many submissions on the same theme, too many submissions from the same school or city, inappropriate format, or too long. Sometimes, unplanned themes bump articles or stories slated for an issue, or the editorial staff and/or focus of the publication gets changed. And, once in a while, your piece might get misplaced and thus not receive proper attention until it's too late. At times, the same submission will score better (or worse) in the editor's opinion, depending on the day and time it was read. An overworked editor working against deadlines *can* make a bad decision. As you can see, most of the reasons do not have much to do with the quality of the writing. So, do not let a rejection letter ruin your day or stop you from creating new compositions.

If you are sure that you're a winner, try other publications. There are many that actively seek youth submissions. Exceptional writing usually comes out when you are writing for yourself, when you are in touch with your own self. Keep on writing about topics that are close to your heart and themes that spark your imagination. Write in your journal, write a letter to yourself or your friend (but don't mail the letter). You don't have to share your writing with others unless you choose to do so.

About *Skipping Stones* Magazine

Skipping Stones is a nonprofit children's magazine, now in its fourteenth year of publication. It encourages cooperation, creativity, and a celebration of cultural and ecological richness. It features original art and writing by youth all over the world. *Skipping Stones* does not shy away from addressing difficult issues. It strives to nurture diverse perspectives and welcomes student contributions. Sometimes we feature bilingual writing—sometimes even trilingual. Published bimonthly during the school year, the magazine has a widely scattered international readership. Winner of four national awards, *Skipping Stones* is a unique multicultural education and nature appreciation magazine attempting to bridge the waters that separate people and nature, cultures and generations.

For submissions and subscription information contact:

Skipping Stones
P.O. Box 3939
Eugene, OR 97403-0939
Phone: (541) 342-4956
E-mail: skipping@efn.org
Website: <http://www.efn.org/~skipping>

Appendix B

Publications That Publish Student Writing, Poetry, and Art

In elementary schools, teachers might have a few students who want to submit their work to outside publications. In middle and high school, more and more students become interested in seeking out and participating in other publishing opportunities. At any age, they need to have realistic expectations about just how difficult it is to be published. I am upfront with my students, telling them to look at it as a learning experience where they participate in the submission process and take the risk all writers take. Moreover, I urge them to feel good about their writing and proud of their best effort regardless of what the rejection letters say.

Arun Narayan Toké's article "Giving Voice to Your Students' Dreams" (Appendix A) has good, solid advice about the submission process. Another great resource is the fifth edition of *The Market Guide for Young Writers*, by Kathy Henderson.

Detailed descriptions and information about three well-known, respected publications make up the first part of this appendix. The information about *Merlyn's Pen*, *Skipping Stones*, and *Stone Soup* is reprinted with permission from each of these publications.

Read and seriously consider the subsequent list of magazines and newspapers that specialize in teen and children's writings (I have read some, and they are excellent—many have won awards) and share this list with your colleagues and students. It may be that these publications end up being the ones that publish your students' writing. Believe me, I have had students published by smaller, lesser-known publications, and they were very proud and ecstatic! Being published is being published.

Three Tried-and-True Publications

Merlyn's Pen: Fiction, Essays, and Poems by America's Teens

Merlyn's Pen is perhaps the oldest of all publishers devoted exclusively to teens in grades 6–12 (or the home-school or international equivalent). Art is not considered. Its staff responds to every contributor, published or not, and read from eight thousand to fifteen thousand contributions each year. For a fee, they also offer a "Comprehensive Critique," which gives the student a lengthy, detailed, personal critique from one of the editors. They are quite selective; about 1 percent of all submissions are selected for publication. They purchase the copyrights to works they publish and pay the writers from $20 to $200, depending on length.

Some five thousand classrooms in the United States use either *Merlyn's Pen* or its anthologies—*The American Teen Writer Series*—in their English and writing curriculum; all their materials have teacher guides, regular and ESL/EFL levels.

Most students appearing in *Merlyn's Pen* have contributed many times before being accepted. Often, a student is asked to revise and resubmit a work—with the editor(s)' suggestions—to be considered a second time.

Merlyn's Pen is published annually, but it is contemplating a relaunch that brings the magazine to homes and schools six times each year, each issue featuring a theme.

P.O. Box 910
East Greenwich, RI 02818
Phone: (401) 885-5175
Fax: (401) 885-5222
E-mail: MerlynsPen@aol.com
Website: <http://www.merlynspen.com>
Publisher: R. James Stahl

Skipping Stones: A Multicultural Children's Magazine

Skipping Stones is a nonprofit children's magazine that encourages cooperation, creativity, and celebration of cultural and environmental richness. It provides a playful forum for sharing ideas and experiences among children from different lands and backgrounds.

Skipping Stones is an award-winning resource in multicultural education. It is timely and timeless. *Skipping Stones* publishes bimonthly during the school year. They accept art and original writings in every language and from all ages.

In *Skipping Stones*, you will find stories, articles, and photos from all over the world: Native American folktales, photos by kids in India and Ukraine, letters and drawings from South Africa and Lithuania, cartoons from China . . . Non-English writings are accompanied by English translations to encourage the learning of other languages.

Each issue also contains international pen pals, book reviews, noteworthy news, and a guide for parents and teachers. The guide offers creative activities and resources for making the best use of *Skipping Stones* in your home or classroom.

P.O. Box 3939
Eugene, OR 97403-0939
Phone: (541) 342-4956
E-mail: skipping@efn.org
Website: <http://www.efn.org/~skipping
Executive Editor: Arun Narayan Toké

Stone Soup: The Magazine by Young Writers and Artists

Stone Soup is made up of stories, poems, book reviews, and art by young people through age thirteen. Although all the writing is published in English, work is accepted from all over the world. To get an idea of the kind of writing and art its staff likes, please look through the sample issue they provide on their website at <http://www.stonesoup.com>.

Send its editors writing and art about the things you feel most strongly about! Whether your work is about imaginary situations or real ones, use your own experiences and observations to give your work depth and a sense of reality. Writing need not be typed, as long as it is legible. They are happy to consider writing in languages other than English; include a translation if possible. Please do not send work you are also sending to other magazines.

Illustrators: If you would like to illustrate for *Stone Soup*, send editor Gerry Mandel samples of your artwork, along with a letter saying what kinds of stories you would like to illustrate. Be sure to include your name, age, address, and telephone number.

Book Reviewers: If you are interested in reviewing books for *Stone Soup,* write Ms. Mandel for more information. Tell her a little about yourself, why you want to be a book reviewer, and what kinds of books you like to read. As always, be sure to include your name, age, address, and telephone number.

All contributors whose work is accepted for publication receive a certificate, two complimentary copies, and discounts on other purchases. In addition, contributors of stories, poems, book reviews, and artwork are paid $25 each, illustrators are paid $15 per illustration, and the cover artist is paid $50.

P.O. Box 83
Santa Cruz, CA 95063
Phone: (800) 447-4569
Website: <http://www.stonesoup.com>
Editor: Gerry Mandel

Magazines and Newspapers That Specialize in Teens' and Children's Writings

The following list is reprinted with kind permission from R. James Stahl, publisher, *Merlyn's Pen: Fiction, Essays, and Poems by America's Teens.* You can also go directly to <http://www.merlynspen.com/publish.html>, and from that webpage, you can click on the various publishing links.

As the *Merlyn's Pen* site informs you, most of the publications listed below prefer that you contact them first—to learn about their submission procedures and requirements and to better understand their editorial preferences—before you send your writing to them. It is not advisable to send your work to magazines and newspapers that you have not seen for yourself.

Some of these publications produce both online and hard copy versions of their publications. Many of the websites provide submission guidelines, samples from past issues, writing tips, subscription forms, and more.

Blue Jean Magazine

Blue Jean Magazine is an alternative to the fashion and beauty magazines targeting teen girls. It is the only magazine written and edited by young women around the world between the ages of 13 and 19. They publish teen fiction, poetry, art, commentary, and nonfiction works. Its mission is to publish what young women are thinking, saying, and doing.

P. O. Box 60
Rochester, NY 14609
Phone: (716) 288-6980
Fax: (716) 288-3417
E-mail: editors@bluejeanonline.com
Website: <http://www.bluejeanonline.com>

Creative Kids, The National Voice for Kids

This magazine contains games, activities, puzzles, photographs, artwork, stories, poetry, plays, cartoons, songs, and editorials by and for kids ages 8–14.

P.O. Box 8813
Waco, TX 76714-8813
Phone: (800) 998-2208
Fax: (254) 756-3339
E-mail: Creative_Kids@prufrock.com
Website: <http://www.prufrock.com>

Foster Care Youth United

Foster Care Youth United is a bimonthly magazine written by and for young people in foster care. FCYU is designed to give a voice to young people living in the system by providing a forum for an open exchange of views and experiences by those most affected by foster care. The magazine is written by a core staff of fifteen youngsters in their Manhattan office, but it accepts and receives submissions from throughout the country.

Youth Communication
224 W. 29th Street
Second Floor
New York, NY 10001-5204
Phone: (212) 279-0708
Fax: (212) 279-8856
E-mail: Youthcomm@aol.com
Website: <http://www.youthcomm.org>

How on Earth! Youth Supporting Compassionate, Ecologically Sound Living

This is a quarterly newsletter by teens, with a focus on animal, global, and environmental issues.

P.O. Box 339
Oxford, PA 19363-0339
Phone: (717) 529-8638
Fax: (717) 529-3000
E-mail: HowOnEarth@aol.com

In 2 Print

A literary and art magazine for and by young Canadians between the ages of 12 and 20, *In 2 Print* features short stories, poetry, illustrations, editorials, reviews, cartoons, and interviews.

P.O. Box 102
Port Colborne, Ontario L3K 5V7
Canada
Phone: (905) 834-1539
Fax: (905) 834-1540

LA Youth

LA Youth newspaper is a countywide, teen-written publication with a readership of three hundred thousand youth and adults in the Los Angeles area. *LA Youth*, an independent nonprofit organization, was founded in 1988 to train, inform, and provide a voice to Los Angeles youth through journalism.

5967 W. Third Street
Suite 301
Los Angeles, CA 90036
Phone: (323) 938-9194
Fax: (323) 938-0940
E-mail: layouth@worldsite.net
Website: <http://www.layouth.com>

New Expression

Written by, for, and about Chicago teens, this publication exists through the diverse voices of Chicago youth who want to educate the world about issues that are important to them. The teen staff makes a conscious effort to invite teens of all ethnicities and beliefs to contribute their ideas about all issues.

Youth Communication
Columbia College Chicago
600 South Michigan Avenue
Chicago, IL 60605-7151
Phone: (312) 922-7150
Fax: (312) 922-7151
E-mail: newexpress@aol.com
Website: <http://www.newexpression.org>

New Moon: The Magazine for Girls and Their Dreams

New Moon is the magazine created by girls for all girls who want their voices heard and their dreams taken seriously. It's completely edited by the Girls Editorial Board (sixteen girls ages 8–14).

P.O. Box 3620
Duluth, MN 55803-3620
Phone: (800) 381-4743
Fax: (218) 728-0314
E-mail: newmoon@newmoon.org
Website: <http://www.newmoon.org>

NYC New Youth Connections

This is a general-interest magazine written by and for New York youth, with a readership of two hundred thousand teens and adults.

Youth Communication
224 W. 29th Street
Second Floor
New York, NY 10001-5204
Phone: (212) 279-0708
Fax: (212) 279-8856
E-mail: Youthcomm@aol.com
Website: <http://www.youthcomm.org>

Potluck Children's Literary Magazine: The Magazine for the Serious Young Writer

Writers from ages 8–16 fill each issue with their poems, short stories, fables, and book reviews.

Box 546
Deerfield, IL 60015-0546
Phone: (847) 948-1139
Fax: (847) 317-9492
E-mail: nappic@aol.com
Website: <http://www.hometown.aol.com/nappic>

Potato Hill Poetry

This bimonthly magazine (not published in July and August) is for teachers and students in grades K–12. They publish students' poems along with writing exercises, interviews with poets, book reviews, contests, and other poetry-related material. Its staff is also interested in submissions of cartoons, writing exercises, artwork (black ink on plain white paper), essays on the writing process, and black-and-white photographs.

361 Watertown Street
Newton, MA 02158
Phone: (617) 965-0484
Fax: (617) 965-6508
E-mail: PotatoHill@aol.com
Website: <http://www.potatohill.com>

Teen Voices

Teen Voices is a magazine written by, for, and about teenage and young adult women, ages thirteen to nineteen. Regular features include sections about family, health, arts and culture (music, Web, and book reviews); an advice column; and creative writing. This magazine honors young women's potential as leaders.

Women Express, Inc.
P.O. Box 120-027
Boston, MA 02112-0027
Phone: (888) 882-TEEN
Fax: (617) 426-5577
E-mail: womenexp@teenvoices.com
Website: <http://www.teenvoices.com>

TeenInk

TeenInk is a national magazine, a book, and a website featuring teen writing, information, art, photos, poetry, discussions of teen issues, and more. All articles are written by teenage authors.

P.O. Box 30
Newton, MA 02161
Phone: (617) 964-6800
E-mail: submit@teenpaper.org
Website: <http://www.TeenInk.com>

The Apprentice Writer

This publication features short fiction, poetry, and personal essays by students in grades 9–12 throughout the United States and Canada. Also uses black-and-white photography and high-contrast artwork. Deadline each year is March 15.

Gary Fincke, Writers' Institute Director
Susquehanna University
Selinsgrove, PA 17870
Phone: (717) 372-4164
Fax: (717) 372-4310
E-mail: GFincke@susqu.edu

The Claremont Review: The Best International Magazine to Showcase Young Adult Writers

The editors of this magazine look for exemplary fiction and poetry by young authors between thirteen and ninteen years of age. They publish those slice-of-life stories that also focus on language and character, not simply plot. They prefer free-verse, nonrhyming poetry.

4980 Wesley Road
Victoria, British Columbia V8Y 1Y9
Canada
E-mail: aurora@home.com
Website: <http://www.members.home.net/review>

The Concord Review

This is a quarterly journal of exemplary history essays by high school students. The editors ask that students submit essays approximately five thousand words in length.

P.O. Box 661
Concord, MA 01742
Phone: (800) 331-5007
E-mail: fitzhugh@world.std.com
Website: <http://www.tcr.org>

The Elementary School Writer
The High School Writer, Junior High Edition
The High School Writer

Each publication accepts submissions of essays, poems, and short stories from students of subscribing schools only. They publish six times per year from September to May.

Writer Publications
P.O. Box 718
Grand Rapids, MI 55744
Phone and Fax: (218) 326-8025
E-mail: *writer@mx3.com*

The McGuffey Writer

Published three times a year, this magazine publishes short stories, poems, and songs by students K–12.

5128 Westgate Drive
Oxford, OH 45056

The Writer's Slate

The Writer's Slate comes out three times a year and publishes original poetry, exposition, and narration from students enrolled in kindergarten through twelfth grade.

P.O. Box 664
Ottawa, KS 66067
Phone: (785) 242-0407
Fax: (785) 242-0407
Website: <http://www.writingconference.com>

VOX

About sixty teenagers from around metro Atlanta are actively involved as staff members to create the peer-to-peer educational and self-help newspaper *VOX*. This teen publication of writing and art is distributed free to more than eighty thousand youth during the school year. Their mission is to raise youth voice by providing forums for youth-led training, sharing of information, and free expression to empower teenagers as active builders of a stronger community.

229 Peachtree Street, Suite 203
Atlanta, Georgia 30303
Phone: (404) 614-0040
Fax: (404) 614-0045
E-mail: dear_vox@youthcommunication-vox.org
Website: <http://www.youthcommunication-vox.org>

Writes of Passage, The Literary Journal for Teenagers

This literary journal, published twice a year, contains the poems and short stories of teens nationwide as well as special features by established authors offering insight into writing.

817 Broadway
Sixth Floor
New York, NY 10003
Phone: (212) 473-7564
E-mail: WPUSA@aol.com
Website: <http://www.writes.org>

YO! Youth Outlook: The World Through Young People's Eyes

YO! is a monthly newspaper by and about young people, which also syndicates articles to newspapers across the U.S. YO! connects young people with each other and gives adults a window into the constantly changing cultures of youth.

450 Mission Street
Suite 204
San Francisco, CA 94105
Phone: (415) 243-4364
E-mail: CLMitch@aol.com
Website: <http://www.youthoutlook.org>

Appendix C

Display Your Students' Writing and Art on the Web

If your students cannot or do not want to have their work published in books or magazines, then have them try the Internet. It holds unlimited opportunities for young writers to display their work with a larger audience. While your students begin exploring the following links, encourage them to have fun reading students' writing and viewing their artwork. Perhaps one day, other students will be enjoying your students' work on the Web.

Many of these links and their descriptions are displayed on *Stone Soup*'s "Young Writers on the Web" page: <http://www.stonesoup.com/main2/ywriters.html>.

Online Publication Sites

Global SchoolNet

<http://www.gsn.org>
GSN provides online collaborative projects and resources.

Inkspot for Young Writers

<http://www.inkspot.com/young>
Inkspot is a superb resource and community for writers eighteen and under, including articles, contests, critiques, links, and a chat room.

Just Write

<http://justwrite.org>

Just Write provides children with opportunities for creative expression on the level of their abilities and interests. Children ages 5–18 are invited to share their creative writing with a larger audience.

Kids on the Net

<http://152.71.0.105/kotn/gokids.htm>
Kids on the Net features writing by children, ages 6–16, at home and at school all over the world. This site is based in Nottingham, England.

KIDLINK

<http://www.kidlink.org>
KIDLINK is a nonprofit, grassroots organization working to help children and youth through the secondary school level be involved in a global dialogue. Also, students can submit their artwork to the Kidlink Gallery of Computer Art.

Kid News

<http://kidnews.com>
Kid News is a free news and writing service for students and teachers from around the globe; it has published thousands of young authors from every continent except Antarctica.

Let's Go Around the World

<http://www.ccph.com>
Provides wonderful learning adventures to various geographic regions around the world.

MidLink Magazine

<http://longwood.cs.ucf.edu/~MidLink>
This is an electronic magazine for kids ages 10–15; its mission is to highlight original, exemplary work from creative classrooms around the globe.

NickNacks Telecollaborative

<http://home.talkcity.com/academydr/nicknacks>
This site provides an opportunity to participate in ongoing projects or publicize your own.

Schoolworld Internet Education

<http://www.schoolworld.asn.au>
Schools K–12 engage in a wide variety of programs and projects.

Storybook Online

<http://storybookonline.net/main.html>
Storybook Online presents novels and short stories for children ages 4–13, including work by young writers.

Student Showcase

<http://forum.swarthmore.edu/students/showcase>
This site lists math projects of all kinds by U.S. schools.

The Canadian Broadcasting Corporation for Kids

<http://www.cbc4kids.ca>
CBC for Kids offers a portion of their huge, colorful website for young writers to share work with one another.

The Young Writers Club

<http://www.cs.bilkent.edu.tr/~david/derya/ywc.html>
The Young Writers Club aims to encourage children ages 7–15 to enjoy writing as a creative pastime by getting them to share their work and help each other improve their writing abilities. Based in Turkey.

U.N. Voices of Youth Page

<http://www.unicef.org/voy>
Students can share their opinions, ideas, and art about what affects children in the world today (e.g., children and work, children's rights, children and war).

Young Girl Writers

<http://home.talkcity.com/WooHooWay/scanner_death/index.html>
If you are a girl who likes to write and wants to link up with other girls around the globe who also love to write, or if you are looking for tips to refine your writing and get published, this is the place for you.

ZuZu

<http://zuzu.org>
ZuZu describes itself as a forum for expression for those explorers who stumble upon it. It began as a print newspaper in New York City but went completely online in 1995. Lots of fun for kids of all ages.

Online Student Newspaper Sites

Internet search engines provide listings of online student publications. For example, a wonderful set of links appears on Yahoo's webpage about K–12 newspapers: <http://dir.yahoo.com/Education/K_12/Newspapers>.

Appendix D

Educational Organizations as Resources

The following excellent educational organizations can serve as resources to teachers interested in helping their students publish.

Bread Loaf School of English

<http://www.blse.middlebury.edu>
Bread Loaf hosts a graduate studies program each summer on four campuses located in the United States and England.

Columbia Scholastic Press Association

<http://www.columbia.edu/cu/cspa>
CSPA is an international student press association uniting student journalists and faculty advisors at schools and colleges through educational conferences, idea exchanges, and award programs. Its staff critiques and provides awards to outstanding student newspapers, magazines, and yearbooks. The site contains lists of both individual and schoolwide winners in middle school, high school, and college newspapers, magazines, and yearbooks for the past four years.

Community of Writers (COW)

<http://www.communityofwriters.com>
COW is a wonderful Portland, Oregon, organization of writers that should be a model for other communities around the nation. Their website not only serves the participating writers, teachers, and students but anyone interested in planning writing lessons, stimulating their own writing, networking, or sharing ideas.

COW helps improve students' writing by training teachers and bringing professional writers into classrooms. Since 1997, COW has trained hundreds of teachers in the Portland Public Schools system, and COW writers have worked with thousands of PPS students. COW is a sponsored project of the Portland Schools Foundation <http://www.portlandschoolsfdn.org> and receives generous financial support from many foundations and individuals.

COW offers teachers and schools an array of services to support their writing instruction, including:

- A weeklong summer writing institute. COW and Portland State University offer this four-credit course to help teachers improve their own writing and to learn new techniques for teaching their students. By immersing themselves in the writing process, teachers gain a firsthand perspective on what their students experience when they are asked to write.
- Writers-in-residence. Dozens of local writers enter COW classrooms for weeklong residencies. The writers work together with the teacher to help students express themselves on the page. COW is proud to offer writers who are persuasive not only on the page, but in the classroom as well.
- Family Write Nights. COW makes sure parents are aware of the writing skills their children are learning. Family Write Nights give students and their parents the opportunity to participate in writing activities together. At these events, COW writers lead families in a variety of writing activities. Each COW classroom receives four Write Nights during the year.

National Council of Teachers of English

<http://www.ncte.org>
NCTE advocates the improvement of English and language arts education in the schools; their site includes related links, publications, awards, conference information, and discussion groups for teachers of English.

National Elementary Schools Press Association

<http://www.nespa.org>
This organization is dedicated to helping elementary and middle schools start new or improve existing class and school newspapers. The association serves as a clearinghouse for schools interested in sharing information and newspapers with member schools from coast to coast.

National Scholastic Press Association

<http://studentpress.journ.umn.edu./nspa/nspa.html>
A national membership association for high school publications (e.g., newspapers,

magazines, yearbooks), offering conventions, contests, and other valuable resources. They give Best of Press Online Pacemaker awards to online student publications, as well as Pacemaker awards for printed publications.

National Writing Project

<http://www.writingproject.org>
This is the national connection for teachers seeking to improve student writing and learning in the classroom through professional development. NWP has an extensive network of teachers working to promote exemplary writing instruction in the United States.

Oregon Students Writing & Art Foundation

Contact Chris Weber at chriscarlweber@earthlink.net for future URL.

"Clearly, the Oregon Students Writing & Art Foundation is establishing a level of excellence not only for Oregon but for the entire country," wrote Donald Graves, author of *Writing: Teachers & Children at Work,* and many other books on teaching.

In 1985 the Oregon Students Writing & Art Foundation, a nonprofit tax-exempt organization, was founded by Chris Weber with the support and encouragement of the Oregon Reading Association. The Foundation publishes writing and artwork by students to enhance literacy and to promote cross-cultural understanding. It is an affiliate of the Oregon Reading Association.

The Foundation has published three books. Student editors have been involved in every aspect of production except the printing. With the assistance of teachers and students in Oregon, the Foundation published *Treasures: Stories & Art by Students in Oregon* and *Treasures 2: Stories & Art by Students in Oregon.* Students, teachers, officials, and businesspeople in the United States and Japan worked together to publish the English and Japanese versions of *Treasures 3: Stories & Art by Students in Japan & Oregon.*

Chris Weber has been working with his Japanese counterpart, Takao Mimura, an instructor at the Graduate School of Education in Joestu University of Education (in Joetsu, Japan), on an international student publication that will result in a book of impressions. It will contain students' impressions of stories they read in *Treasures 3* and stories they were inspired to write. Students from France, Guam, Japan, Malaysia, Russia, and the United States are represented. For more information and guidelines about this and other upcoming projects, please e-mail Chris Weber at chriscarlweber@earthlink.net.

Teachers & Writers Collaborative of New York City

<http://www.twc.org>
TWC runs a writers-in-the-schools program, as well as offering other resources for teachers.

Write to Change

<http://www.strom.clemson.edu/teams/literacy/write.html>
This is a nonprofit organization with the mission of promoting school and community projects that encourage action research, writing, and public service.

Appendix E
Award Programs and Writing Competitions

I love the fact that some organizations critique student publications and recognize the outstanding ones. Of course, it's the publishers themselves who know just how good their publication is. The organizations listed here have well-established reward programs and competitions. You will get all of the resources, information, guidelines, and entry forms you and your students need by visiting each organization's website. (Additional information about some of these organizations can be found in Appendix D.) If your publication is eligible, talk with your students and see what they think about submitting their publication(s) for recognition or an award. Then go for it!

Award Programs

Columbia Scholastic Press Association (CSPA)

<http://www.columbia.edu/cu/cspa>
CSPA lists the "awards to recognize excellence in student media" given to both individual and schoolwide winners in middle school, high school, and college newspapers, magazines, and yearbooks for the past four years. CSPA's services include written evaluations (conducted by mail) of individual student publications. CSPA also sponsors the "Gold Keys" awards to recognize excellence in people (e.g., educators, members of the professional press, and others for their support of excellence in teaching journalism, in student media advising, and for significant contributions to student journalism). This organization sponsors several other award programs.

National Council of Teachers of English (NCTE)

<http://www.ncte.org>
NCTE sponsors the Program to Recognize Excellence in Student Literary

Magazines. The program is intended as a means of recognition for students, teachers, and schools producing excellent literary magazines; as an inducement for improving the quality of such magazines; and as encouragement for all schools to develop literary magazines, seeking excellence in writing and schoolwide participation in production. Magazines are evaluated and ranked. Critiques of individual magazines are not provided.

Eligibility: The student literary magazine program is open to all senior high, junior high, and middle schools throughout the United States and Canada, and to American schools abroad. Only one entry may be submitted per school. In cases where a school publishes more than one magazine or more than one issue per year, a selection committee should be formed at the school to select the best entry. Two or more schools may not join to submit one entry. Districtwide magazines produced by student staff are eligible if such magazines are developed in a district that does not have individual school literary magazines. Note: The following types of magazines are not eligible: kindergarten and elementary magazines and other kinds of publications, e.g., newspapers, yearbooks. Evidence of plagiarism will disqualify a magazine.

For information on how to enter a magazine in this program, click on the awards and grants category in the "NCTE links" section on the NCTE's website: <http://www.ncte.org/grants>. There you can learn more about the NCTE's annual Achievement Awards in Writing program and its Promising Young Writers Program for Eighth-Grade Students.

National Scholastic Press Association (NSPA)

<http://studentpress.journ.umn.edu./nspa/nspa.html>
NSPA strives to help students and teachers improve their publications. It also assists students to become better reporters, writers, editors, photographers, designers, desktop publishers, and advertising and business staffers. They help advisors as well.

Entry forms are available for download in PDF format for their annual Magazine, Yearbook, and Yearbook CD-ROM Pacemaker awards, plus Online Pacemaker awards.

Quill and Scroll, International Honorary Society for High School Journalists

<http://www.uiowa.edu/~quill-sc/index.html>
Quill and Scroll sponsors a number of writing, newspaper, and yearbook competitions each year. You may request entry forms be sent to you by e-mailing <quill-scroll@uiowa.edu>. Quill and Scroll's purpose is to encourage and recognize individual student achievement in journalism and scholastic publication.

To be eligible for a Quill and Scroll charter, your high school must publish a magazine, newspaper, or yearbook. When a charter is granted, the publication advisor automatically becomes a member of Quill and Scroll. Only charter member schools may submit student names for nomination as Quill and Scroll members.

The Society also sponsors The International Writing, Photo Contest and the Yearbook Excellence Contest. *Quill & Scroll* magazine is filled with articles, pictures, news items, and helpful hints for students and advisors. There is a Quill and Scroll Junior High School website <http://www.uiowa.edu/~quill-sc/junior-high /junior-high.html> where, for a fee, the society evaluates and offers suggestions for improvement to junior high schools submitting their newspapers or magazines. The Society gives awards to outstanding newspaper, yearbook, and magazine staffs.

Writing Competitions

As an elementary school teacher, I am inclined not to involve individual students in writing competitions. However, some of my colleagues and I encourage entire classrooms to participate in contests, such as the "Brief Message from the Heart" Letter Writing Contest (more information on p. 199). Find a select few competitions (one to three per year) you want your students to enter and make it a classroom project where everyone is involved, including the teacher. The Letter Writing Contest is open to all ages, so I enter along with my students. I model for my students my approach and revision process to the pieces I am submitting.

It's a different ball game with middle and high school students. More contests are available to them, and they are more mature and able to handle rejection. The older students are able to participate in one competition after another throughout the year, although, I recommend that they have strong knowledge of the characteristics of past winners and understand the high standards and guidelines.

Writing Competitions and Publishing Opportunities

This list, compiled by Linda Denstaedt, Clarkston High School, Clarkston, Michigan, includes school, local, state, national, and international competitions. Each competition has specific guidelines for submission. The postmark deadline may change from year to year. Some competitions require a fee or try to sell books to students. Adult competition and publication markets are open to advanced students.

The following books and magazines offer additional information on competitions and publications: *Writers Digest* and *Poets and Writers* magazines, and the books *Writer's Market* (several different volumes organized by genre and age), *Market Guide* for Young Writers: Where and How to Sell What You Write, and *The International Directory of Little Magazines and Small Presses*.

Try the following contests:

Ayn Rand Institute

Grades: 9–10
Genre: *Anthem* Essay
Contact: <http://www.aynrand.org/contests>
Prize: Cash
Postmark deadline: April 2

Ayn Rand Institute

Grades: 11–12
Genre: *The Fountainhead* Essay
Contact: < http://www.aynrand.org/contests>
Prize: Cash
Postmark deadline: April 16

Brief Message from the Heart Contest

Most of my students enjoy this contest immensely and submit multiple entries.
Grades: all ages
Genre: Letter of twenty-five words or less
Contact: < http://www.briefmessage.org>
Prize: Cash, certificates so beautiful that they should be framed and hung on the
    wall
Postmark deadline: November 30

Fulbright

Grades: 7–12
Genre: Essay
Contact: Fulbright Young Essayists Awards, c/o Alliance for Young Artists &
    Writers, 555 Broadway, 4th Floor, New York, NY 10012
Prize: Savings bond
Entry fee required
Postmark deadline: January 18

Hemingway Writing Awards

Grades: 9–12
Genre: Journalism—features, news, sports, commentary
Contact: <http://www.kcstar.com/aboutstar/hemingway/hem2.htm>
Prize: Scholarship
Postmark deadline: January 15

Holocaust

Grades: 9–12
Genre: Essay
Contact: Children of the Holocaust Survivors Association in Michigan
P.O. Box 339614
Farmington Hills, MI 48333
Prize: Cash
Postmark deadline: March 1

The International Television Video Association (ITVA) Festival

Grades: All levels
Genre: Video and production
Contact: <http://www.beaweb.org/96news/itva.html>
Prize: Cash, trip
Postmark deadline: November 16

Lawrence Technological University

Grades: 11–12
Genre: Poetry, short story, essay
Contact: (248) 204-3520
Prize: Cash
Postmark deadline: January 15

MADD

Grades: 1–12, 4–12, 7–12
Genre: Poster for 1–12, essay for 4–12, photography for 7–12, Public Service
    Announcement video for 7–12
Contact: Local chapter
Prize: Cash
Postmark deadline: January 31

Merlyn's Pen

Grades: 6–12
Genre: Poetry, fiction, nonfiction
Contact: Merlyn's Pen Submissions, P.O. Box 910, East Greenwich, RI 02818
(401) 885-5175 <http://www.merlynspen.com>
Prize: Cash, publication
Postmark deadline: Continuous

Oatmeal Studios

Grades: Open
Genre: Greeting cards
Contact: (802) 767-3171
Prize: Cash
Postmark deadline: Continuous

Olive Garden

Grades: Ages 7 and up
Genre: Essay
Contact: <http://www.olivegarden.com/ourcommunity/pastatales.asp>
Prize: Savings bond
Postmark deadline: December 3

Penguin Putnam Inc.

Grades: 11–12
Genre: Essay
Contact: <http://www.penguinputnam.com/scessay>
Prize: Scholarship
Postmark deadline: April 15

Poetry.com

Grades: 9–12
Genre: Poetry
Contact: <http://www.poetry.com>
This is an amazing site of over 3.1 million poets, superb links, and resources. It also
sponsors the Poetry in Motion contest, a haiku contest, and an online poetry
contest.)
Prize: Cash (except for haiku contest)
Postmark deadline: Continuous

Potato Hill Poetry

This is an annual poetry contest for students and teachers.
Grades: Teachers K–12, students 1–3, 4–6, 7–9, 10–12
Genre: Poetry
Contact: e-mail: info@potatohill.com; (888)5-POETRY;
    <http://www.potatohill.com>
Prize: Cash awards
Postmark deadline: June 4

Princeton University

Grade: 11
Genre: Poetry
Contact: (248) 204-3520
Prize: Recognition
Postmark deadline: March 1

River of Words

Grades: K–12
Genre: Poetry, artwork
Contact: <http://www.irn.org>
Prize: Trip, book and website publication, T-shirt
Postmark deadline: February 15

Skipping Stones *Annual Youth Honor Awards*

Grades: Ages 7–17 years old
Genre: Essays, poems, short stories, songs, travelogues, artwork (drawings, cartoons,
    paintings, or photo essays)
Contact: e-mail: skipping@efn.org; <http://www.efn.org/~skipping
    /youthhonor.htm>
Prize: Publication, honor award certificate, five multicultural and/or nature books,
    one-year subscription to *Skipping Stones*
Postmark deadline: Continuous

TeenInk

Grades: 9–12
Genre: Poetry, nonfiction, fiction, review, interviews, photography
Contact: < http://www.TeenInk.com>
Prize: Publication
Postmark deadline: Continuous

Veterans of Foreign Wars

Grades: 7–9
Genre: Essay
Contact: (816) 756-3390
Prize: Cash
Postmark deadline: March 15

Veterans of Foreign Wars

Grades: 10–12
Genre: Essay, speech
Contact: (816) 756-3390
Prize: Cash
Postmark deadline: November 1

Writer's Digest Short Short Story Competition

Grades: 9–12
Genre: Short story
Contact: The Writer's Digest Short Short Story Competition, 1507 Dana Avenue, Cincinnati, Ohio 45207
Contact: <http://www.writersdigest.com/catalog/contest_frame.html>
Prize: Cash
Postmark deadline: December 1

Appendix F
The Authors

I apologize for the fact that some authors were not included in the appendix. I was unable to contact those authors or get any response from them.

Alma Flor Ada is a renowned author, translator, scholar, educator, storyteller, and advocate for bilingual and multicultural education. She has written many distinguished books for children in both English and Spanish. She has also written and edited numerous textbooks, education materials, and journal articles and was the founder and served as editor-in-chief of the *Journal of the National Association for Bilingual Education*. She is a professor of international-multicultural education at the University of San Francisco and travels throughout the United States and abroad facilitating workshops for educators.

Drawing upon the inspiration of the great storytellers from her childhood and her own unique gift for writing, Ada has written many memorable books for young readers—most often about the themes of identity and self-discovery. Some of her literary awards and recognitions include the 2000 Pura Belpré Award Medal, the Latina Writer's Award (1996), the Parent's Choice Award (1994), and the Christopher Award (1991).

GaBrilla Ballard, a performance poet and activist, has worked with the Students at the Center program at Frederick A. Douglass Senior High School for two years. Her poetry appears in *From a Bend in the River* published by Runagate Press.

Celeste Barker is currently a student of French and English literature at Western Oregon University and has had her poetry published in *Northwest Passage,* the campus literary magazine. She spent her junior year studying French culture and authors in Lyon, France. While there, she also developed an interest in Irish literature, and returned home later to complete her senior honors thesis on James Joyce. In the future she plans to become an English professor specializing in non-British literature of the United Kingdom. Through teaching, she hopes to create an awareness of the role of the English language in the world and to introduce students to authors not explored in typical English literature classes. Her interests are in Irish history and culture and in U.S. foreign relations, particularly the impact of American culture on the rest of the world. She still deeply enjoys writing and anticipates future publication projects.

Richard Barrow started his early career as an assistant film editor for the BBC in London. During a break for a year, he traveled around Australia visiting all the major sites. After returning to the UK, he found he couldn't settle down. So, after saving up enough money, he went backpacking across Asia. His intention was to only go for a year, but one thing led to another and he found himself settling down in Thailand. He is now the head of the computer department at Sriwittayapaknam School. His student webmasters run some of the most successful English-language websites in Thailand.

Address: c/o Sriwittayapaknam School
                58 Tetsaban 4 Road
                Amphoe Muang, Samut Prakan, Thailand 10270
E-mail: webmaster@thaistudents.com

Marion Dane Bauer is the author of nearly thirty books for young people, from picture books and early readers through novels and writing guides. She has won numerous awards, including a Jane Addams Peace Association Award for her novel *Rain of Fire* and an American Library Association Newbery Honor Award for another novel, *On My Honor,* and the Kerlan Award from the University of Minnesota for the body of her work. She was the first Faculty Chair and continues on the faculty at Vermont College for the only Master of Fine Arts in Writing for Children program in the country. Her book, the American Library Association Notable Book *What's Your Story? A Young Person's Guide to Writing Fiction,* is used by writers of all ages. Her books have been translated into more than a dozen different languages.

Harold "Butch" Beedle is a sixth-grade social studies teacher at J. C. McKenna Middle School. He has been active in rain forest education throughout the nation. He has written various articles, helped develop curriculums, and acted as a resource on rain forest education.

Address: J.C. McKeena Middle School
            307 South First Street
            Evansville, WI 53536
Telephone: (608) 882-4780
E-mail: bbeedle@ehs.k12.wi.us

Jennifer Block is currently attending Cornell University. She is studying Human Biology, Health, and Society, and is planning to attend medical school next fall. She is involved in research and peer advising and volunteers at a nearby hospital. Other interests of hers include traveling, exercising, and spending time with friends and family.

Joe Brooks teaches at Guilford Central School in Vermont, working with middle school students who publish a community newspaper, *The Guilford Gazette*, and serves as an advisor to the school's website. He is as a consultant for service learning to Vermont's Department of Education.

   Joe Brooks is also the founder and executive director of Vermont Community Works, a nonprofit organization dedicated to assisting K–12 schools and teachers in developing service and community based learning activities. Joe has worked with many schools throughout New England since 1993 providing technical assistance and workshops on service learning and community based learning. Community Works has developed a number of resources for teachers that can be accessed through their website at: <http://www.vermontcommunityworks.org>.

Address: P.O. Box 1075
            Brattleboro, VT 05302
Telephone: (802) 254-7795
E-mail: jbrooks@vermontcommunityworks.org

F. Isabel Campoy is the author of numerous children's books in the areas of poetry, theater, stories, biographies, and art. She is a scholar, educator, and translator. She is also a researcher and author of several books on the culture and civilization of the Hispanic world. Songwriter and storyteller, Isabel's goal is to provide children the key to interpreting the world in a fun, challenging, and affirmative way.

   Her poetry has appeared in eleven anthologies published by Harcourt and Alfaguara in the U.S. and abroad. Poetry has been her way to communicate to children the wonder of life and words, the joy and magic of creativity.

   She is a scholar devoted to the study of language acquisition, a field in which she started publishing in 1978. About herself, she says: "From my mother I inherited a robust pride in my roots, a wealth of folklore through her storytelling, and an abundant sense of humor. From my father, the passion for learning and the art of teaching."

Angie Cheek is the English Department chair at Rabun County High School in Tiger, Georgia. She and a business teacher facilitate the *Foxfire Magazine* class. Angie received her bachelor's degree from Georgia Southern University and her master's from Piedmont College. With twenty-five years of teaching experience, Angie has been a system Teacher of the Year twice and was selected as STAR (Student-Teacher Achievement Recognition) teacher five times.

In 2000, Angie was the recipient of the Rotary Professional Service Award and received the Honorary Teacher Award from *The Atlanta Journal-Constitution*. She has also been recognized by the local chapter of Retired Georgia Educators as Educator of the Year and was selected to membership in Delta Kappa Gamma, an honorary international organization for key women educators, and Kappa Delta Pi, an international honor society in education; she was also included in Who's Who Among American High School Teachers. Angie has worked with *Foxfire Magazine*, a student-produced, student-managed publication, since 1992.
E-mail: angiedcheek@yahoo.com or acheek@rabun.k12.ga.us

Anna Citrino, a teacher since 1985, has worked both as a public high school English teacher in Santa Cruz County, California, and as an English/reading, language arts, and social studies teacher in international schools in Turkey, Kuwait, and Singapore. She has coordinated and worked with students and teachers on a variety of online international exchange projects. Additionally, she has served as an advisor and editor for several different student publications. She especially enjoys writing poetry and has had her work published in a book and in a number of small press publications. Ms. Citrino has also coauthored a chapter about online publications that previously appeared in *Electronic Networks*, published by Heinemann. She received her M.A. from the Bread Loaf School of English, and has been teaching at Singapore American School since 1996, where she continues to enjoy both life in the tropics and the vivacity of her students.
Address: P.O. Box 1167
            Soquel, CA 95073
E-mail: Anna_Citrino@breadnet.middlebury.edu

Matthew Cohen was editor-in-chief of *Erehwon*, Winston Churchill High School's literary arts magazine, during the 1999–2000 school year. He is presently a sophomore at Penn University.

Emily Coutant is a student in Redlands California. She loves to sing, write poetry, and help people work out their problems. She's aiming toward a career in radio broadcasting or as a therapist.

Linda Denstaedt is a National Board Certified teacher who is the Director of Writing K–12 for Clarkston Community Schools, Clarkston, Michigan. She coauthored *The Creative Writer's Craft: Lessons in Poetry, Fiction and Drama* with her adult writer's group. She was named Creative Writing Teacher of the Year by Michigan Council Teachers of English and currently coordinates the writing competition for Michigan Youth Arts Festival. Linda serves on the advisory board and facilitates the Teachers as Writers Program for the Oakland Writing Project, an affiliate of the National Writing Project.
Telephone: (248) 623-3600 ext. 3060
E-mail: denstalg@clarkston.k12.mi.us, ldenstaedt@hotmail.com

Peter Elbow is Professor Emeritus of English at the University of Massachusetts at Amherst, where he directed the writing program. He has written: *Writing Without Teachers*, *Writing with Power: Techniques for Mastering the Writing Process*, and *A Community of Writers* (coauthored with Pat Belanoff). He is also author of *Embracing Contraries*, a book of essays about learning and teaching. Other works include *Oppositions in Chaucer* and *What Is English?* as well as numerous essays about writing and teaching. His most recent book is *Everyone Can Write: Essays Toward a Hopeful Theory of Writing and Teaching Writing*, Oxford University Press, 2000. He has taught at M.I.T., Franconia College, Evergreen State College, and SUNY Stony Brook, where for five years he also directed the writing program.
E-mail: elbow@english.umass.edu

Katia Fedorova is presently studying at Moscow's State Social University in Moscow, Russia. Her hobbies include swimming, gymnastics, and track-and-field.

Peter Frost is originally from Seattle, Washington. He has been living overseas now for three years, first in Singapore and then in the Netherlands where he goes to high school at the American School of the Hague. He enjoys writing free-style poetry as well as short stories. "Coral" is his first published writing piece.

Elizabeth Bridges Hammond served as advisor to *LAUREATE* for seventeen (1980–1997) of her twenty-five years as a teacher of English at Brookland-Cayce High School in Cayce, South Carolina. She taught journalism workshops and judged magazines for the Southern Interscholastic Press Association, the Virginia High School League and the South Carolina Scholastic Press Association. In addition she served as president of the South Carolina Writers Workshop. She received her Masters in English Education from the University of South Carolina.

Lisa Jobson has worked as Program Coordinator for iEARN-US since 1997. Before that, she taught writing and social studies in South Africa, and history in Providence, Rhode Island, where she also worked at the Coalition of Essential Schools and Annenberg Institute for School Reform. She received her B.A. and social studies teaching certification at Brown University in 1995.

Address: I*EARN-USA (International Education and Resource Network)
            475 Riverside Drive
            Suite 540
            New York, NY 10115
Telephone: (212) 870-2693
E-mail: iearn@us.iearn.org
Website: <http://www.iearn.org>

Adrinda Kelly, an English major at Harvard University, plans to be a writer and publisher. She was in the original Students at the Center class at McDonogh #35 Senior High School.

Dr. Eric A. Kimmel is Professor Emeritus of Education at Portland State University in Portland, Oregon. He is a member of the writing faculty at Vermont College's MFA program in Writing for Children. Dr. Kimmel is the author of over fifty children's books and numerous articles and short stories. His books have won numerous state awards as well as prestigious honors in the field of children's literature, including the Caldecott Honor Medal. He is a frequent guest on the Loose Leaf Book Company's children's book radio program, hosted by Tom Bodett. Dr. Kimmel and his wife, Doris, live in Portland, Oregon.

Address: 2525 NE 35th Avenue
            Portland, OR 97212-5232
E-mail: kimmels@earthlink.net

John Kissingford spent a decade or so teaching English, EFL, and theater at schools in Connecticut, California, Saudi Arabia, Mexico, and Colorado. The more he taught, however, the more he discovered that the most powerful way for students to connect with literature was to explore ways to embody the text; this led him to study methods of integrating theater into the discipline of English. Of course, the more he studied theater, the more he realized that what he truly wanted to be is an actor. He holds a B.A. from Princeton, an Ed.M. from Harvard, and an M.A. from the Bread Loaf School of English, and is presently studying for his M.F.A. in acting from Florida Atlantic University.

E-mail: jfkonthenet@yahoo.com
Website: <http://photos.yahoo.com/jfkonthenet>

Mark Levin has been a classroom teacher for over twenty years. Currently he teaches fifth-grade language arts and science at Carolina Day School in Asheville, North Carolina. Levin, a Certified Journalism Educator, is the founding director of the National Elementary Schools Press Association.

Levin is the author of: *Real-World Publishing For Kids, Kids in Print, Publishing a School Newspaper, The Reporter's Notebook—Writing Tools for Young Journalists, Taming the Wild Outdoors—Building Cooperative Learning Through Outdoor Education,* and *ExP3 Journalism—A Handbook for Journalists.* In addition to teaching and writing, Levin presents workshops around the country based on his classroom ideas.

Address: c/o Mind-Stretch
              3124 Landrum Road
              Columbus, NC 28722
Telephone: (828) 863-4235
E-mail: markL@teleplex.net
Website: <http://www.mindstretch.com>

Louise Parms is currently a teacher at the Horace Mann School in New York City, where she directs the Publishing Center at the Lower Division. She earned her B.A. in creative writing at Vermont College. She regularly takes courses at the Center for Book Arts in New York City and enjoys learning new bookmaking techniques to bring to her students. Parms loves poetry and art and finds the book arts a perfect place to bring these avenues of expression together.

Telephone: (718) 432-3300
E-mail: Louise_Parms@horacemann.org

Jim Randels, a teacher in the New Orleans Public School System since 1984, currently codirects the Students at the Center (SAC) program at eight secondary schools in New Orleans. He also teaches at McDonogh 35 and Frederick Douglass High Schools. He was named Teacher of the Year for the New Orleans Public Schools in 1998.

Randels' interest in developing students as educational and community resources dates to his work from 1988–94 as a Ph.D. student and instructor in curriculum and instruction at the University of New Orleans and as an instructor in and director of the Writing Center at Tulane University's A. B. Freeman School of Business. During this tenure, he developed a peer tutoring program that is documented in his article "Peer Tutor Training: A Model for Business Schools" in the July 1992 issue of the *Journal of Business and Technical Communications.* Randels also has strong interest in interdisciplinary, community-based approaches to education.

Address: c/o Frederick A. Douglass Senior High School
                3820 St. Claude Avenue
                New Orleans, LA 70117
                c/o McDonogh #35 Senior High School
                1331 Kerlerec Street
                New Orleans, LA 70116
E-mail: jimrandelssac@earthlink.net

Denise M. Reagan is an art director and designer at the *Star Tribune* in Minneapolis, Minnesota. She has won several awards from the Society for News Design for her work on features and news pages, and she speaks regularly about typography and design across the country. She has worked in newspapers since graduating from the University of Florida journalism school. Although her professional career has taken her to newsrooms from Fort Wayne, Indiana, to Detroit, Michigan, to Minneapolis, some of her best memories are of long days and nights spent laboring over her college newspaper, the *Independent Florida Alligator,* in Gainesville, Florida.

Telephone: (612) 673-7286
E-mail: dreagan@startribune.com

Romi Sussman is currently an English and creative writing teacher at Winston Churchill High School in Potomac, Maryland, and she is the sponsor of Churchill's nationally acclaimed literary magazine, *Erehwon.* In addition, Romi sponsors an underclass magazine, *Polliwog,* that has won state awards. Romi received her undergraduate degree in mass communication from the University of California at Los Angeles and her Master of Arts in Teaching English Education from Boston University.

Address: c/o Winston Churchill High School
                11300 Gainsborough Road
                Potomac, Maryland 20854
E-mail: rojo108@aol.com

Dick Swartout has been a teacher for thirty-three years. He received a B.A. from Oakland University in 1967 and an M.A.T. from Oakland University in 1970. His primary teaching responsibilities include accelerated language arts (ninth grade); newspaper and yearbook advisor; department chair; and varsity boys and girls tennis coach. Swartout has served on various district committees: K–12 curriculum, language arts, curriculum, and teacher mentor.

E-mail: rswart@speedlink.net

Sam Swope is a teacher and writer. His award-winning books for children include *The Araboolies of Liberty Street, The Krazees, Katya's Book of Mushrooms,* and *Gotta Go! Gotta Go!* Sam is a cofounder of Chapbooks.com. It was his idea to bring chapbooks technology into the classroom, and the first chapbook prototypes were written by his students in Queens, New York.

His essays on teaching have been published in the *Teachers & Writers Collaborative Magazine, The Threepenny Review,* and elsewhere. Swope does teacher workshops and author visits to schools throughout the country, and is also a consultant for Nickelodeon and the National Assessment of Education Progress. He is an Individual Project Fellow for the Spencer Foundation and the Open Society, funded by George Soros.

Arun N. Toké, a native of India, has written two books: *Song of Winter Wonderland* (Greenhill Books, 1982) and *Energy, Economics, and the Environment* (Prentice-Hall, 1984). He has previously worked as an Associate Professor of Electrical and Electronics Engineering Technology at Vermont Technical College, Randolph Center, Vermont, and as the editor and publisher of *Cookstove News* at Aprovecho Institute in Oregon. Arun speaks four languages and has traveled extensively in Europe, India, Mexico, and Central America. He founded *Skipping Stones* magazine in 1988.

Address: c/o Skipping Stones
             P.O. Box 3939
             Eugene, OR 97403-0939
Telephone: (541) 342-4956
E-mail: skipping@efn.org

Mark Wagler teaches in a multiage fourth- and fifth-grade classroom in Madison, Wisconsin, where he is a cofounder of the Heron Network and *Great Blue*. Earlier, as a professional storyteller and folklorist, he performed and developed projects in over seven hundred schools and was cochair of Heads & Tales, an international conference on storytelling in education. In the past several years he has codirected a video exchange project, helped create the *Teacher's Guide to International Collaboration on the Internet* <http://ed.gov/Technology/guide/international>, presented Wisconsin culture at the Smithsonian Folklife Festival in Washington, D.C., and received a Presidential Award for Excellence in Mathematics and Science Teaching.

His recent publications include two locally published action research articles and excerpts in *Tales as Tools: The Power of Story in the Classroom* and *Best Classroom Practices: What Award-Winning Elementary Teachers Do.*
E-mail: mwagler@facstaff.wisc.edu

Chris Weber has been an ESL teacher for the Portland public schools for twenty years, where he coteaches in the classroom with mainstream teachers. He has been involved with student publications throughout his teaching career. In 1984, he founded the Oregon Students Writing & Art Foundation and has since supervised the making of: *Treasures: Stories & Art by Students in Oregon*, *Treasures 2: Stories & Art by Students in Oregon*, and *Treasures 3: Stories & Art by Students in Japan & Oregon*.

He has written articles for books and magazines and plans on writing a second book explaining everything teachers want and need to know about making books with students, from planning to publicity.

Chris has presented at many conventions and given numerous teacher workshops at schools.

Address: 1826 SE 54th Avenue
                     Portland, Oregon 97215-3334
Fax: (503) 236-1992
E-mail: chriscarlweber@earthlink.net
Website: <http://www.home.earthlink.net/~chriscarlweber>

Tom Wisniewski attends school in Ann Arbor at the University of Michigan, where he studies music and writing. Former publications include poems anthologized by the *Detroit Free Press*, Michigan Youth Arts Festival, Western Michigan University, and the National Textbook Company. He plays the saxophone, likes to drive, and in his spare time, he writes.

Appendix G
I Also Wish to Thank

There were many that worked so hard and very long to produce superb pieces that, unfortunately, because of space limitations could not be included in *Publishing with Students*. I wish to show the following people my heartfelt appreciation by acknowledging them on this page. I sincerely apologize if I have accidentally left out any names.

Judy Barr

Russell Bauman

Sharon Bishop

Jane Blystone

Judy Bryson

Susan Bonthron

Tola Cohia Brennan

Karen Bunnell

Angela Carone

Mee "Christine" Chang

Diane Clark

Rhonda E. Day

Nattawud Daoruang

Margaret Forst

Doug Frisina

Nancy Gorrell

Donna Graves

Carole Griffin

Dori Griffin

Chris Gustafson

Jack Harkrider

Chanrithy Him

Ernae Klepper-Windham

Ken Klepper

Nicole Cecilia Koenig

Evgenia Koptyug

Nina M. Koptyug

Shannon LaFlam

Jeannie Le Blanc

Paul Linnman

Danielle Logan

Dan London

Kathy Lowe

Clifton Manahan

Leah Meijer

Di McWhirter

Takao Mimura

Rosetta Morse

Sharman Murphy

Christina Ongley

Ramiel Papish
Hope Parker
Patricia Parrish
Natalia Petriaeva
Laura Ramseier
Lucille Rossbach
Anthony Roy
Janika Ruusmaa
Seth Selleck
Randee Silverman
Cary Smith

Nicole Speulda
Chris K. Soentpiet
Kazusa Takahashi
Joanne Tate
Zsuzsanna Tubakos
Tamara L. C. Van Wyhe
Prudence Vincent
Pamela Whitmore
Natalie Wight
Stephanie Windham

Appendix H

Students Keep Me Teaching

by Elizabeth Bridges Hammond

Elizabeth B. Hammond, the teacher-contributor who died while the book was in progress, wrote the following article. Elizabeth's words will give you a glimpse of what a wonderful teacher and human being she was. ■

High school can be a cruel place for teens who aren't athletic or members of the popular crowd. I went into teaching because I wanted to make a difference in the lives of such young people: the creative students, the scholastic underachievers, and the loners. However the traditional, often overcrowded, classroom didn't allow the time or opportunity for developing a trusting relationship between teacher and student.

A magazine journalism class gave me that chance because in the journalism room I was not an all-powerful teacher with the right answers to every question. I was truly just an adviser, one who offered suggestions and stepped in when needed to help solve problems. In that setting, I was able to focus on individual strengths and weaknesses so that students became more important than lesson plans, deadlines, test scores, or any of the myriad things school officials deem sacred. My reward came from watching them gain confidence as they developed new skills in writing, art, photography, and design. In an age when we worry about disengaged students shooting other students, helping adolescents see themselves as worthwhile people is an important reason to be an adviser.

One year, before we had a computer lab, the students and I were sitting on the floor of my classroom cutting and pasting as they learned to design. When we heard a knock at the door, the editor got up and peeked through the glass. "Get up, Mrs. Hammond," she whispered. "There's a real teacher coming in here. You don't want her to see you sitting on the floor." She wasn't being disrespectful. She'd just been conditioned to believe high school teachers were normally more dignified. That incident made me consider why journalism class was more relaxed and fun than my regular English classes.

Working informally with students put me in a unique position to know them as individuals and talk with them as friends. I frequently found myself giving advice about afterschool jobs, dates, and problems at home as well as showing them how to fit copy or size pictures. Sometimes the tables were turned, and they helped me find better ways to deal with a misbehaving student or offered advice about what to tell my daughter when she came home from middle school saying, "Nobody likes me." Knowing we enriched each other's lives provided the incentive to give up lunch periods and afterschool hours so we could meet publishing deadlines.

Since there were no other courses similar to the magazine class, I had the freedom to design a curriculum that fit their needs without worrying about meeting district goals and standardized test objectives. From the beginning, the curriculum was student centered. Editors set long-term goals and decided what needed to be accomplished each week. Although I developed a staff manual outlining the process of creating a magazine, it was always a work in progress as staffers came up with new ideas and creative ways to deal with problems. I realized I was less uptight about meeting goals because students cared about the magazine and motivated themselves to get the work done. In turn, they were happier and actually enjoyed what they were learning. I soon realized other classes would benefit from the same techniques if I were willing to relinquish authority and allow students to be in control of their own learning. Discovering how to be a better teacher from my work with the magazine staff provided another powerful incentive to keep me advising year after year.

Although students were my main source of inspiration as an adviser, adult friends also offered support and helped maintain my sanity, especially during those last busy weeks before the staff and I relinquished our manuscript to the printer. English teachers pitched in to proofread, the art teachers patiently answered questions about who painted which picture, and the graphics teacher gave up afternoons to solve perplexing computer problems. I also made good friends at the journalism conferences we attended several times a year and found it invigorating to commiserate with other advisers who faced similar problems. These usually involved administrative decisions and lack of funding rather than students. Except for one, the principals I worked for supported the magazine, sometimes financially, but mainly by trusting us to make responsible decisions about content and produce a publication the school and community could be proud of. I could not have remained as an adviser without that kind of help.

Throughout my years as an adviser, I worked with a lot of staffs and principals and watched talented students come and go. Looking back, sometimes the years blend together, and I can't remember which editors worked on which edition. However, 1996 is a year I won't forget. A junior art student painted a beautiful picture for the cover, depicting a nighttime view of our city from a bridge leading to the downtown area. Our principal loved that magazine so much he gave a copy of it to everyone who visited the school, eventually giving away so many I had to hide the last ten copies in a locked desk drawer. When we told him there were no more available, he said, "That's too bad. You and your magazine make me look good."

As I remember his words, I feel a bit sorry for him because, having never been a publications adviser, he doesn't understand the real magic of journalism. He hasn't experienced the pleasure of shepherding students through a yearlong creative process, nor seen the joy on adolescent faces as they tear into boxes from the printer and pull out a hot-off-the-press magazine. A compliment here and there and an award or two don't mean much until you've watched students' faces light up when they first see their names in print and you realize those fledgling staffers from August have taken a giant step—into adulthood.

Index